Praise for *Escaping Enemy M*

In a time characterized by unprecedented divisiveness and self-promotion at the expense of others, retired Brigadier General Chaplain Ray Woolridge and Dr. Jim Wilder have written a must-read book for every person who seeks to experience more meaningful relationships. The authors insightfully describe the relational problems caused by enemy mode, instruct how to recognize when we are in enemy mode, and give practical advice on how to transform from being stuck in a destructive enemy mode to a life-giving mode that builds engaging community.

JULIANA LESHER, Former National Director of Veterans Affairs Chaplain Service; author of *A Heart That Sings for Jesus*

For almost everyone, anger and enemies seem everywhere. Which is why it's so important that you read this book—*today*. I wish I'd have known what Jim and Ray share here about "enemy mode" being a default lifestyle. I started my "enemy mode" training by hating my father. He bailed on our family when I was two months old. I spent years perfecting being angry at him and others, not knowing or wanting anything to do with "loving my enemy." But leave it to a Christian neuroscientist and a West Point General to team up and talk about those "enemies" we all have—both in our past and present. Helping us know how to reverse that curse that is swamping our culture and communities—and ruining our everyday lives. Your marriage, your memories, your relationships with those around you will be stronger and more loving when you understand "enemy mode." Especially how there really is an escape clause from adding so many enemies and so much anger—in relationally living out God's love.

JOHN TRENT, Coauthor of *The Blessing* and *Where Do I Go from Here?*; president, StrongFamilies.com and TheBlessing.com

Using the wisdom gained from brain science, *Escaping Enemy Mode* is a breath of fresh air that provides insightful pathways for those seeking to create sustainable peace in their individual life, family, business, and larger community. A must-read for anyone seeking to create life-giving and flourishing spaces for humane connection and healing. I especially recommend this book for churches and organizations invested in peacebuilding initiatives across communities that have been divided by economic, social, and political differences.

JULIA ROBINSON MOORE, Associate Professor of Religious Studies, UNC Charlotte; author of *Race, Religion, and the Pulpit: Rev. Robert L. Bradby and the Making of Urban Detroit*; cofounder of Moore Grace Ministries

When you understand enemy mode and learn to recognize when you are in it, then you can start practicing how to avoid it. On the street I have often found myself in a rapidly deteriorating exchange with a suspect. One of my best techniques, if I catch things early, is to say, "Wait, let's start over. This doesn't have to be adversarial, I'm not like those other cops!" Whether I agree with the suspect's evaluation of what other cops are like is irrelevant, I am forming a bond by acknowledging their reality. I've learned to recognize pitfalls in myself that will take me into enemy mode in a heartbeat. It is easy to ignore the feelings of others when we have white knight syndrome and are fighting for a "worthy cause." It is my hope that by applying the techniques presented in this book you will grab hold of the best version of you, achieve win-win solutions, and strengthen your relationships with those around you.

MIKE BELLER, Assistant Chief of Police, Chamblee, Georgia, and former army ranger

Escaping Enemy Mode is a powerful and desperately needed book. Easiest to address are those unwitting or unintentional times when we shut off relational circuits and harm those we care about. More challenging are the times when we (or friends) allow descent into the destructive behaviors that are increasingly hard to stop. Worst of all are the times when we, or those around us, step into the grip of coldhearted predatory "intelligent enemy mode," and act destructively on purpose. Jim and Ray offer winsome and often painfully transparent examples of their own shortfalls, and amazingly hopeful guidance of how to be our best selves who not only prosper in relationships but make the world better. It is an important read.

BILL ATWOOD, Anglican Bishop and author of applied neuroscience books, including *The General, The Boy, and Recapturing Joy*

Jim Wilder and Ray Woolridge clearly dive into the multidimensional complexity of our natural tendencies toward enemy mode versus fulfilling relationship with others. In today's world, we're continually faced with enemy mode in every realm of our existence. With great clarity, *Escaping Enemy Mode* provides extraordinary, practical action steps to escape the challenges of enemy mode that we encounter and, instead, seek to serve, love, and care for others in our sphere of influence. While we strive to live life by design, and not by default, it is increasingly powerful to return to joy in our daily lives in order that we should endure hardships well and impact the lives of others around us more extraordinarily.

JEFF REETER, Entrepreneur, business leader, speaker, author

JIM WILDER & RAY WOOLRIDGE

ESCAPING
ENEMY
MODE

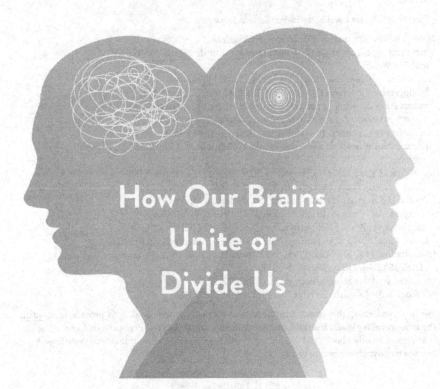

How Our Brains
Unite or
Divide Us

NORTHFIELD PUBLISHING
CHICAGO

Edited by Amanda Cleary Eastep
Interior design: Brandi Davis
Cover design: Erik M. Peterson
Cover illustration of two heads copyright © 2022 by melitas/Shutterstock (1771185044). All rights reserved.

Library of Congress Cataloging-in-Publication Data

Names: Wilder, Jim, author. | Woolridge, Ray, author.
Title: Escaping enemy mode : how our brains unite or divide us / Jim Wilder and Ray Woolridge.
Description: Chicago : Northfield Publishing, [2022] | Includes bibliographical references. | Summary: "Enemy Mode is a brain state that occurs every day where a person experiences others as adversaries. The authors put years of research to the test in assessing the possibility of loving one's enemies. This book is for all who desire harmonious relationships at home, at work, and in their communities"-- Provided by publisher.
Identifiers: LCCN 2022027133 (print) | LCCN 2022027134 (ebook) | ISBN 9780802425034 (paperback) | ISBN 9780802475381 (ebook)
Subjects: LCSH: Interpersonal relations--Psychological aspects. | Interpersonal relations--Religious aspects--Christianity. | Hostility (Psychology) | Brain. | Neuropsychology. | BISAC: RELIGION / Christian Living / Leadership & Mentoring | PSYCHOLOGY / Interpersonal Relations
Classification: LCC BF1045.I58 W55 2022 (print) | LCC BF1045.I58 (ebook) | DDC 158.2--dc23/eng/20220729
LC record available at https://lccn.loc.gov/2022027133
LC ebook record available at https://lccn.loc.gov/2022027134

We hope you enjoy this book from Northfield Publishing. Our goal is to provide high-quality, thought-provoking books and products that connect truth to your real needs and challenges. For more information on other books and products that will help you with all your important relationships, go to www.moodypublishers.com or write to:

Northfield Publishing
820 N. LaSalle Boulevard
Chicago, IL 60610

1 3 5 7 9 10 8 6 4 2

Printed in the United States of America

To my wife, Deborah,
whose love and courage are helping me
become a more relational man every day.

Ray

———————————

To the memory of my dear wife, Kitty.

Jim

CONTENTS

CONTENTS

FOREWORD

Despite a society that appears bent on seeking individual or group control and a "win," can we find our best selves and help others do the same? Jim Wilder and Ray Woolridge have provided us with that very hope in *Escaping Enemy Mode*. They look at the world as it is, describe how it has changed us, and explain how enemy mode in its various types is increasingly affecting all of us. They complement their poignant examples of enemy mode in the lives of prominent leaders and ordinary citizens with insightful descriptions of the science of the brain. More importantly, they show us how to recognize enemy mode in our own lives, and they provide practices that can help us learn the process of "refriending," a skill that will help each of us to be better leaders, followers, spouses, parents, and citizens.

We have a problem in American culture: we are losing the sense of community we once had. We are increasingly at odds with each other and frequently identify those who are different from us as being wrong, less valuable, less worthy, and, ultimately, the enemy. This does not happen just for some distant group we identify as "them." As we become more used to criticizing others—anyone other than our self-centered selves—even our coworkers and family members can, to our minds, go from being one of "us" to one of "them" . . . people we react to as we would an enemy.

While this is not new behavior for human beings, many changes in American society have prompted us to be less relational, more interested in defending *our* rights and opinions, and increasingly prone to tearing down others. Our thoughts and words, once limited to our communities, now can reach millions and live forever—for good or ill—on the internet. The great proliferation of media sources has enabled us to select media that aligns with our specific view of the world. Content providers maximize profit by reinforcing one perspective and demonizing others. The efforts of many well-intentioned parents to protect their children from emotional distress has increasingly led to children being coddled, protected, and always rewarded. Children seldom learn how to constructively overcome disappointment or conflict with others.

More recently, the global pandemic has widened the gaps, masked us, and made us much less relational. Remote work has deprived us of common and casual office interactions—those frequent encounters at the coffee pot, in the hallway, or in the margins of meetings where learning, mentoring, modeling, and professional development most frequently took place. Online meetings are efficient, but the two-dimensional screens make it easier to misperceive others as the enemy.

American politics has exacerbated a "win at all costs" mentality. Political discussion has devolved into rancorous and vitriolic name-calling and scandal mongering instead of coherent discussions about what is best for America. As biases, newsfeeds, suppositions, or other stimuli raise suspicions, we increasingly default to the "foe" assumption, enter enemy mode, and "unfriend" others. Our reactions can seem natural, self-justified, and rational.

When I first read *Escaping Enemy Mode*, I was taken aback by the term "enemy," a word that seemed unduly harsh and off-putting. But I've come to see the accuracy in the term, especially in light of the way the brain functions. Having earned my undergraduate degree at West Point (as Ray's classmate) and serving thirty-two years in the Army, I've experienced how the mind, without even consciously thinking of someone as the enemy, naturally identifies people as "friend or foe," and then reacts accordingly.

After retiring from the Army, I joined the American Armed Forces Mutual Aid Association (AAFMAA), the oldest nonprofit assisting the military and veterans. Because of my leadership there, in 2016 I was called in to lead a team for the Department of Veterans Affairs (VA) during the transition between the Trump and Obama administrations. It was not hard to find people in enemy mode among the incoming and outgoing administrations, VA officials, and the transition teams. This did not bode well.

However, the Chief of Staff of the Department of Veterans Affairs, Bob Snyder, was a former West Point classmate of mine. We'd also served together in the 1990s. He had been severely wounded at the Pentagon on 9/11, earning a Purple Heart. There was no way that I could see him as the enemy. Nearly every evening throughout the transition, he and I would meet. We used our personal relational capital to counteract the enemy mode of the teams because we all had a common objective: provide great service to veterans on behalf of the American people.

Escaping Enemy Mode is an enlightening and inspirational book that America needs now. It clearly explains the challenges that trigger enemy mode, the brain science behind it, and how to recognize, admit, and escape enemy mode to become our best self . . . and a better leader, spouse, and friend.

MICHAEL J. MEESE
Brigadier General, US Army (Retired)

There was a poor man
who by his wisdom could have saved the city
but
no one listened to him
because he was a poor man.

—————

**—Ancient Jewish wisdom
often attributed to Solomon**[1]

ABOUT THE
AUTHORS

RAY WOOLRIDGE (MDiv, Southwestern Baptist Seminary, and MSS, The Army War College) is the executive director of Life Model Works. The Life Model is helping Ray escape enemy mode in his life, work, and personal relationships every day.

Ray is a retired US Army Brigadier General. He is a 1981 graduate of the United States Military Academy. He is a graduate of the Army Airborne, Ranger, and Chaplain Schools. His military career culminated as Assistant Chief of Chaplains, guiding fifteen hundred Army Reserve chaplains and chaplain assistants across the world.

Ray and his wife, Deborah, started and pastored a church in Georgia for eleven years, and he later served as associate pastor in a church in Colorado. After 9/11, he deployed to the Middle East as a chaplain and had the privilege of supporting military personnel full-time in two major commands in Colorado.

Ray and Deborah have been blessed by thirty-six years of marriage. They enjoy life in Colorado and their family and four grandchildren. A disabled veteran, Ray is a malignant melanoma cancer survivor, avid skier, coffee aficionado, and mentor to leaders.

JIM WILDER (PhD, Clinical Psychology, and MA, Theology, Fuller Theological Seminary) is a clinical psychologist and neurotheologian at Life Model Works who applies brain science to needs in communities and cultures. He has authored or coauthored twenty books with a strong focus on maturity and relational skills. Wilder is the thinker behind the Life Model, a lifespan guide to being fully human.

Wilder grew up in villages tucked into the Andes mountains of Colombia and travels to learn and teach resilience in places like Southern Sudan, India, Bhutan, Sri Lanka, Eastern Europe, Mexico, Korea, Thailand, Chile, Brazil, Alaska, and Canada. Wilder has been training leaders and counselors for thirty years on five continents.

Wilder takes a second look at what we often accept as reality. He is good reading for those who would rather be alive than simply comfortable. Wilder examines life and tells stories through a lens formed from years of providing therapy for trauma victims, a background in neuroscience, and his travels through many cultures. Transparency, humor, and a passion for joyful life guide his writings about brain science.

INTRODUCTION

A QUEST BEGINS

THIS BOOK TOOK FORM DURING a period of increasingly obvious family and community alienation over immigration, race, religion, police authority, the US presidency and elections, LGBTQ topics, social media viewpoints, cancel culture, and federal, state, and local management of the COVID-19 pandemic. People were becoming alienated at a rapid pace. While their families and friends were sick and dying from a variety of causes, Dr. Jim Wilder, a psychologist with a brain science background, and retired Brigadier General Ray Woolridge suddenly found themselves working together for the same not-for-profit social agency created to improve relationships globally.

Wilder's work involved applying newly developing, relational brain science to rehumanizing people after the damage done by violence, wars, disasters, and human predators. His goal was teaching people to be their best selves using the way the brain learns.

Woolridge retired from the military the day before starting his not-for-profit work, which is aimed at helping the world's largest religious group—the approximately 2.4 billion Christians[1]—to build strong, protective, and life-giving relationships with the individuals inhabiting this planet. This target group was, instead, increasingly alienating huge numbers of people. Ray was particularly interested in why some church leaders were so adept at alienating others.

This book is not a research paper but the story of a quest.

Wilder and Woolridge undertook this two-part quest together. Wilder would explore how the brain came to see others as enemies—and sometimes hate them. Based on these patterns, Wilder would create brain-based escapes from enemy mode thinking and ways to "refriend" those who'd been alienated. Woolridge would approach leaders in this expansive faith community and find out if they would understand, value, and lead an effort to escape enemy mode thinking and behavior.

The same brains that can unite us can also divide us. What could be discovered about enemy mode from current research? How does enemy mode impact human relationships in various settings: family and community conflicts, police violence, military training and recovery for veterans, medical care, corporate offices, corrections, race relations, and spiritual life?

Enemy mode has touched every life and institution. Can we escape?

ENEMY MODE
IN DAILY LIFE

THE GROCERY STORY WAS NEARLY EMPTY when Jim heard metal hit metal. He turned to see a woman in her seventies repeatedly smashing her grocery cart into the cart of a woman half her age. It was the early 2020s—a global pandemic was raging, and enemy mode was spreading more rapidly than COVID-19. The older woman's shouting was muffled by the mask she wore. The younger woman wore no mask. The younger woman glared silently, but belligerently, at her assailant. A man in his twenties intervened almost instantly. "Get away from her," he told the older woman. "She is going to get you sick. Stay away from her."

All three brains were in enemy mode. Because of Jim's background in neuropsychology, he suspected that a specific brain state was causing a rapid transmission of alienation from person to person. The human brain is a natural amplifier, easily detecting unfriendly signals and returning them with more intensity. Enemy mode feels as if "you are not on my side." We don't like people being against us. We don't like the way enemy mode feels. Suspicion, wariness, and hostility toward others, even those trying to help, follows. Relational joy levels drop drastically.

Most shoppers would have recognized the COVID symptoms as a fever and dry cough. Few would recognize the symptoms of enemy mode in the brain as they stared at the banging carts, angry faces, and rapidly escalating hostility that was sucking them into the conflict. Instead, bystanders blamed the conflict on differing beliefs about COVID between the two ladies. Yet, shoppers who were not banging carts also held differing beliefs.

ENEMY MODE SYMPTOMS VARY

Could one brain state explain why we hate, stop listening, stop talking, start blaming, raise our voices, see others as against us, want them to lose, unfriend, post nasty remarks online, sue others, fall out of love, divorce, stop caring, abuse, bully, feel alienated, despise a politician, race or religious group, start wars, or carry out a genocide? Those reactions may be hot and cold, attacking and withdrawing, silent and loud. The elderly woman with the demolition derby grocery cart was in a hot and angry enemy mode. The younger lady in the store without a mask was in a cold and calculating enemy mode. The same person can be in either at different times. Opposite beliefs and both sides of an issue can react alike. Could one brain state create a whole range of social issues from genocides to lynchings, from domestic violence to confrontations in our local supermarkets? What can these social issues have in common? If there is a brain state behind these symptoms, then knowing how it starts, spreads contagiously, and lingers could help us escape enemy mode.

Characteristics of a Brain in Enemy Mode

- wants the "enemy to lose"
- can't discern when others are trying to help
- recruits others to attack the enemy
- feels justified in hating
- sees other people's motives as "bad"
- turns people into objects (not fellow humans)
- feels alone (no one on "my" side)
- will often attack or withdraw from allies
- sees enemy mode as a strength

After Jim witnessed the altercation at the supermarket, he realized that recognizing enemy mode did not help him stop it. Enemy mode spreads quickly but dissipates slowly. Words easily escalate enemy mode but are rarely enough to disarm it. As soon as people in enemy mode start talking, they can more easily lose friends. People want the other person to lose and find it rather hard to "let go" or "move on." Battles can be long and expenses huge. Sometimes people die.

Law enforcement is often called into enemy mode situations to try and stop the damage, so Jim went to see what his friend Ed Khouri knew. Khouri served in law enforcement for years and saw police officers face, and also exhibit, both cold and hot enemy mode. Either kind could escalate dangerously. For instance, domestic violence calls inevitably put officers between people in enemy mode. A brain in enemy mode cannot tell when others are trying to help. For those involved, having officers present felt like a threat, not a help. If the officers themselves went into enemy mode, they increased the use of force rather than de-escalated the situation. Khouri's stories made it clear that engaging people who are in enemy mode should only be attempted by people who are not.

Neutralizing enemy mode was sounding like disarming a ticking bomb. Jim worked for Life Model Works, an organization that aimed to solve such problems. When the shopping carts began colliding, Jim recognized enemy mode quickly, but was unable to help anyone escape. That bothered him, but that was also his job. Jim felt his shoulders getting tight. He needed to know what made the bomb tick.

The Army General Joins the Quest

Jim's Board of Directors informed him that Ray Woolridge, a retired US Army Brigadier General, had been hired as Executive Director of Life Model Works. The General should know something about enemy mode, but would Ray endorse getting *out* of enemy mode? Would a General consider enemy mode a weakness or an asset?

Most of Jim's childhood friends, neighbors, and teachers had been Mennonites or Brethren pacifists. These traditions, along with "plain people" like the Amish, refused military service during the religious wars between Protestants and Catholics that spread across Europe for centuries. Would the General be on his side, Jim wondered? Of course, feeling that someone is not on your side could be a symptom of enemy mode starting between him and the General.

Jim's job was converting the best brain science and theory into the simplest real-life applications. Ray joined Jim's work applying neuroscience to build resilient people and cultures. On the trauma recovery side, they helped people recover from damage that family, tribe, race, religion, and nationality had done to them through people in enemy mode. On the resilience side, they taught relational skills that built joyful relationships.

Ray admired Jim's work and was beginning to grasp that staying relational was the opposite of enemy mode, but could he live that out? Ray didn't know if he could stay relational in his personal life, much less while leading an organization. Ray was about to be working on himself.

He knew he could get things done by ignoring relational cues. Ray sensed an inner impression: "Rush to relationships; the tasks will take care of themselves!" Could he embody this impression? Could Ray lead a nonprofit organization dedicated to helping people become more relational?

The world's 2.4 billion Christians constitute one of every five people on earth. The Life Model Works' "big hairy audacious goal"[1] was training these Christians to form caring attachments with their enemies sponta-neously—a seemingly impossible mission. According to their founder, Christians should be distinguished by their ability and eagerness to form good relationships with people who act like enemies. "Love your ene-mies," Jesus said.[2] The Life Model Works strategy was to teach this largest religious group on earth how to do what they claim to believe. Jim and Ray were aiming to help the world stop living as enemies. The question was "How?" Were there helpful solutions that actually worked?

What is your impression of Christians? The US has a higher per-centage of Christians than most of the world. Statistically, two out of every three people in enemy mode at the grocery store would consider themselves Christian. Yet, Jim saw no one get out of enemy mode or, for that matter, seem to even try.

John Lennon imagined a world without religion. Ray and Jim imag-ined a world where people did what they said they believed. What would life be like if one out of every five people actively, skillfully, and enthusiastically loved their enemies? This book is for all who hope our best selves will become friends, not enemies.

ENEMY MODE CREATES RELATIONAL BLINDNESS

The trouble is that enemy mode produces relational blindness and keeps us from seeing people as fellow humans with value. Some peo-ple succumb to this more easily than others. Jim needed to know much more about the process. He decided to observe everything he could about enemy mode. Since enemy mode doesn't dissipate quickly, it proves easy to observe. Could careful study reveal a way to slow or even prevent its spread?

Jim knew that signals pass through the brain in a specific order. Damage along the path will block the signal flow. Visual blindness happens for several reasons: no light gets into the eyes, the eye is damaged, nerves to the brain are damaged, the occipital lobe of the brain is injured, or signals from the visual cortex do not reach other parts of the brain. In this last case, people might be blind but are still able to avoid obstacles they could not consciously see.

Jim's mother suddenly lost her vision in half of each eye when she was in her seventies. The problem was not in her eyes, but rather down the signal path beyond the optic chiasma on one side of her head. X-rays revealed that a cyst filled with cerebral-spinal fluid was putting pressure on the right side of her brain. She would need brain surgery.

Jim's dad called the doctor as soon as these symptoms appeared. He recognized that having only half of one's vision was not normal. Several years before, however, he'd also noticed that his wife had stopped seeing other people's points of view. She only had "vision" for her own opinion and perspective. When it came to dealing with others, she only "saw" one side—her own. The growing cyst was causing both her visual and her relational blindness. Jim's dad did not call the doctor. To him this self-oriented, self-absorbed, and relationally blind half-vision seemed normal enough even though his wife hadn't always been that way.

If seeing both sides is normal, that means people who don't have that capacity are experiencing some kind of pressure, not usually from a cyst, but rather from emotional and relational sources. The inability to see other people's points of view is a symptom of something abnormal in the brain.

MEANWHILE, BACK AT THE GROCERY STORE . . .

After the initial altercation between the two women, Jim became aware of other shoppers showing symptoms of enemy mode. A man walking down Jim's aisle glanced with contempt at the traffic flow arrow—a product of early COVID protocols—taped to the grocery store floor. His face said, "I dare you to say something to me." A brain in enemy mode is blind to others' motives and thinks everyone else is in enemy mode as well. A brain in enemy mode sees other people's motives as "bad" without the slightest curiosity about what is in the other's mind. Helping others out of enemy mode can be dangerous; helpers are frequently attacked.

In another section of the store, the cart-crashing woman was agitatedly telling her side of the mask issue to anyone who would listen. A brain in enemy mode recruits others to resist or attack the enemy. Sometimes a brain in enemy mode feels like "I'm fighting for my life" and escalates a conflict, blind to the damage created.

The younger woman without a mask passed Jim while avoiding eye contact, thus increasing her relational blindness. Her expression would have melted asphalt. A brain in enemy mode wants the other side to lose. Making others lose is a "win" in enemy mode, regardless of the cost.

As Jim neared the checkout, a middle-aged man with earphones pushed past. He was not angry but was relationally blind at the moment; he simply didn't notice that the obstacles in his path were human. A brain in enemy mode turns

A brain in enemy mode:

- sees other people's motives as "bad"
- recruits others to resist or attack the enemy
- wants the other side to lose
- turns people into something like inanimate objects

people into something like inanimate objects. Annoyed looks shot his way didn't register with him. He had created a mild enemy reaction in others.

Since enemy mode sees other people more like objects than humans, shouldn't we suspect something went wrong in the brain? The brain uses the posterior cingulate cortex to recognize members of our species. The cingulate is one of the most vulnerable areas of the brain when it comes to injury or toxins. It is also vulnerable to fatigue and stress. When impaired, the cingulate fails to respond to members of our species and cannot distinguish them from objects like rocks, hats, or chairs.

Just as there is a pathway for visual signals passing through the brain that converts light into vision, there is a pathway for signals that reveal we are with another sentient human being. This social awareness pathway travels directly through the cingulate. If cingulate processing fails, we become relationally blind. While the cingulate is only one part of the pathway we need for relational vision, as we will see, the practical question is how we get the pathway working once again when something goes wrong.

ESCAPING ENEMY MODE

We might think the solution is to avoid enemy mode in the first place. The problem is, simple avoidance doesn't work. Slipping into enemy mode is too quick and easy, and it spreads just as quickly and easily. And once the brain has identified a specific person or topic as the enemy, it responds even faster the next time. We can become increasingly lonely and depressed . . . unless we get faster at "refriending." The brain systems that detect potential danger can "unfriend" others before we are even conscious that we have seen them. This speed can be protective but very reactive and unfair. The speed is meant as a warning to the brain and not as a final rejection of others. While this warning is hardwired in the brain, the refriending process must be learned.

While going into enemy mode is like falling down a hill, refriending is more like walking up the hill. Refriending is the process of changing how we react to others, from antagonism to finding the best outcome for both sides.

That day in the grocery store, Jim left feeling frustrated. Despite everything he knew as a neuroscientist, he was unable to help anyone in the store refriend their "enemies." Recognizing the different styles of enemy mode and knowing how people got there wasn't helping anyone refriend. Could he "reverse engineer" enemy mode and find practical ways to escape it? The brain is a learning machine . . . now if he could just teach escape in the way the brain learns. If refriending became contagious, fewer people would leave grocery stores in enemy mode.

While the fast warning systems in the brain that trigger enemy mode are mostly visual and nonverbal, the most common approach to recovery is through talking about our beliefs. However, beliefs and words develop far later in the brain's relational pathway than where enemy mode starts. How well does "talking it out" work to refriend?

Talking through conflict with friends and family members can offer some relief. Even then, we continue to be a bit more guarded with one another. We've all been surprised the next morning when loved ones who are still in enemy mode continue the attack. We thought the disagreement had been resolved. There we are, right back in enemy mode!

Talking things through might even speed the next enemy mode episode. The warning systems in the brain will fire to warn us to anticipate an enemy when we see the people involved in painful conversations that drag on and on. Talking can even escalate enemy mode. Marriages and in-law relationships frequently deteriorate while talking.

Another common attempt to get out of enemy mode is to let some time pass. The time that passes is always longer than the time it took to get into enemy mode. The next enemy mode episode can begin before we get out of the last one. The brain starts into enemy mode more easily and quickly each round.

If we keep falling down the same hill with someone or a certain kind of person and have the hardest time climbing back up, we default to enemy mode with them. Is it even in our best interest to learn to escape enemy mode quickly? We will resist escaping enemy mode because it feels like a kind of protection. Refriending will then sound like a bad idea. Watch children being told to say they are sorry, kiss, and make up. The women crashing shopping carts were not asking for anyone's help either.

Few people see enemy mode as a problem or weakness. Some people even see enemy mode as a sort of body armor or strategy for victory. Since enemy mode produces a degree of relational blindness, it facilitates conflict. Jim, the pacifistically inclined neuropsychologist, was concerned when Ray, the retired Army general, commented that enemy mode operations might be necessary when real threats were present.

HOW RAY DISCOVERED HIS OWN NEED TO REFRIEND

While Jim was watching the pandemic produce enemy mode reactions in the grocery store, Ray was beginning to see his own enemy mode reactions manifesting at home. During the pandemic, Ray's entire family was living together for the first time in ten years. Most of Ray's family had moved in for the holidays and were working in his home where he worked as well. Another son, with his wife and three children, visited often. Ray and his wife Deborah's four-bedroom home was constantly filled with ten adults, four children aged five and under, plus five pets. Despite the chaos, it was a fun family reunion with a lot of late nights and good food.

Ray had just started as executive director and could not take a vacation. Could he stay relational with his family while getting his work done? Some days he could. Other days, he found his mind racing, urging him to get back to work. He fought his hardwired brain the whole month.

"Several times one of the kids would ask my wife, 'What's wrong with Dad?'" Ray recalls. "In the past, my wife, Deborah, would have said, 'Dad has to work.' Back then, I would quickly disappear to my office without another word. This time, neither of us did that."

Ray was getting his relational vision restored. Partnering with Jim began to open Ray to change, even if he didn't know where to begin.

But Ray still observed his enemy mode while at work. For three months, Ray found his new job was like a carnival "whack a mole" game. Ray had learned to decide quickly, often without collaboration, and then later inform his team of the decision. He thrived making decisions in this "whack a mole" manner. That had worked in his military career, but what about now?

Ray was leading a meeting of his new team when an executive questioned two decisions Ray had made unilaterally. The executive told him, "You were nonrelational when you made these decisions." Ray readily agreed with the executive but was stunned by his recurring relational blindness under stress. He knew he had to learn to lead collaboratively and stay relational.

When Ray used enemy mode as his best tool, he was not being relational. His neural pathways became hardwired so that he responded quickly to challenges in the way he always had. Could Ray learn a new way to lead in his sixth decade of life? A successful leader usually doesn't change, especially in their sixties. Could he become relational and collaborative and escape the transactional and controlling ways of enemy mode?

THE BIG WHY BEHIND THE QUEST

Ray and Jim's interest in escaping enemy mode was professional. After all, it was their job. But the mission was also fueled by deep personal pain and a longing for life change.

Two Phone Calls

Two surprising phone calls in 2008, twelve years before Ray began his work at Life Model Works, opened his mind to his need for change. The first was a dream fulfilled.

The US Army Major General and Chief of Chaplains called to say, "Ray, congratulations on your selection for promotion to Brigadier General!"

Ray and his family were overjoyed. He felt elated by news of his promotion and was eager to make a difference for the Army. They held a party to celebrate with their five children. He would serve three years as the Assistant Chief of Chaplains assigned to the Pentagon.

The second phone call soon after was a nightmare. Ray's doctor interrupted the celebration: "I am sorry to tell you that malignant melanoma has returned, and it is in three of your lymph nodes. We will have to do surgery and chemotherapy or radiation."

Ray and Deborah didn't know how their lives would change after these two phone calls. Ray was terrified, angry, and began having trouble sleeping. Not long afterward, he decided to do all he could to beat cancer and succeed as Assistant Chief of Chaplains. He only knew one way to do that: focusing on his work. With a real threat present, Ray became relationally blind to his wife and family. He didn't see how his focus was empowered by enemy mode. Ray's enemy mode cost them a lot.

Treatment began immediately and continued for the next six years with multiple surgeries, immunotherapy, and radiation. Meanwhile, Ray "soldiered on" and traveled as Assistant Chief of Chaplains half of each month. Time to connect relationally with his wife and family was not a priority.

Deborah was extraordinarily supportive. She selflessly served him and their family while he battled cancer and served in the Army. She became Ray's hero! Deborah carried him when Ray couldn't take another step. She was also a homeschooling mother and had to care for herself, her sick husband, and their family of five children without losing herself in the process. In that season, two sons suffered serious injuries. A daughter and son graduated from high school. Two sons graduated college, got married, and began serving in the Army—both deployed to Afghanistan the same year.

While Ray fought melanoma and traveled for the Army, Deborah suffered emotionally. She had a husband who could not feel and validate her pain, isolation, and fear. Ray's relational blindness cost them both dearly.

The General's Enemy Mode Surrenders to Deborah's Refriending

During that painful season, Deborah began to communicate honestly about how Ray's actions had made her feel, not just during his career change and health challenges, but for three decades. Ray's dangerous cancer diagnosis had fueled her determination to live the rest of her life without regret. She was a relational person in ways Ray was not.

Cancer and Deborah became Ray's wake-up calls. Ray knew that career success was meaningless if the cost was making his wife and children feel unseen and unheard.

The couple had many hard conversations. Eventually a pattern emerged that is common for communication-based efforts to climb back up the hill after slipping into enemy mode. Deborah would speak about the pain Ray made her feel. His mind would immediately switch into enemy mode. Ray would be distant for a few days. Deborah would refriend Ray, and they would start again.

Slowly, Ray realized that Deborah might not be an enemy. She was actually very good at refriending because she kept helping him escape enemy mode. She gave Ray hope that refriending was possible. She provided powerful working examples. Now when Ray thinks of Deborah, he feels warm gratitude, admiration, anticipation, and the unworthy sense of being treasured. In a word, he feels love. Ray is forever indebted to her.

Ray Discovers His Enemy Mode

"As a direct result of being refriended," Ray says, "three discoveries changed my life."

Ray's first discovery was how thoroughly nonrelational he had learned to be. He remembers, "I treated others, even my loved ones, as transactions. My brain was focused on doing rather than being. I found it hard to be present in the moment with others."

Deborah would frequently say to Ray, "I don't feel connected to you," and he would have no idea what she meant. Ray would answer, "We've been doing things together all day! I don't understand. How can you feel that way?"

Deborah's understandable longings continually collided with Ray's relational blindness and lack of emotional intelligence—both symptoms of enemy mode in the brain. He mistakenly concluded the problem was with her, but he was wrong. He was beginning to understand and share what Deborah felt when he locked her out like she was the enemy. The problem was his.

"My second discovery," Ray says, "was how early in life I learned to operate in what I now know is enemy mode. Good grades brought approval at home and so I worked harder to achieve. Achievement drove me early in my career in the infantry and later as a pastor and senior chaplain in the Army. In the military I learned to win the argument, hold my ground, dominate the opposition, and get things done, no matter who or what stood in my way. Back then, I was a husband and father in enemy mode. I pastored a church the way I had led in the military—nonrelationally. That may sound odd, but I didn't know any other way to be."

"Once I became aware of enemy mode, I saw it everywhere in my life. I discovered that even though I had thought I was physically and spiritually mature, I was emotionally and relationally still a child in some areas."

While researching with Jim, Ray remembered a typical moment of enemy mode. "One night at home the Apple TV remote was missing, and our oldest granddaughter wanted to watch *Daniel Tiger*. I was frustrated and I blamed everyone in the room. I knew that someone else was at fault! My heart was racing, and my vision was narrowing. I didn't know it, but I was in enemy mode and everyone else was the enemy. There was no one on my side. I said and did things I would regret."

Most painful to Ray was his third discovery. What had living to win cost him? He usually acted as if mission and task were everything. He got the mission accomplished without staying relationally connected. Ray turned on the charm to win key people to his mission. As we'll see later, this is enemy mode at its intelligent worst.

Ray's beliefs were not the source of his enemy mode. He genuinely believed people had value and worth because of who they were, not what they did. But his manipulations made others feel like cogs in a machine, not friends and partners. Ray would feel lonely in leadership and wonder why he had no deep relationships. He told himself, "That's just the way it is, let's get back to work."

Christians and Jim's Enemy Mode

Jim grew up in Colombia, South America, where his Protestant mother did literacy work with women and children in Catholic villages. She began teaching before Jim was born while World War II raged around the world. It was a time of violent civil unrest in the country where an estimated quarter of a million people were killed by their neighbors. The old antipathies between Catholics and Protestants— hatred that had caused so many European wars—still raged in Colombia. Protestants were denied medical treatment in Catholic hospitals. When Jim's mother developed appendicitis, the local Catholic doctor saw his opportunity to kill her and, after she survived, to cause her pain and suffering.

Jim's mother belonged to a little missions group made up mostly of Mennonite pacifists who rejected violence, so the Wilder family did not leave. Jim cannot remember how young he was when he learned what the local doctor had done. As he grew up, anything Catholic set off fierce amygdala alarms in his brain. His mind flooded with anger, fear, and attachment pain for what his mother had suffered. Catholics horrified him; Catholic symbols panicked him. Every Saturday morning at 5 a.m., a priest brought a procession and stopped in front of Jim's window. The priests knew where the Protestants were. The crowd outside was not on his side. He looked out his window at their torches, knowing Catholics had burned Protestant churches with everyone inside. Jim went deeply into enemy mode each Saturday morning.

Centuries of disagreements about beliefs had separated Protestants and Catholics, but given that the relational processing pathway in the brain did not start with beliefs but rather with alarm systems, the solution to enemy mode did not lie in discussing beliefs. Since most of the 2.4 billion Christians in the world are Catholic, Jim knew he needed to face his own enemy mode. Teaching others to escape enemy mode meant some brain changes for him as well.

Escaping enemy mode needed to start with Jim and Ray making their personal escapes. The trouble in the grocery story made it clear that some method of helping others out of enemy mode was also needed. It was becoming increasingly clear that much talking, discussing, and changing beliefs was not the path forward. How could the science help Jim—and the rest of the world—escape enemy mode?

THE QUEST FOR ESCAPE

Ray was an expert at working and living in enemy mode without knowing it. Enemy mode felt like an asset. Leaders, entrepreneurs, politicians, ambitious pastors, and even parents eager for their children to excel unknowingly employed enemy mode for the win. Ray was not about to give up being a winner, but might there be a way to stay relational throughout the last season of his life? As Ray talked with Jim, who was already working on the brain science involved, he saw the relational cost he was paying for distancing his wife and children emotionally. Ray's growing compassion made him long for an alternative way to excel without slipping into enemy mode at home and causing harm to his family relationships.

But outside the home, could Ray actually lead a mission to change how Christians operate in the world without operating in what he had come to realize was enemy mode? If enemy mode was a necessary asset, how did that square with Jesus' command to love even our enemies?

Ray and Jim met to see where they stood. Jim asked if Ray could explain enemy mode to Christian leaders he knew; Ray asked if Jim could explain how the brain escapes enemy mode. Neither one could. This intersection of spiritual life and brain science remained elusive. But Ray liked the relational challenge, and Jim was going to figure out the science if he could.

Escaping enemy mode and taking the world with them became their quest.

ESCAPING NEEDS TO SPREAD

The more Ray researched his own experience, the more he wondered: Could he get church and ministry leaders to recognize enemy mode and then see it as a weakness? Would leaders see the harm enemy mode was doing to them and the people in their organizations? Why were so many Christians continually in enemy mode?

Ray was determined to find out why so many impressive leaders were disappointing in private. Many acted like winning was all that mattered. Some compelling speakers led beneficial projects, acquired social media followers, and influenced thousands but could be unbearable up close and personal. Like they say in Texas, they were "all hat and no cattle."

Ray had a vast network of influential leaders, mostly Christians, he counted as colleagues and friends—retired military generals, a former congressman, police officers, CEOs, business coaches, chaplains, pastors, entrepreneurs, and nonprofit leaders. As the list grew of those he might enlist to help, Ray was overwhelmed but eager to find out who would join the quest.

Ray's first attempts to describe enemy mode felt like speaking in an unknown language. After all, his colleagues and friends were in the winner's circle. Many of them also worked nonrelationally and had developed a relational blindness to other options. Giving up a favored way of working in exchange for an unknown relational way made no sense: How could they win at work and stay relational? No one was willing to lose productivity.

Refriending was not only for his personal life but also his professional life. Even if he had always thought enemy mode was sometimes needed, refriending would always be needed. Ray's new goal was living and leading relationally both at home and at work.

The Problem with Winning

A brain in enemy mode is all about the win. Enemy mode lacks compassion. Enemy mode lacks attachment. Enemy mode fights for status. At the same time, the human brain is deeply relational, so why not become more relational people? We would find the least harmful solution to conflicts and escape enemy mode more quickly. A rehumanized life would see us bring out our best selves—and the best in others—rather than making others lose. Rehumanized means to be fully human, living with our whole brain. Enemy mode dehumanizes because the person in enemy mode is not living as their best self with their whole brain.

Jim observed enemy mode during the 2016 and 2020 presidential elections. Both Hillary Clinton and Donald Trump declared themselves Christians; the same was true for Trump and Joe Biden. However, it would be difficult to look to these three leaders as examples of loving our enemies and easy to see their interactions, instead, as illustrations of enemy mode.

In enemy mode, making the other side lose is a win. This desire to see the other side lose was quite strong among voters, many of whom perpetuate enemy mode thinking for their "side." Many voters were not too keen on their candidate but clear about who they opposed. Several of Jim's relatives proudly posted who they hated on social media, encouraging everyone to join the hate. The contagious nature of this thinking provided clickbait for the media.

Jonathan Haidt, a social psychologist at New York University, had grave concerns about the corrosive effects of social media. Twitter and Facebook had become the modern public square with the power to shape news coverage, government policy, and interpersonal relationships. Haidt said: "When our public square is governed by mob dynamics unrestrained by due process, we don't get justice and inclusion; we get a society that ignores context, proportionality, mercy, and truth."[3] A hate pandemic does not build herd immunity—except for immunity to other points of view.

The soldier and the chaplain in Ray were having a talk. Was life about winning, or about becoming a better person? When Ray looked around, he noticed most people chose winning. Making winning the *only* value in life was a symptom of both enemy mode and sociopathic thinking. Ray was looking for his best self and wondering what fueled the need to win.

Can Ray Stay Relational and Get Work Done?

Once he addressed enemy mode and refriending in his own home, Ray wondered how to embody refriending at work and how to ensure that his leadership was doing the same. At Life Model Works, Ray was leading an organization that aimed to provide practical and advanced tools to help people in their relationships, yet the leaders had inconsistently embodied escaping enemy mode. Ray discovered some broken relationships, narcissism, and relational blindness among both leadership and staff. Would the organization embody refriending? How Life Model Works operated, collaborated with partners, and engaged supporters and the rest of the world was at stake. Could this organization reform and then raise the funding needed to develop a solution that worked well enough to spread?

Training the world's Christians to escape enemy mode would need to start internally. Ray took direct action. He set up a meeting with staff. The staff regretted their history of enemy mode and lamented how widespread enemy mode was with Christians. In general, most Christian groups were relationally blind to each other as allies. Some groups attacked while others withdrew. A brain in enemy mode attacks or withdraws from allies.

Ray doubted Christians would actually embrace loving our enemies, even though that is what Jesus taught. Managing distrust, disagreements, or even hate would not be enough. Refriending needed real relational attachments where none existed. Jim suspected that, as a strategist, Ray had calculated the chances of success correctly. There were six people working for his organization against 2.4 billion scattered around the world.

TWO INVESTIGATORS ON A QUEST

As early as grade school, Jim was fascinated by diseases and famous scientists who solved how illness spread and did its damage. Understanding causes led to prevention. Jim studied Anton van Leeuwenhoek's work with bacteria and Louis Pasteur's work with anthrax, chickenpox, cholera, and rabies. He also studied Alexander Fleming, Jonas Salk, and the Mayo brothers. Alfred Nobel and Madame Curie inspired Jim to believe he could make a difference by figuring out the things that were killing people.

As a teenager, Jim drew diagrams of the cranial nerves. His prize possession was a microscope. When hemorrhagic Lassa fever broke out in Africa, he dreamed of finding the cause. As Oliver Sacks used L-Dopa to awaken encephalitis patients, Jim followed the weekly updates in the *Science Newsletter*. Dr. Sacks went on to become the storyteller of brain science for his generation.

In graduate school, Jim built research equipment, learned neurofeedback, and trained at VA hospitals before brain scan machines existed. He learned to read EEG brain waves and test for brain damage using A. R. Luria's methods. Luria had refined ways to check the function of each brain element in a processing pathway. Tracing brain signals was very similar to the electronic system diagnosis Jim had studied in college. Knowing what each stage of a television should do allowed the symptoms to reveal the part that was not working. A signal would be damaged or missing beyond the point of failure. Now Jim was eager to trace the source for enemy mode processing in the brain and discover where the symptoms started and how they got passed forward through the brain's processing streams.

Damaged brains dropped easily into enemy mode. Jim worked in a brain injury unit for patients with brain tumors, strokes, or motorcycle accidents. He expected to help restore memory function and muscle usage. The patients' families were more concerned by how easily the patients went "postal" and treated their families as instant enemies. Knowing where the damage had been done explained the behavior but provided few solutions.

Jim and Ray, a pacifist and a military man, a scientist and a pastor, fellow workers with their own enemy mode issues, agreed that what they wanted was to see the whole world refriending with the same speed that people were slipping into enemy mode. Gandalf and the General, their friends dubbed them. Impressive monikers, but now they needed a solution that actually worked.

As they began strategizing, Ray turned his attention to his many influential friends. He wanted to know who would back his fight against enemy mode. Would people in power understand it and realize how it had impacted them? Would enemy mode be a necessity or a weakness in their eyes? Would they open doors for refriending?

This wasn't how Ray had pictured his new job. The idea of enemy mode was fairly new to him. He seemed to be planning a peaceful takeover of the world, or at least the badly divided Christian segment, with only six troops. The General needed backing and allies.

Jim wanted to develop a written plan. He argued that people didn't even try refriending enemies because solutions were too difficult and didn't work. Could refriending become contagious enough that people who "caught it" could pass it on? How far would it spread?

Jim would also need better science. Enemy mode killed more people than the anthrax Louis Pasteur had faced. First, he needed to understand what caused the symptoms. As Jim laid out the evidence and brain science, he observed three patterns. Not all enemy mode activity looked the same, as we will see in the next chapter.

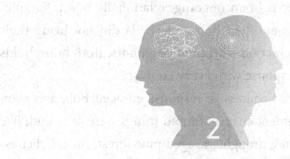

THREE TYPES OF ENEMY MODE

"IT'S TOO EARLY FOR MUSIC! TURN IT OFF!" Bob yelled at his next door neighbor, Sheila.

Sheila retorted, "I can play my music when I want."

Bob was a forty-something professional with three children still at home. His wife, Natalie, served on the neighborhood homeowners association board. They had lived in the community a long time, knew the HOA rules, and had status in the community.

Sheila's husband, Joe, was retired military. They bought their dream home right next door to Bob and Natalie in a location near their adult children and grandchildren. Sheila and Joe resented how Bob and Natalie "weaponized" the HOA covenants. It was common for Bob and Natalie to appear at neighbors' doors citing rule violations, with no apparent interest in building a neighborly relationship. Many other neighbors also felt unwelcome. Bob and Natalie avoided relationships and kept everything about the rules.

The two families lived in an ongoing, relationally blind, "simple" enemy mode with one another. Bob and Sheila did not bring their best selves to their interaction with their neighbors. Both households anticipated a hostile response with every contact.

That Saturday, Sheila's aggressive response enraged Bob, and soon an out-of-control argument ensued. Stupid things were said, and, like lightning starts a fire in a drought-ravaged pine forest, the conflict escalated when Bob threatened Sheila: "You better get your idiot husband out here to defend you."

Sheila called the police instead. "Stupid" enemy mode is intense and usually short-lived. People say things that don't reflect their best selves or long-term interests. The police are often called during stupid enemy mode escalations.

Bob and his wife, Natalie, retaliated by aiming their security cameras at Sheila and Joe's house. The two began a campaign to convince neighbors that Sheila and Joe were dangerous and crazy. *Joe might even have PTSD. He was retired military.*

A careful campaign such as Bob and Natalie's signals "intelligent" enemy mode. Enemy weaknesses are scouted and analyzed for places to attack. Attacks are pre-planned so that enemies will have the least chance of defending themselves and will lose. Bob and Natalie wanted Joe and Sheila to lose.

Sheila and Joe countered by verifying the city ordinances and proving that their music was within the permitted decibel level. The dispute escalated. A restraining order was threatened but did not receive police support. Most neighbors quietly developed simple enemy mode toward both families, hoping someone would move.

Simple enemy mode had people expecting the worst of others. Stupid enemy mode was lighting fires with long-term consequences. Intelligent enemy mode was fighting a status-and-control war. Even an open discussion could, in the presence of intelligent enemy mode, be used to plan damaging future campaigns.

Fred, the president of this HOA, had not gone relationally blind. As a retired Army colonel, he had worked for decades helping people change through Bible study and discipleship training in a nonprofit. He was a naturally positive and optimistic leader who now worked as a professional leadership coach.

How was Fred to help his neighborhood escape enemy mode? He had relational skill training and saw the need for a relational solution to this expanding conflict, so he consulted with Ray. But Ray was stumped. He didn't know how to advise Fred but did know an enemy mode solution: Fred could overcome Bob and Natalie by viewing the HOA fight as something to "win" by making them lose.

A common powerful enemy mode solution for Ray would have been to "power up" and overwhelm the opposition with logic and his forceful personality. After all, Ray had always aspired to be a powerful person who got things done. His achievements had come through enemy mode, but so had his losses. The more Ray studied enemy mode, the more tangled his life seemed. His relational blindness was a common occurrence. He only knew an enemy mode way to win here.

To Think Like, but Not Be In, Enemy Mode

If Fred had been operating in simple, stupid, or intelligent enemy mode, his brain would not be capable of building community. But—and this was a big one—Fred would need to understand how people in enemy mode think, and his brain would need to simulate the three types of enemy mode he was facing. Fred needed to think as if he were in enemy mode. His mental simulator could then work out the least harmful solutions.

Ray realized he would need to avoid enemy mode solutions as he helped Fred, so he called Jim. Meanwhile, Jim needed to figure out the difference between a relational brain that understands and escapes and one that falls into enemy mode. There would not be much difference, but the difference would be crucial.

OUR BRAINS ARE RELATIONAL

Even people who don't think of themselves as particularly relational are still running relational brains. The central relational areas of the brain have been called the social engagement system, attachment system, limbic system, right brain, control center, relational circuits, master system, and the fast track depending on which functions are being studied. The relational circuits provide our identity.

Jim and Ray built on a brain model that traces, in large part, to Dr. Allan Schore's work on how the brain develops an identity, a self. For Dr. Schore (and this book), the working self (identity) develops through relational attachments. The right brain is dominant for our identity, using systems that run faster than conscious thought.

Jim pondered the brain science and realized that Ray's powerful enemy mode solutions were learned behavior that arose from deep in his brain. To find solutions, Jim needed to dig deep into the science of how the brain works. How do our brains unite or divide us?

The Brain's Relational Circuits (RCs)

The identity master system has four levels of integration we will call the relational circuits (RCs).

Level One: As the brain processes the experience of "me here now," the activity begins deep in the brain. The structures involved are the thalamus and basal ganglia. Level One quickly determines how much energy our body is about to need and sends out the orders to pump the necessary chemicals. The brain determines whether something in the input stream is personal to me—a smile, a snake, an angry look—or not, like paint drying. Each moment has its own energy needs. Level One starts the energy response and passes the input stream to Level Two for evaluation. Simple enemy mode does not produce sufficient brain activity and thus Level One lacks arousal. When most dogs see a person, they will run over to sniff and be greeted. In the HOA scenario, neither of the couples in conflict saw the other as humans to "greet." Their Level One response stayed off.

Level Two: Level Two divides the input into pleasurable (good) and unpleasurable (bad/scary) streams. The structures involved are the amygdala and hippocampus, where memory associations are stored. The amygdala labels the input stream as good, bad, or scary using memories as a reference. These implicit memories produce no sense of being "remembered." We just "know" we hate broccoli without recalling when we learned how it tastes. Level Two's opinion—GOOD, "love that broccoli," or BAD, "hate disgusting broccoli!"—is added to the input stream on its way to the brain's cortex. The energy launched by Level One is now focused into the good, bad, and scary clusters.

Historically, the brain's energy management was called *drives*. Doctors a century ago cleverly remembered these drives by words starting with "F." Most people have heard two of these Fs: fight or flight.[1] When Level Two detects pleasurable input, energy enters the GOOD stream. We seek these joy-related experiences. Doctors remembered these pleasurable drives as feeding, fornication, and fun. Most medical attention was given to fight, flight, frown, feed, and fornicate as those seemed more like drives.

When Level Two detects unpleasurable input, adrenaline energy becomes:

FIGHT = Bad + Scary, so run toward it and make it stop
FLIGHT = Scary, so run away
FROWN = Bad, so lower energy as this will waste my effort,
         but I cannot get away

Level Two does more than direct the body's energy responses; it tags the brain's energy systems using the seven hardwired emotions: joy, anger, sadness, fear, disgust, hopelessness, and shame. When either of the HOA couples thought of the other, Level Two said "bad" and added anger, hopelessness, and likely other emotions.

Level Three: The input stream now enters a very relational Level Three. The central structure is the right cingulate cortex. From this point on, processing through the cortex runs more slowly. Even so, the right brain RCs run much faster than conscious thought.

Level Three is a convergence zone. The temporal, parietal, occipital, and even frontal cortices feed signals into the cingulate. This diagram

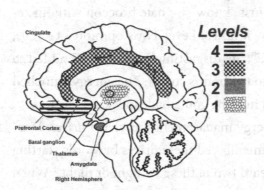

of the cingulate cortex helps us picture how it starts deep in the middle, back, and bottom of the cortex and wraps itself around and forward along the centerline of the brain before heading toward the bottom once again at the front of the brain. The cingulate gathers and integrates a huge amount of relational data as it goes forward.

Unlike the lower two pathways, the Level Three (cingulate) pathway is quite vulnerable. Processing can break down at numerous points along the way and for quite different reasons. No matter where the brain is damaged, the region most likely to suffer impairment is Level Three. Poisons, such as heavy metals, also impact the cingulate more heavily. You may have heard the expression "mad as a hatter." Hat makers once used mercury in the manufacturing process. As the poisonous heavy metal built up in their cingulate, their relationships with others became bizarre.

If emotions become too intense, the cingulate will "cramp" and block processing. With Level Three blocked, we get stupid and say and do irrational things. We also fail to understand others.

The relational objective for Level Three is understanding what another mind knows. When another person is present, the cingulate tries to figure out what the other mind is thinking by using its own experience and any cues from their face, body, and voice tone. When the two minds understand each other, they feel connected. This is a mutual mind moment. When two minds cannot connect, either can feel alone, misunderstood, ignored, rejected, or even attacked. Level Three then wonders: *Am I alone? Is this person against me? Does anybody understand? Does anybody really care?*

The emotional "flavor" of the input stream coming from Level Two makes huge demands on the cingulate. We may wonder: *What will be in other minds if I am angry, sad, afraid, disgusted, joyful, hopeless, or ashamed? Will they like me and want to be with me?* Our emotional memories predict whether people will be on our side (relational) or against us (enemies). When Sheila opened her door and saw Bob, her brain did not wait to hear what he had to say. Both brains predicted the other was "not on my side."

Like previous levels of the brain, Level Three uses implicit memory to interpret the current input stream. Implicit memories feel like "it is happening again now." Thus, the memories of the past can put the brain into enemy mode even when we do not have an enemy in sight. Sorting out our current reality is possible at Level Four but is not achieved when the cingulate is overwhelmed with intensity. The result of this intense confusion is doing and saying stupid things. (In chapter 4, we will explore stupid enemy mode.)

> **The memories of the past can put the brain into enemy mode even when we do not have an enemy in sight.**

Level Four: Level Four takes the two points of view developed at Level Three— my mind and another mind—and works to add a third perspective: an internal observer. The structure involved is the right prefrontal cortex (rPFC), sometimes also called the right orbital prefrontal cortex. Our internal observer provides our values, desires, and what the people in our identity group will think. Our identity group is determined by noticing whose examples we follow with our language, expressions, styles, values, and desire to be included. By using the perspective of how "our people" see this situation, the rPFC determines what it would be like us to do, how this reflects our values, and how this feels in our bodies. The rPFC calculates the least harmful options that are then submitted for the conscious mind's consideration and implementation.

The least harmful options may still be harmful. We should note that if our people or family or tribe have established only harmful patterns, then Level Four must pick between the fire and the frying pan. We may find ourselves doing what our parents did that we swore we would never do or say.

The way the rPFC calculates the least harmful alternative is through its ability to mentally simulate outcomes before we actually do them. This simulator can help us understand enemy mode without being in it. Unfortunately, without attachment, the simulator also produces intelligent enemy mode. We will examine that topic in chapter 5.

Fred could understand how his neighbors thought while they were in enemy mode and want to help them; he stayed out of enemy mode. When Ray heard the story, his first reaction was to help Joe and Sheila defeat Bob and Natalie. Ray did not feel attached to all four of these humans.

A CLOSER LOOK AT THE THREE ENEMY MODES

Now that we have a basic understanding of what's happening in the brain, let's take a closer look at each of the modes occurring in the people in the HOA story.

Simple Enemy Mode

Simple enemy mode is basic relational blindness: *I don't feel a connection to "it." It is not a welcome fellow human.* We do not feel like we are on the same side. An uneasy tension develops when relational connection signals are being missed, ignored, mistrusted, or feared. When we want to ignore a call that just came on our phone, we are likely having an enemy mode moment. When that unknown caller rings our doorbell and we feel instant distrust, we have entered simple enemy mode. When Jim's wife said, "Jim, we need to talk," fear started in his stomach, and his mind told him, "I am in trouble." Jim was in simple enemy mode.

Enemy mode starts with the feeling that someone is not on our side. Some people withdraw or "shelter in place" by hiding their thoughts and feelings. When others become upset by our relational blindness, simple enemy mode says, "What are you upset about?" This response can range from no awareness to feeling blindsided. There are tasks to do, schedules to keep, video games to play, sports to watch, children to help, and dogs to walk. What is all this upset about? Nothing has happened!

When two nonrelational minds work together on a task, it is not enemy mode. They are neither friends nor enemies. One orders a burger and the other serves it. The fact that the participants are human does not enter their expectations. But, as soon as someone begins looking for a human connection, both the lack of response and the seeker's upset become the beginning of enemy mode.

In the 1990s, Ray and Deborah started a new church in Georgia. Ray had no work boundaries and averaged sixty to seventy hours of church work a week. Back then, the Woolridge household was glorious chaos with a full basketball squad of five children, ten and under, at the kitchen table.

One night, Ray was exhausted. After the children were in bed, Ray ignored Deborah and withdrew to read the paper and a book.

Deborah surprised Ray by saying, through tears, "I am not important to you."

Ray was shocked and felt ambushed. Ray justified himself saying he was tired, needed downtime, and wanted to disengage. They were doing all they could to survive. The realization dawned on him that she was right. Connecting with Deborah had not been his priority. He had been ignoring her and felt ashamed. Ray's relational blindness had left Deborah in tears.

When Ray told the story, Jim responded, "You were being non-relational that night. That is simple enemy mode. Simple enemy mode leaves the people around us feeling unseen, unheard, and unimportant."

From a brain perspective, simple enemy mode is a failure to connect that results in creating distance. One person signals, "I want your attention," and the other does not respond. People looking at us, calling our names, and smiling warmly provide verbal and nonverbal cues for a desire to connect minds. That moment of connection and understanding can be called "mutual mind." We are both thinking the same thing at the same moment. These mutual moments build trust and relationships.

The absence or even repeated delay of mutual mind moments lowers trust while inducing a kind of attachment "ouch." Deep in the subcortical brain, below the level of direct conscious awareness, the brain responds to the attachment "ouch" by remembering who hurt us. For instance, a needy girlfriend or boyfriend goes there quickly anticipating that a delayed response means rejection: "I texted you over a minute ago! Where are you?"

Can you guess how the brain reacts to people who hurt us? *People who hurt us are not on our side.* The subcortical brain doesn't consider if they meant to hurt us. Other systems much higher in the brain figure out people's intentions. The brain records the "ouch" before any explanations are made.

For now, we can conclude that simple enemy mode can be produced in many ways, but they all involve some failure to "awaken" a brain to see that some other mind wanted a connection. Minds became "enemies" during omissions where "nothing happened." Simple enemy mode is an unintended relational blind spot—a low energy moment. Escaping simple enemy mode requires increased energy.

Stupid Enemy Mode

Stupid enemy mode is a high energy moment energized by "hot" anger. Stupid enemy mode says and does things that we regret later. What makes this mode "stupid" is that when we calm down or sober up we realize that the person we attacked wasn't our enemy. We destroyed things or people we valued or needed. We damaged relationships we depended upon. We were not our best selves.

The brain in enemy mode sees others as enemies whether they are or not. But why would we damage things and people we value? The answer is one of limited capacity in brain systems. To lift a rock, we need to be stronger than the rock we want to lift. To handle the brain voltage created by hot anger, we need to have strong enough circuits. If the hot anger gets too intense, we overload the flow of thoughts that move us toward intelligent actions, creating a sort of mental "cramp" that blocks the way. We are about to turn stupid.

The excessive emotional activity overloads the mutual mind processing in the brain. When our emotions are burning down the barn, we lose the opportunity to understand what others are really thinking and feeling. Without shared feelings, others turn into "enemies" who don't respond to what I feel is important.

Shared emotions are mutual mind enhancing when we have the capacity to share them. Blocked mutual mind can happen when our feelings become too intense or when our mental capacity drops. Either way, the chemical/electrical intensity of the signals passing through the brain is greater than those circuits can handle at the moment.

Many factors can reduce our capacity to handle hurtful feelings that may feel like threats when they are not. What makes our capacity drop can be a lack of training, chemicals, fatigue, or pain. Did you ever see someone get upset and say something stupid after drinking? While being overly tired? After not eating for a long period of time? When they stubbed a toe? After anesthesia? When they turned two years old?

After developing Alzheimer's or returning from war? In a situation they didn't know how to handle?

When important consequences are at stake, we need others to show understanding (mutual mind) and respond quickly. However, strong feelings can accelerate so quickly that we cannot tell if others are with us. With a blocked ability to know, our brain feels alone. There is no one on our side. The people in front of us become enemies. The feeling that becomes too intense does not have to be anger: we might hit our thumb with a hammer, be badly startled, watch someone get hurt, or even fear that something bad is going to happen.

Ray has a fair share of stupid enemy mode stories, like the night he couldn't find the Apple TV remote mentioned in chapter 1. Ray felt all alone. Everyone was his enemy because no one was helping. Ray said things he soon regretted and hurt his wife's feelings. The whole family watched the tirade. Once he cooled down, he apologized, but the damage was done.

Solutions to stupid enemy mode involve "quieting." Solutions to simple enemy mode involve increasing our energy levels. When either over- or under-aroused, the brain is not at its best. What about intelligent enemy mode? The brain is alert and running cool but has captured our intelligence to make others lose.

Intelligent Enemy Mode

Intelligent enemy mode grows out of "cold" anger—the anger that can fill the brain with thoughts, plans, revenge, resentments, lawyers, hired guns, deceptions, and even fake friendship. Intelligent enemy mode is not getting stupid or missing cues. Cold anger can turn into hate but can also last for years as a cold indifference to the pain others feel. Intelligent enemy mode can be taught and passed from one generation to the next. At the extreme end of the spectrum, intelligent enemy mode takes over communities for a drug cartel, marches people to gas chambers, waits for opportunity in prison blocks, and defends gang turf. Intelligent enemy mode recruits new members for hate groups, victims for serial predators, and followers for oppressive governments, terrorist cells, opposition groups, and radical religious groups.

While these intense forms of intelligent enemy mode feel creepy to most of us, it is not difficult to become infected with a milder version. Observe almost any workplace, divorce, affair, real estate transaction, car purchase, telephone solicitation, or traffic stop, and you will find intelligent enemy mode operations. Even common family interactions can involve plot lines and motives that are hidden and not in other family members' best interests.

Intelligent enemy mode, like the other forms of enemy mode, reveals impaired brain function. We cannot actually tell if the other person is really an enemy. Enemy mode lacks the mutual mind functions that help us know when to trust others. The result is a chronic distrust, a suspicion that others will hurt us.

The key to maintaining intelligent enemy mode is not feeling the pain others feel. At the same time, to be effective, intelligent enemy mode, is very aware of pain and uses the pain others feel for a win. Painful emotions are needed for the "success" of intelligent enemy mode provided others experience the pain while the person operating in enemy mode does not. There is no room for compassion here.

Personal insensitivity to emotions, pain, and attachments becomes a value for intelligent enemy mode operators, who live by ideas and principles, not emotions. This tendency is shared by quite a number of Christians.

While the work Ray and Jim do focuses on motivating Christians to escape enemy mode, they face a challenge: Might they trigger intelligent enemy mode opposition from Christians simply by trying to help them feel and share emotions? Could they be received as enemies? It was common for conservative Christians to distrust emotions, fearing they lead to temptation. But the tendency to think instead of feel creates its own vulnerability—developing intelligent enemy mode.

HOW DOES ENEMY MODE IMPACT ME?

All three forms of enemy mode are forms of diminished brain function. In simple mode, the brain is not sufficiently engaged. In stupid enemy mode, the brain is overdriven and not moving signals where they need to go. Intelligent enemy mode blocks pain signals. Is that how we like to feel and live, particularly when our enemies might only be in our own heads?

Enemy mode is fear-driven, constantly using our brain to calculate threats. Do we want to stay in fear? Fear motivates avoidance but not creativity. Fear drives the back of the brain to avoid pain and problems. But avoidance does not take us where we want to go.

"Don't upset your mother!" was the principle that steered Jim's childhood family. That warning might not sound like fear at first. When Jim's mom got upset, she recovered slowly. The family feared their long misery if she got upset again. It was not that Mom would explode, but the house would be a dreary place to live. Smiles would be rare. Anything that might upset her immediately produced warnings from any family member nearby. Mom's anger meant the rest of the family were her enemies (not on her side) in everyone's mind. The family appeared to be close, although it was less about being glad to be together and more about their shared fear of Mom in enemy mode.

How Does Enemy Mode Work Against Me?

Most of us know about airplane mode for phones. In airplane mode, both incoming and outgoing signals are blocked. The phone is locked into its own "reality." Enemy mode operation is like airplane mode for the brain's relational system. We lose input signals and become isolated in our own perceptions.

Enemy mode is a weakness, producing a brain that is too shut down or overloaded. Both extremes produce the same result—the perception of being isolated in a hostile environment. Worse yet, enemy mode is relatively contagious. Once one brain in a cluster of people goes into enemy mode, others tend to follow. One person ignores others, and soon more people are ignoring one another. One person starts saying and doing stupid things, and almost everyone will think of something stupid to say or do in return. One person begins to track and hunt down the weaknesses in others, and before long everyone is seeing weaknesses to exploit.

Don't we want to be the first person to escape enemy mode—the one proud to be our best self? Don't we want to get others out also? Don't we all wish our enemies could be brought out of enemy mode too and thus be surrounded by best selves and not enemies?

What Is in It for Me to Get Out of Enemy Mode?

We feel miserable until we get out of enemy mode. *Don't I want to be the one who gets out first?* Healthy friendships, creativity, options, movement toward satisfaction, and a better mood are some of the incentives to escape quickly.

Jim doesn't remember what started the fight.

"Why don't you just get a divorce?" Jim's wife, Kitty, was angry. She knew it was a stupid thing to say.

Jim felt hurt, misunderstood, and quite certain that his wife was not on his side, so he marched into the backyard. The midday sun and 105-degree temperature made him miserable standing outside and thinking of stupid things to say back to her.

Three times in a row, this middle-aged couple repeated the cycle. During Jim's third time standing under the hot California sun, a thought crossed his mind. He was hurt and angry because he really didn't want a divorce; he wanted a good relationship. Jim wanted to refriend his wife and be refriended. He wanted them both on the same side.

When we drop into enemy mode, our brain gets focused on the "win," or more accurately, making the other person lose. Leaving enemy mode feels like we are going to lose. We have a tendency to think, *This is important. I need to stay in enemy mode.* That would mean trying to solve problems while running on a partially disabled brain. Problems are not easily resolved by thinking others are against us when they might not be. But, since the mind in intelligent enemy mode cannot read others' good motives, we will hide from, reject, or even attack our helpers. That is not too intelligent, is it? Intelligent solutions require using our whole brain.

Suppose I Want to Escape—What About Others?

Ray began interviewing leaders, many of whom were Christian, about enemy mode. He asked, "Do you think enemy mode exists? Does the term even make sense to you?" The questions sparked fascinating conversations, a good bit of pushback, and some indifference.

A retired oil executive said he didn't believe it existed. It's not hard to understand how he could say that. He didn't see enemy mode in himself, but people close to him said he was in it during every meeting! His goal was always focused on solving problems or "fixing" people. That was simple enemy mode in action.

A young executive coach said, "Why call it 'enemy mode'? Maybe call it confrontational mode, or something like that?" The term seemed too inflammatory. Yet a brain in enemy mode views other people as enemies. Another responded, "Why not call it 'preservation' or 'self-protection' mode?" He felt we were trying to be provocative with the term "enemy" but couldn't see how a relationally blind brain makes enemies of others.

For these people, what was being coined as enemy mode seemed more like a common mode of operation in their various roles. Is it possible that this brain state is actually needed at certain times in our lives?

Ray, for example, felt he could do his best work when he could simply focus, not engage with other people, and let them know he was busy. When he was a pastor, his wife used to tell their children, "Don't bother Dad. He is studying and getting ready to preach!" Deborah had learned to say nothing controversial to him on a Saturday night. Why?

She wanted to support him but also instinctively knew that Ray would react negatively.

When Ray started the church, the only way he knew how to work was in simple enemy mode. If there was a problem, he worked harder. The people in his life would understand, he told himself. He did good work but did not bring out his best self in those days. Even in his sixties, as executive director of Life Model Works, Ray found himself wishing he could isolate, work fourteen-hour days, and get stuff done.

As Ray pointed out the benefits of an undistracted focus, Jim shared a different perspective. "You make a good case that performance can be achieved by ignoring the relational half of our brain, but doing that reduces performance because the fastest and brightest part of our brain is disabled or malfunctioning. We can get to the front of the line fastest by knocking over everyone in the way. But, have we answered the question of whether we achieve the best outcome? Is the cost-to-benefit ratio as satisfying as we could achieve using our full brain instead of the over-focused part? Did you consider any alternatives? What are the costs that Deborah and your family paid for your performance?"

Ray answered, "I didn't know there was another option. A lot of circumstances set me up. I didn't know I was working in enemy mode at the time. All I can tell you is that my success under pressure came when I was in enemy mode. I paid a big price for that."

"Well, Ray," Jim said, "I have noticed that Christians and their leaders spend a lot of time in simple enemy mode. Their relational systems are off. They are not tuned in to their own feelings or those of others. It is almost as if they are enemies with their own emotions.

"I have seen Christians rely on beliefs and conscious choices to live the Christian life, while expecting that emotions like anger, shame, disgust, sadness, and hopelessness would lead them to sin. That lack of emotional awareness contributes to all three types of enemy mode. Could generations of Christians who distrust and avoid emotions in favor of beliefs actually be making it harder for themselves to escape enemy mode?"

Ray responded, "I think you are right, Jim. I used to say, 'Don't trust emotions, trust the facts.' Trouble is, emotions are telling me something important. I pay attention to them now."

THINGS GET COMPLICATED

Seeing three different enemy mode patterns bothered Jim. In simple enemy mode, the brain needed energizing; stupid enemy mode needed quieting; and intelligent enemy mode would receive neither. He thought it would be excessively complicated to teach people to identify three different patterns with three different solutions. Finally, he posed these questions to Ray: "Do you think that intelligent enemy mode might hide under the other two? Intelligent mode works by not feeling pain others are feeling. Do you think that the shut-off emotions of simple enemy mode could be intelligent enemy mode taking a nap? Then, if you wake it up, something stupid comes out?"

Ray didn't have the answer but had a question of his own: *How can I stay out of enemy mode and help others get out of enemy mode once it strikes?*

Ray and Jim needed to find better solutions. When Jim tried helping others out of enemy mode, they saw him as the enemy. His actions were interpreted as an attack. His motives were seen as hostile. He didn't like being misunderstood or accused. These "ouch" experiences set up his brain to declare war on whoever saw him as an enemy and sent him back to his own enemy mode. Ray was wondering if he could perform well without enemy mode; after all, his simple enemy mode had been with him as long as he could remember.

Jim's mind was pretty blank. Forget teaching others! It was time for a detailed study of each type of enemy mode. Perhaps a common solution might emerge. Simple enemy mode was first on the list.

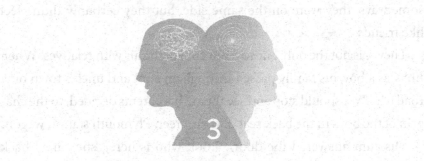

SIMPLE ENEMY MODE

NO ONE REMEMBERED SEEING THEM FIGHT, but ever since Lucy could remember visiting, her grandparents only spoke to each other when necessary. When either Martha or Homer came into the same room, the other one rarely looked up. Their life together was sort of a mutual convenience. When their children planned a fiftieth anniversary celebration, the couple agreed without great enthusiasm. When asked why they were still married, Martha once answered in a monotone, "Better the devil you know than the one you don't." Separately, each of them was enjoyable to be around. Homer was surprisingly funny when he was out fishing. He talked to store clerks he didn't know like they were old friends. Martha started baking cookies and inviting people over once Homer passed.

Whenever Lucy spent time with her grandparents, she felt their silent tensions rise and fall. There was some kind of enemy mode in the air. There wasn't much life going on between the long-married couple. In some ways, they were on the same side, but they certainly didn't feel like friends.

Lucy was not the only one to feel a chill in the air with relatives. When Jim was a boy, his family passed through an aunt and uncle's town on a road trip. "We should stop and see them," his parents decided, to the chagrin of the boys in the back seat of their green Plymouth station wagon.

His aunt answered the door. "Look who is here," she called back into the house. "Come in," she told them without a smile.

No cross words were spoken during the evening meal, which seemed to last a decade. After dinner, the cousins stayed in their rooms. The men discussed gas mileage on one side of the room, while the women compared the children's ages on the other. By morning, everyone was more than ready to leave. Jim felt like he had spent a night in an enemy's camp, but, no, they were family, not enemies!

Signs of Simple Enemy Mode

- No response except "What do you want?"
- No "flavor" to meaningful relationships
- Not curious about what the other person is thinking
- Feeling ignored, manipulated, or misunderstood
- Abrupt end to interactions
- We or they are distracted (do not feel "present")
- Dimmed awareness of the body
- Focusing on rules, procedures, and policies
- Wondering what he/she is getting so upset about
- Relational circuit test shows RCs are off

Enemy mode in the brain does not depend on whether we use the term "enemy" for another person. Governments are not the only ones who attack each other. The people we allow close to us attack as well—even ones we consider our friends. For some people, each morning brings the expectation of an attack. We behave differently when we expect others to be against us. Consider what goes on inside our minds when coming home a few hours later than promised.

CHECKING OUR RELATIONAL CIRCUITS

Our relational circuits create our social engagement with others, as well as regulate our emotions when something is going wrong during an encounter. One moment we might want to share our connection, and another we may prefer to be left alone. Our readiness to connect involves many factors besides what the other person means to us. There are many subtle signals that we don't want to be connected with someone at the moment.

Below are some simple ways Jim developed to know when our RCs are not running smoothly:

Relational Circuits (RCs) Test

- I just want to make a problem, person, or feeling go away.
- I don't want to listen to what others feel or say.
- My mind is "locked onto" something upsetting.
- I don't want to be connected to _____ (someone I usually like).
- I just want to get away, fight, or freeze.
- I more aggressively interrogate, judge, or try to fix others.

Typically, we have a default reaction when we don't want to connect. Once we figure out that symptom, we can catch our RCs shutting down fairly quickly.

Early in their marriage, Jim and Kitty drifted into a chronic simple enemy mode. Kitty stopped bringing up topics that seemed to upset Jim. Jim did the same by dropping any subject he anticipated would elicit an unfavorable reaction from Kitty. Life at home became quiet and low joy. They were unknowingly avoiding stupid enemy mode by living in simple enemy mode. Trying to avoid trouble was creating trouble. Unless we learn to escape enemy mode, our best self will not emerge.

At that time, Jim was attending a graduate school that had a 70 percent divorce rate by graduation. The psychology faculty attributed these divorces to couples drifting apart as the spouse in the program outgrew their partner emotionally. Kitty and Jim decided that they should both be in therapy and grow together.

While Jim and Kitty recognized the need to change course, Jim's friend John and his wife, Meg, didn't. John and Meg loved cooking and having people over for parties on their deck. John always seemed to have the latest release on vinyl. One day, John suggested listening to music in the garage so it would not bother Meg. She had seemed a bit preoccupied recently. Over the next few months, Jim saw less and less of Meg. John rarely said much about her until one day when he told Jim, "Meg moved out, and I have decided to drop out of school."

John was sad but fairly matter-of-fact as he explained to Jim that he and Meg had had a few fights and were going in different directions. Meg had her work and friends, and John no longer believed in "this psychology stuff." He wasn't expecting any big upset from Meg. Simple enemy mode is a rather low energy affair. Their spark was gone and not expected back. John and Meg were soon divorced.

LEARNING TO REFRIEND SOMEONE

We must be friends, or at least friendly, before we can refriend. A person with a friendly disposition sees relational possibilities with people who are in simple enemy mode. It is easier to imagine being glad to

be together again when relational joy is our
usual experience. Joy is relational and built
when people are happy to be with us.

In his book *The Joy Switch*, Chris Coursey
explains how joy switches the brain out
of simple enemy mode. His book was one
of the first to use the term "simple enemy
mode" and provide exercises for escaping
enemy mode.[1] We will examine ways to get

**We must be friends,
or at least friendly,
before we can
refriend.**

ourselves and others out of simple enemy mode later. Coursey lays
out practices that build resilient, "high joy" people. People who have
practice building relational joy will be far ahead when it comes to refriending their way out of the three enemy mode states.

IS IT US OR THEM?

Mutual understanding, developed through our brain's relational circuits, tells us what is going on in another mind. A brain in enemy mode
cannot tell if other people are in enemy mode or not. In the case of simple enemy mode, the brain is simply not "on" enough to engage. Our
brain is relationally blind because it is relationally asleep.

Are we the ones in enemy mode, or are they? We can feel ignored,
disconnected, hurt, or offended and think someone is not paying attention, yet we are the ones in simple enemy mode. Once this irritation sets
in, our irritation can increase if we detect signs that the other person is
distracted: they look away, check the time, speak to someone else, pay
attention to the children, or shift their weight. Are they not interested in
us, or are we in enemy mode and not connected?

The Vietnam War was a daily topic at the college TV studio where
Jim worked part-time. His boss was a religious pacifist. William had
been raised a Quaker, and his quiet ways made Jim curious about that
tradition. One Sunday, Kitty and Jim picked a Quaker church near their

house for a visit. The parking lot was fairly empty when they arrived. As soon as they entered the church, an older couple ran excitedly to greet them.

"What is your name?" the man asked. They told him.

"That is not a Quaker name," he said, and his wife nodded. The couple turned and walked away, leaving Jim and Kitty standing there, astonished. They held no relational status in this place.

Jim and Kitty exited out the door they had just entered, feeling the sting of simple enemy mode.

WHAT SIMPLE ENEMY MODE DOES TO THE RCs

Simple enemy mode is a low energy state. It could be argued that this lack of activity is not a mode of thinking at all because almost nothing is happening. But, if any household appliance did not come on when we wanted to use it, we would realize that doing *nothing* is *something* we don't like. When we look at the effect that being uninterested, unresponsive, apathetic, and indifferent have on others, we see what *is* happening: people don't like it. We don't even need to know the person we are ignoring to get a bad reaction. An unresponsive waiter, ticket agent, or clerk—someone we have never met before—can set off an enemy mode interaction.

When it's someone we know, we discover people like it even less!

Ray was driving a rented twenty-nine-foot-long, thirteen-foot-tall recreational vehicle across the high desert of Idaho. He was nervous because winds were buffeting the RV. Ray was also focused on the latest episode of his favorite podcast. He was so focused on driving and listening that he missed a question from Deborah. She asked him again. Ray replied, "I really want to listen to this podcast."

Ray was in his "driver's podcast brain" and relationally blind. Deborah felt unseen and unimportant. He had slipped into simple enemy mode. Had Ray stayed relational, he would have paused the podcast, kindly answered her question, and then hit play.

The brain has more than one way to enter a non-responsive sort of simple enemy mode. Since activation energy is closely tied to the first two levels of our relational circuits, let us look there.

Level One: The thalamus and basal ganglia normally produce excited energy we call joy when we see someone significant. This excitement might be personal, like seeing our parents after school. Our excitement could be situational, like seeing anyone we don't know when we are lost in the woods. We tend to feel energy from Level One in our bodies with an uptick of heart rate and breathing. Level One makes our heart pump, and Level Two makes us jump. While Level One controls the body response of a racing heart and heavy breathing, Level Two stimulates the nerves that make us move, fight, or flee.

Cultures regulate when we can or must show a response to others. Jim has set off enemy mode frowns in strangers by not smiling when the dog at the end of their leash came to greet him. The lack of response was all it took.

A lack of response can also reflect emotional injuries. A chronically low joy existence during infancy can deaden the thalamus's response to people.[2] Fatigue, distraction, and other factors can also deaden our responses.

Level Two: The amygdala and hippocampus memories energize the nervous system directly but also amplify or deaden the body's response. Joy (GOOD) grows through activating the energetic *sympathetic* system. But the amygdala can also suppress our energy. When the input stream delivers something BAD, Level Two activates the *parasympathetic* system, dropping our energy. If the memories in the hippocampus signal that being around people, or a particular person, feels BAD, we may enter simple enemy mode.

Level Two can color our energy with the parasympathetic emotions of sadness, shame, disgust, and hopelessness. Without energy from these two levels of our relational circuits (RCs), we barely notice the presence of someone else. We might have the energy to frown, but we are not interested in an interaction. This is simple enemy mode.

An energized response from the RCs when encountering significant people is normal, but a lack of response does not always mean the person is in simple enemy mode. Sometimes we don't respond because we are fatigued. Some people have their RCs damaged in ways that impair their responses. What makes a muted response into simple enemy mode is the brain's anticipation of an unpleasurable outcome. In simple enemy mode, the brain is suppressing energy. (Details of how to distinguish low energy from simple enemy mode can be found in the appendix.)

All four levels of the RCs run in the brain's "fast track." Reactions happen very quickly in the right brain before we have time for conscious thought. When meeting another person, the RCs in their fast track know immediately if we are really glad to see them before either of us is aware we have seen each other in our conscious left brain "slow tracks." This fast track exchange took about a sixth of a second, and we are already headed for either joy or simple enemy mode.

THE VERBAL LOGICAL EXPLAINER (VLE)

The left brain is dominant for conscious, focused analysis. While our right brain is being relational, our left brain is analyzing what just happened. Our right brain operates quickly and our conscious left brain runs a step slower. Our left prefrontal cortex (lPFC) must provide explanations. That is its function. Dr. Karl Lehman has called this the verbal logical explainer (VLE).[3]

Since RCs run too quickly for the explainer to watch, the lPFC searches the environment and consults autobiographical memories for clues. The VLE generates explanations using patterns it has seen before. When one explanation doesn't fit, the VLE rapidly switches to another one. The VLE quickly comes up with the most logical sounding explanation it can justify.

Jim's basement office has a great view of the Rocky Mountains. This is where he studies and writes books about relational brain science. Sometimes Kitty would come down the stairs while he was concentrating. In Jim's brain, this registered as a BAD interruption, wasting his time. If she spoke, he missed what she said. Jim's VLE didn't have a clue that his RCs were off but would justify his simple enemy mode. Kitty called this Jim's "computer brain."

Kitty's interaction with Jim could run like this:

K: "Why didn't you say hi?" (Her VLE adds) "Don't you want me around?"

J: (His VLE) "I didn't see you there."

K: "I told you I was here!"

J: (His VLE changes justification/explanation) "I was busy finishing what I was writing."

K: (Her VLE) "You never have time for me. You know I live in this house!"

J: (His VLE) "You are the one who comes around, interrupting my work and starting fights."

Self-justifying responses escalate simple enemy mode into a conflict. While simple enemy mode begins with the lack of relational energy, many people take offense at the lack of a response. People in enemy mode, even simple enemy mode, cannot tell that others want to relate and will feel attacked. When justifying themselves, people energize enemy mode, usually with anger. Kitty and Jim tried that, and neither cared for it.

Kitty adapted creatively. She began coming in and standing quietly where Jim could see her. In response, Jim followed a short process to wake up his attachment center at Level One and get some relational energy going. It took a few seconds to find his best self, but it was worth it.

First, Jim noticed his simple enemy mode reaction and asked himself, "Do I want a good day with the person standing there? Yes, obviously. Then, what do I appreciate about her?"

The answer in Jim's mind was immediate. "I appreciate that she is giving me a few seconds to finish my sentence and to get my RCs started." By the time he looked her way, his attachment was activated and he was already smiling.

This was a two-part solution. First, he needed to keep his VLE from justifying his enemy mode. Second, he needed to get his attachment (RCs) started. On the other side of the room, Kitty also had two parts. First, she needed to keep her RCs on. Second, she needed to keep her VLE from escalating Jim's delayed response into a conflict. Learning this process took some work for both of them.

As Jim reflected on their solution, he had doubts it would work for most people. A single step solution is simple to teach and promote. But 1) suppressing any VLE accusations/justifications while at the same time 2) activating the RCs attachment response was more complex. Enemy mode was quite contagious. Contagious solutions would need to be intuitive and simple to learn.

Ray and Jim focused on one-fifth of the world's population (Christians) as their target audience, so solutions for escaping enemy mode would need to spread easily and rapidly. Could they teach this group how to activate their RCs while suppressing self-justifications and hope they would put their learning into action once they found themselves in simple enemy mode?

Relational Joy in the RCs

Our brains generate joy when we are glad to be with someone. Let us compare two experiences we have all had. Following these two experiences through the four levels of our right brain relational circuits (RCs) will help explain joy.

Experience one: I see the joyful smile and happy eyes of someone I like. Level One finds this personal and pleasurable. Level Two adds, "This is good," and reminds me of good times of safety and closeness. Level Three concludes, "This person is looking at me, likes me, understands me, and we have growing relational joy as our smiles get bigger." Level Four knows our people like to hug and so we do. With this first experience, most of us think, "You make me smile." Joy and peacefulness are generated by two minds who are glad to be together.

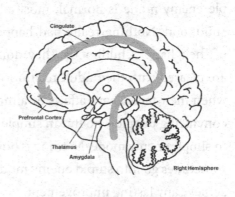

Experience two: I see an angry face with snarly lips and a flared nose coming at me. Level One starts to pump adrenaline to fight or run. Level Two pulls up my memories with angry people and adds that this is bad and scary. Angry people make me mad, so the angry brain system is activated. Level Three gets the input stream and adds that angry people invade my space, don't listen, and can hurt me. I "know" already that this angry person will not be on my side. If the feelings are too intense, Level Three might actually have a meltdown, thus blocking the input stream from going farther. Now I am in stupid enemy mode. If the experience manages to get to Level Four, I imitate what I have observed, said, and done to angry people by angry people. With this experience we will think, "You make me mad." Anger, fear, and suspicion are generated when there is no eagerness or ability to be together.

HOW DOES SIMPLE ENEMY MODE IMPACT ME?

We can survive under many conditions, but that doesn't mean our body is going to thrive. We can breathe polluted air, drink contaminated water, absorb lots of chemicals, and smoke tobacco, but in the end it catches up with us.

Growing up under toxic conditions can seem normal. When simple enemy mode is normal, most adults will report, "I had a happy childhood. Nothing really bad happened." When pressed for details of their happy childhoods, they don't remember many. Often, they are pleased with their adult relationships as well and totally surprised when their mates have affairs or announce they are leaving. It is hard convincing people who live in simple enemy mode that they might be in simple enemy mode. Nothing is bothering them! Their partners will sometimes go into stupid enemy mode to get their attention but rarely achieve any lasting improvement.

Simple enemy mode produces chronic stress. Chronic stress damages our bodies. Chronic stress is an unnatural condition created by low-level threats that do not go away. Being alone to face our problems and having people upset with us are two such low-level threats. In these low joy states, we anticipate that people will not be glad to be with us. For the relational brain, this anticipated lack of status, rejection, or isolation generates bad chemistry.

Simple enemy mode produces chronic stress. Chronic stress damages our bodies.

Increasing levels of stress are matched by increasing blood serum levels of the stress hormone cortisol. Normally, our bodies take a break from making cortisol overnight so we can heal. As nighttime cortisol levels rise, so do brain cell deaths. Going to bed in enemy mode is a sure way to pump cortisol all night. Any distress that lasts overnight will negatively impact our brain. New growth (learning) will have the greatest losses. Stress that does not resolve before we go to sleep damages our brain and our health.

Take a couple who recently fell in love. Their brains are growing new connections, forming wonderful memories, and circulating enough joy chemistry in the blood to feel a little dizzy at times. Each one has discovered the perfect person who is always on their side. They are in love.

Now comes the moment when one of them goes into simple enemy mode. This takes longer to notice in online dating, but face-to-face it is unmistakable. Once in enemy mode, that person is relationally blind and will not be able to tell if the other is in enemy mode or not. Usually, people do not give others the benefit of the doubt, so soon they will both be in enemy mode. Enemy mode begins generating cortisol. If they cannot refriend before bed, the cortisol pump stays on. Cortisol in the blood begins dissolving and eventually killing new growth in the brain. The new growth could be many things, but for sure it will include the "in love" feelings. By morning, the feeling of being in love is eroding.

Simple enemy mode easily becomes routine. One person is tired, distracted, and simply forgets to engage because of work. Perhaps, one of the six hardwired unpleasant emotions—anger, sadness, fear, shame, disgust, or hopelessness—triggers saying something stupid. Given enough episodes of enemy mode that run through the night, our couple will have "fallen out of love."

Falling out of love is not inevitable. The joy that generates love must be restored each time we are in enemy mode and before we go to bed. Enemy mode and the resulting loss of joy contribute heavily to falling out of love and its consequences. The consequences of falling out of love are both painful and very costly.

Adding to our losses and loneliness, when we are in simple enemy mode, we miss knowing that others want to be with us—if there is someone interested. Enemy mode blinds us to relational potential and reality.

This was Joel's experience. Joel lived alone, and he rarely participated in social activities; when he did, he was often one of the first to leave. Joel would say that people weren't interested in the same things he was. When people did talk with him, he thought, "They just want something from me." Joel spent time on his computer but not on social media. He held lively discussions with anyone interested in fly fishing, tying flies, seasonal variations in fish habits, riverbeds, waders, and the geology of rivers. But, in the end, Joel was lonely and believed no one was that interested in him. If you asked people around Joel if they were his friends, you would hear, "We met doing (this or that), and he seemed like an intelligent and interesting person, but he just never seemed interested in more of a relationship." Joel's mind passively informed him that there was no one out there who was really "with" him. Sooner or later, people left, just as his brain predicted. Joel lived in simple enemy mode.

What Is in It for Me to Get Out of Enemy Mode?

Most of us end up in simple enemy mode without noticing when or how we got there. Sure, we may feel misunderstood, intruded upon, or ignored while our VLE says that others are in our way or just "don't get it." We drift along in simple enemy mode because we do not notice that we are in enemy mode. No one enjoys that state. Escape starts with learning to notice simple enemy mode.

The brain in enemy mode almost always thinks our mood and reactions are about "them" and what is wrong with them. There will always be people who are not on my side. Owning my simple enemy mode enables me to regain control of what state my brain is in, even when people are not on my side.

Our happiness and well-being are tied to how long we stay in that deactivated and nonrelational simple enemy mode. While we stay in enemy mode, we become about as popular as a cellphone that doesn't keep a charge. There are usually people around us interested in connecting. Our enemy mode is the buzzkill.

Simple enemy mode is a lonely place to be. Being lonely ranks with health risks like obesity, anger, or smoking cigarettes. Loneliness increases our risk for dementia. Simply put, we have relational brains.

Harold provides an example. Harold's lonely life was littered with relationships that started quickly but were lost in the swamps of enemy mode. Each time Harold hit enemy mode, he felt others were turning against him. His style was to confront others with their flaws and perceived bad intentions. His friends felt misunderstood and even accused. But rather than get himself out of enemy mode, Harold would insist that others admit their faults.

Sustainable relationships require good levels of joy. Positive relationships are not hard to start, but we lose relationships when we cannot refriend once things go wrong. Brains in relational mode want to find creative solutions with others.

Getting out of simple enemy mode restores and reactivates our mutual mind states. Every working family, organization, and culture develops from people who understand one another. Mutual mind states enhance personal development, family life, education, work, and culture.

ARE WE MAKING ANY PROGRESS
WITH CHRISTIAN LEADERS?

While Jim was writing descriptions of how the brain experienced enemy mode, Ray was interviewing Christian leaders. Ray was getting better at explaining and asking questions about enemy mode.

Some people grasped the concept right away. When Ray spoke with former Army ranger Mike Beller, a police chief in the Atlanta area, Beller agreed that enemy mode not only exists, but that he regularly sees enemy mode reactions in officers and in the situations they encounter. Sometimes an officer reacts one way and defuses a situation. Another time, the same officer reacts differently, and the situation escalates, becoming more dangerous by the moment. There was something different about how the officer's mind was working that the chief could observe in the actions and sometimes in the outcome.

Dr. Naomi Paget is a Japanese American who was born just after her family was released from the World War II relocation camps where they experienced firsthand the effects of being seen as enemies. She has led disaster recovery chaplaincy programs during which enemy mode reactions have interfered with services. Dr. Paget told Ray, "I think that we deal with simple enemy mode all the time—with victims, first responders, and chaplains."

Ray's friend James, an African American who has spent his entire adult life worshiping in integrated, evangelical churches, told Ray that he sees too many Christians operating in simple enemy mode around race. Like most people around the world, James found the murder of George Floyd and others like him as evil and worthy of condemnation.[4] Floyd was an African American whose killing by white police officers fueled the Black Lives Matter movement and exposed a great deal of enemy mode thinking. James was shocked by the lack of a clear voice from evangelical churches condemning these senseless murders. James has since devoted time and energy to a local racial reconciliation ministry to build bridges so the church can be part of the solution, not the problem.

Retired Major General Jack Briggs was another Christian leader Ray interviewed who resonated with the brain science behind enemy mode. After retiring from the Air Force, Briggs became the CEO of the Springs Rescue Mission, a homeless shelter in Colorado Springs. Ray asked Briggs how the different types of enemy mode play out every day at the Mission. He had ready examples. Clients came in for food and shelter in simple enemy mode. Simple enemy mode was transactional: "Give me what I want!"

Briggs said the Mission team first engaged clients in simple enemy mode, but the Mission's goal was building relationships. They met clients in the reality of life on the street and leveraged transactions to communicate dignity and worth. Meeting practical human needs raised the client's status and restored their personal dignity.

Briggs added, "A lot of our clients come from corrections. If you really want to see enemy mode, you should interview somebody from there. Yeah! They're the ones who deal with intelligent enemy mode on a daily, hourly, minute-by-minute basis. That's their entire world."

When Ray asked George, a former CEO and volunteer in his church, about the presence of enemy mode, George said, "I'm not sure I have ever noticed this enemy mode you are talking about," and not recognizing the phenomenon, declined to be interviewed. This was the case for other leaders as well, including an executive who emphatically denied the existence of enemy mode and a former congressman who found the concept "complicated."

Similarly, pastors were not immune to enemy mode, nor did some recognize it when Ray pointed it out. Ray knew several pastors who lived in simple enemy mode. When a congregant no longer supported their pastor's mission, that person lost all status in the pastor's eyes. Ray experienced this dynamic when he explained what he was learning about enemy mode to a former pastor. Ray made an extra effort to get him out of simple enemy mode, but the pastor wasn't interested.

The lack of interest by pastor friends bothered Ray. Because simple enemy mode was how he had led at home, in church, and in the military, he couldn't unsee it—in himself or in others. Realizing he had missed all those opportunities to be his best self shattered Ray's reality. He longed to see others discover what was changing his life.

Relationally blind leaders were oblivious to their simple enemy mode lives. What now shocked Ray about himself in simple enemy mode was but a minor irritant. Ray told Jim, "It doesn't feel like I am making much progress convincing leaders who don't think there is a need." Among many leaders, Ray found little interest in change.

"How do you explain water to a fish?" Jim answered, "We might be trying to explain relational thinking to people who live in simple enemy mode like a fish lives in water. These people you are talking to claim to be Christians, don't they?"

Ray nodded, so Jim added, "Even if they don't care about the brain, wouldn't they see the need for loving relationships because they are Christians?"

The question hung in the air a long time.

While simple enemy mode hampered awareness and created road-blocks and apathy with some leaders, the need for change was felt on the streets. The group most interested in change proved to be those who had done or said something stupid.

STUPID
ENEMY MODE

"THIS WAS ONE OF THOSE PUBLIC SITUATIONS where everyone is clearly uncomfortable," Lisa told Jim. "Everyone had a tightness in their chest watching this guy just screaming at this kid." Lisa lived in Minneapolis, where public tensions were high over the killing of George Floyd and the conviction of the officers involved.

Lisa was in a Minneapolis COVID-19 testing center located in a large, empty warehouse. The room provided a cavernous echo chamber where everyone heard the screaming. Everyone! People stared at the ground super uncomfortably.

"I vaguely noticed an argument and raised voices coming from the area by the exit door. I thought nothing of it at first. I had been tested before, so I knew the routine. As the commotion escalated, I saw a dad and two boys about ten years old. The boys were trying to fill the spit sample vials. The dad had totally lost it on one of the boys. He was screaming, visibly frustrated, clearly drowning in emotion and feeling overwhelmed."

The woman behind Lisa said, "That dude needs to *stop* it." Her eyes grew wide.

Lisa was witnessing that enemy mode in which people lose it, "get stupid," and end up saying and doing things they would not like recorded—moments that do not reflect their best self.

A man and a woman wearing volunteer vests approached the man, said something, then quickly walked away. The room was now filled with people in simple enemy mode. Although the Minneapolis media talked about de-escalating tense situations almost daily following the killing of George Floyd, no one did.

"What made you get involved?" Jim asked Lisa.

Lisa recounted her mental impression of Jesus standing there. "I remember saying to Jesus something like, 'Okay, if he flares up again when I get closer, I'm going to do something.' I was a few steps away when, wham! The dad just came unglued with frustration and lit into the boy again."

"I had no formulated plan in my head when I stepped toward them. I think I said something like, 'Can I help out here?' or 'Can I give it a try?' The dad yelled, 'Go right ahead! We've been here trying for so long,' and kept yelling and yelling.

"I asked what the boy's name was. It was Mason." Lisa crouched down about three feet away from Mason and told him she was glad he was getting tested and hoped he was not sick. She connected with his struggle: "Hey, Mason, you know what? The first time I was here I could not believe how hard it was to fill this thing up with spit!"

Lisa noticed the dad bring his yelling down about a decibel. With no other plan than a vague sense of emotional attunement and rela-tional connection, she offered that the dad could go outside and walk a little bit and she would stay with Mason. He declined.

Lisa turned back, trying to connect with Mason, who wouldn't lift his head to look at her. A moment later his dad walked outside. Lisa was grateful and said, "Hey, Mason, you know when I was a kid, my dad screamed at me all the time, and that's why I came over here. I just want you to know I see you, and I get it."

A lady in line tapped Lisa on the shoulder and said, "Thank you!" Just then the dad came back. Lisa suggested to him that Mason get a swab test. Dad agreed and said he had made an appointment. Mason's brother looked at Lisa and said through his mask, "You're the only one who understands."

Then the dad blurted, "The only reason we're here is because Mason's brother has a runny nose. The school can't tell the difference between allergies and COVID! Now Mason can't go to school until he has a negative COVID test. The school won't take them! Daycare won't take them! I'm a single dad and now I can't go to work because these two can't go to school!"

The dad continued, "I just paid $350 to daycare, and now they can't even go! Is anyone going to reimburse me for that? Who's got an extra $350 just laying around for that sort of thing?"

"Oh my gosh, right?" Lisa said to Jim. "This guy was drowning, feeling overwhelmed. I just kept attuning, 'Oh, gosh, man, this is so hard . . . I hear you.' He settled considerably and I could see his humanity returning to his face."

"Okay, Mason. Get your mask on, buddy, and we'll just go now," the dad said, and he headed out first.

Lisa called out, "Hey, Mason!" And then did the motion with her two fingers pointed to her eyes and then his. He paused, then walked toward the door. She reached in her purse, pulled out some money and handed it to the brother saying, "Go give this to your dad." He ran toward the door excitedly, yelling "Dad . . . Dad . . . *Dad!*" She glimpsed his bewildered look when he was handed the money.

"When I got in my car I thought, 'This is the coolest freaking thing ever.' I cannot stop being totally amazed at the beauty of that whole moment," Lisa concluded, smiling at Jim.

"I have some questions, Lisa," Jim said. "I don't know many people who would react like you did. In fact, I know from experience that I would not. I need to know what went on inside of you that helped get that dad out of his stupid enemy mode meltdown. Were you afraid?"

"It is stunning how I did not feel fear when I jumped in," Lisa answered. "I have been the kid being yelled at, the parent 'losing it,' and the onlooker with no idea what to do!

"My dad was a violent, raging man. The fact that I could see a large, raging man and walk straight toward the anger is nothing short of a total miracle. I'm telling every human being I know this story. The transformation of my entire identity is the driving force behind all the things I teach about relational brain science. What if every Jesus follower could bring this kind of life preserver to people in crisis?! Every Wal-Mart in the world with a parent raging at a child would be transformed!" Lisa just sat back and beamed.

Here was evidence of what Ray and Jim were seeking. Lisa's spiritual life motivated her to live as her best self. To her, that meant learning, practicing, and teaching relational brain skills that could bring people out of enemy mode. That Lisa overcame stupid enemy mode in herself was an eye-opener. She obviously helped this dad out of his enemy mode. More importantly still, Lisa was hopeful, and, as we will see, actively teaching relational brain skills to others.

Signs of Stupid Enemy Mode

- We start seeing everyone around us as stupid.
- Our voice is the loudest by quite a bit.
- Everyone seems against us or at least not "with" us.
- We say or do things we later want to take or walk back, deny, or change.

- People with cellphones are thinking about getting a video of us.
- We want "it" to stop.
- We feel overwhelmed and out of control.
- We are usually angry or afraid, but sometimes very excited.
- Often alcohol or drugs are involved.
- We are tired and stretched too thin.
- On reflection, this was not our finest hour.
- We become a different person from our usual self.
- We are focused on something or someone else and lose sight of ourselves.
- We act like our parents or someone we swore we would not be like.
- We use the most "powerful" words, not the smartest words.
- We sometimes "keep it to ourselves" when faced with someone more powerful.
- We think or express contempt, rage, and hatred.
- We immediately notice other people's vulnerability and humiliate them for their:
  - race/nationality/language
  - age/gender/sexuality
  - social status/wealth/education/intelligence
  - weight/clothes/attractiveness
- We insult their mother and people they have attachments to.
- We cause damage to what others value (maybe make it look accidental).
- We may warn people with phrases like: "Don't make me/him/her mad!" "Don't make me get stupid!" "Don't make me get my Irish up!"

How easily a person goes into stupid enemy mode varies substantially from one person to the next. It is equally clear that people learn patterns they use during stupid enemy mode by watching others get stupid. Some people overcontrol until they blow up while others consider getting stupid a sort of life skill that gets them what they want. But people are not together for long before they begin to recognize and predict what will bring out stupid enemy mode in themselves and others.

Stupid enemy mode often leads to domestic violence, child, spouse, and elder abuse, excessive force by law enforcement, and crimes of passion. Stupid enemy mode is often encouraged against selected targets by oppressive groups, gangs, and governments, and during genocides. Stupid enemy mode is learned brain behavior.

HOW STUPID ENEMY MODE WORKS IN THE BRAIN

Speed in the brain is important. If the brain is running too fast, it has lost efficiency. If it is running too slowly, it has lost touch with the world around it. In either condition, areas of the brain might be burning lots of energy (like a muscle in a cramp) but doing no work. Nerves are pathways moving information from one place to another. When a spot on a brain pathway "locks up," the information it is supposed to be processing and passing along gets blocked, and processing breaks down.

Think of it this way: When muscle cells fire but don't rest, the muscle cramps. If nerves in the brain fire together without resting, that's called a seizure. Brain circuits need rhythms of fire and rest, fire and rest. If nerves fire too often and for too long, they die. Nerves in the brain that are firing too fast can lose efficiency and stop being useful, much like a muscle cramp will not help you swim.

One of the most important regions in the brain for processing relational experiences is the cingulate cortex in the right brain. (You may recall from the earlier discussion of relational circuits that this is the central structure referred to as Level Three.) The right cingulate is particularly involved in emotionally charged interactions with other people. When the right cingulate is running cool and smoothly, we remember what other people mean to us, what they are thinking, and how to stay "on the same side," even when we are upset.

Positron emission tomography (PET scans) can identify brain circuits that are too active and have lost their effectiveness. The PET scans of people experiencing emotional control problems and difficulty with their relationships often reveal "hot spots" in the brain's cingulate cortex. These hot spots block people from feeling connected to others even when nothing emotional is happening; they are simply sitting in a brain scan machine. In short, these subjects are already starting to feel a sort of "enemy mode" attitude to a world they experience is not on their side. What will happen if that brain is upset or fired up on some kind of drug? It's not going to be pretty.

What this "overheated" brain needs is a rest cycle before it fires again. Take a breath, wait a bit, rest, pause—these are the serotonin and GABA rest moments for nerve cells. Nerves receive dopamine, adrenaline (from anger or fear), and other "fire starter" chemicals from other nerves and the bloodstream during periods of strong emotions. Without enough rest cycles, something will break down.

The cingulate cortex is a pathway to the right prefrontal cortex (rPFC) and a major pathway for emotional control—when it works. The cingulate adds together the information about what is going on between our mind and another's mind. If and when processing gets through the cingulate and reaches the rPFC, an important calculation about the least harmful solution is made. Calculations take place near the centerline of the brain (medial) at the bottom-central (ventromedial) region of the rPFC (rvmPFC).

If the cingulate gets "overheated," we lose a sense of connection to other people. We misunderstand what they are really thinking and start to see them as enemies. The pathway for emotional intelligence is blocked, causing a drop in activity to the rvmPFC, so the brain is not calculating the least harmful alternative. We see others as enemies and start doing and saying stupid things. Lots of energy, little identity, and no emotional intelligence replace our best self.

When our "least harmful solution" system (rvmPFC function) has its function diminished or blocked by overactivity in the cingulate, we need to quiet the cingulate and provide rest cycles. However, the time to learn quieting exercises that relax the cingulate is before the cingulate is experiencing a cramp. Brains in cramps are not processing correctly and certainly not in the mood to learn at that moment. We will come back to how the brain learns to quiet and see how a secure attachment (relationally safe place) can train the cingulate to quiet itself.

The brain has other pathways outside the relational circuits that do not go through the cingulate. Deep in the brain, a calculator is processing arousal: *How upset should I be, and what kind of energy will I need?* This alternate (energy) pathway sends information to the thalamus, amygdala, and basal ganglion, releasing all kinds of energizing or de-energizing chemical "messages" into the body.

However, these messages aren't going to the "least harmful solution" system (that path is through the cingulate). Instead, they bypass the cingulate, energizing the potential for stupid enemy mode before the conscious mind has even received a signal.

Former police officer Ed Khouri, who is also a coauthor with Jim on a book about ways to stay relational and build joy,[1] explained that he was frequently called upon to stop or even subdue people who were operating in stupid enemy mode. When he was a rookie, the more seasoned officers told him that on calls where deadly force might be needed, he should swear and yell as loudly and angrily as possible to de-escalate the situation. Sounding angry seemed to reduce resistance in many cases. How the de-escalation worked was not known at the time.

As Ray and Jim were discussing how to stop enemy mode, Ray related a story about a former special ops officer who was being threatened at a party by a man in stupid enemy mode. The vet froze the man by uttering an intense "you don't want to mess with me" warning.

How does this work? There is a small, dense pathway between the dopamine activation center (substantia nigra) and the power-calculating striosomes in the striatum of the basal ganglia. This deep brain calculator in the energy and dopamine activation pathway through the thalamus does fast "math" about a superior force. Scientists at MIT showed that "this communication pathway is necessary for making decisions that require an anxiety-provoking cost-benefit analysis . . . between areas that control emotion, decision-making, and movement."[2]

When these striosomes of the basal ganglia calculate that we are about to get our backsides kicked, they shut off the power surge, thus de-escalating the situation. Greater force can shut down the dopamine activation, making us lose interest in the fight. To complete the picture, there is also a pathway to the striosomes from the least harmful solution system in the ventromedial PFC (vmPFC) that can also shut down our "stupid" before it happens if, and only if, the pathway through the cingulate is running correctly.

As we noted in the brain discussion, people in stupid enemy mode still calculate when they are facing superior force (unless they are impaired by chemicals). When their brain calculates that they are the superior force, they can be dangerous. Physical size, number of enemy people, past behavior, perceptual bias (such as seeing all women as weak), spectator silence, emotional intensity, weapons, resources, and backers for aggressive action all enter the calculations. The discussion of stupid enemy mode begins spilling over into intelligent enemy mode at this point. We will consider how intelligent enemy mode calculates winning in the next chapter. Stupid enemy mode calculates the probability of winning preconsciously, not consciously.

It bears repeating that the brain's preconscious calculations of power differentials are greatly impacted by mind-altering drugs, alcohol, and medications. So stupid enemy mode is much more likely to be dangerous when people are intoxicated. Danger also increases with privacy, isolation, social power, or anything that grants a feeling of immunity for this predatory response. The more that others (those within the person's identity group) accept the target as an "enemy" and not "one of us," the more dangerous stupid enemy mode becomes.

So, we find two ways to stop stupid enemy mode. First, we can display enough of a threat to shut down the power system for the brain doing the extremely fast cost-benefit decision in the striatum. Naturally, this "shock and awe" approach does not always work, like when drugs are present, or the guy getting stupid is six-foot-eight and weighs three hundred pounds. Second, we can use the higher pathway out of enemy mode that goes through the cingulate cortex. We saw Lisa take this mutual understanding path with Mason's father. The pathway through the cingulate is the way that brings refriending.

To the thalamus, our attachments to others are very important. Attachment greatly changes the cost-benefit analysis in the basal ganglia's striosomes. In other words, strong love can stop (actually prevent) rage from becoming stupid—right in the fast energy pathway. Strong attachment love can also keep people fighting when all hope is gone. When a mother bear is protecting her cubs from a large male bear, the male's "shock and awe" power displays do not shut down the power system. People will fight like crazy long after hope is gone to save someone they love. Attachment is a powerful force in the brain.

Strong love can stop (actually prevent) strong rage from becoming stupid.

HOW DOES STUPID ENEMY MODE IMPACT ME?

We have all felt the impact of people in stupid enemy mode. In a town where Jim once lived, his neighbor, who worked for the postal service, brought color to the expression "going postal." He threw a gallon of paint through the plate glass window of a neighbor who had complained about him, and he poisoned another neighbor's barking dogs. Jim's sons would come racing through the front door when the postman came outside raging and screaming because he had heard them playing in the front yard. In his fits of rage, he made enemies out of everyone.

When the man divorced and moved away, a lawyer moved into the same house. If anyone crossed him, he threatened them with a lawsuit. Once, when Jim was having some concrete poured in the driveway, the lawyer became angry that the concrete truck made him walk a few extra feet to get into his house. He began screaming at the driver, "I am much smarter than you are. I have a law degree. You are not nearly as smart as I am!" That didn't seem to impress the concrete truck driver, and the driver let him know. All the same, the low spot in Jim's driveway that didn't receive enough concrete forever bore evidence to the distraction caused by the altercation.

Every day, the news provides examples of people saying and doing stupid things that injure others, resulting in consequences that can last a lifetime. Much of this emotional or domestic violence is continued because many people think, "If I say something, it will only make things worse." Yet even stupid enemy mode can be overcome when attachments are strong enough.

STANDING UP TO STUPID ENEMY MODE

Jim and Kitty were planning to attend a book signing by local author Karen Z. Brass, the daughter of Holocaust survivor David Zauder. *Trauma Filters Through* tells her story about living with the impact of Jewish people being seen as enemies by an entire culture. Jim and Kitty joined Karen's family for the book signing and a meal at the Brass home. Karen was candid about her experience and how difficult it was for her to write truthfully about the extent that traumas had changed her father. Karen told a story about her father so others would know that standing up for the vulnerable must sometimes be done at home.

She and her father called themselves "standupsters"—people who would not be silenced. Karen was protective of her family and of her own children. So, when her father, who had lived with Karen for eight years, began to exhibit stupid enemy mode reactions (definitely not his best self) toward the family dog, Karen had to say something. The dog had been his beloved companion while he battled metastasized bone cancer. After four days of enduring Mr. Zauder's verbal abuse, the upset dog had begun growling and snapping at Karen's special needs son.

When Karen addressed his treatment of the dog, Mr. Zauder was not receptive. He responded: "I am going to pretend this conversation never took place." Karen writes:

> In my "mother to my children first" style, I retorted, "I am sorry you feel this way, Dad. Please keep your door closed unless you can maintain control and be nice to the dog." And I walked out, closing his door behind me.
>
> In less than an hour, DZ [her father] had opened his door, and began clanging pots in the sink, his normal way of getting my attention. I asked, "You okay, Dad?"
>
> "Kar, Kar, come here."
>
> I went into his kitchen. He grabbed me and hugged me and did not let go. It was awkward, because he had never done this before. He whispered in my ear, "I'm sorry. You are right. I've lost my control . . . I have had a tight cover on my emotions like a lid on a pressure cooker, for all of my life. I never wanted to let the steam out because I was scared of what would happen. Now, I feel as though the pressure cooker nozzle has come all the way off and I can't control my mouth. I have never sworn like this or been angry for this long before. But it ends now, it ends today. I covered the nozzle and I am good. I can handle this."[3]

We notice how the strength of Karen's attachment to both her son and father helped her stay out of enemy mode and address the issue. In addition, the strength of Mr. Zauder's attachment to both his daughter and grandson was sufficient for him to stop his enemy mode reactions. In this case, what was stronger than the enemy mode was not some kind of external force but an internal attachment.

Is It Always Safe to Speak Up?

Let's take a deep breath and cool down our cingulates. You have been working your mutual mind system as you've followed us through all this brain theory, but the real workout happens when we recall our experiences with stupid enemy mode, that of others and possibly even ourselves. Taking time for some deep breaths, noticing our body relax, and even taking a short walk helps our brains rest.

Are people who stay in abusive relationships also operating in a sort of stupid enemy mode?

Jim wondered if the same circuits that make people excessively aggressive might also make them excessively passive. When the ventromedial PFC fires too little, the result is high energy and people acting dangerously stupid. At normal levels of ventromedial activity, good judgment and the least harmful actions result.

Could it be that if the ventromedial PFC fires too much (similar to a muscle cramp), people become dangerously passive? Does their voluntary activity shut down?

Jim pondered these questions and remembered Oliver Sacks, one of his heroes in neurology. As a boy (in the 1960s), Jim had followed Dr. Sacks's efforts to awaken patients whose brains were damaged during the encephalitis lethargica epidemic of the 1920s. Sacks wrote about his work in *Awakenings*, which later became a movie of the same name starring Robin Williams. His patients were mostly unresponsive in ways that implicate the dopamine energy system we have been examining in the basal ganglia. Sacks decided to experiment with the drug

L-Dopa, which nerves could convert to dopamine. As dopamine levels drop in the basal ganglia, people develop tremors. His patients didn't move voluntarily. Sacks asked the question: If a tremor is taken to the extreme, is the result no motion at all?

Voluntary actions are carried out through the brain's pyramidal neurons. Looking back over articles Jim had filed, he spotted one about Professor Linda Van Aelst at Spring Harbor Laboratory, who had been experimenting with the OPHN1 gene governing the RhoA kinase protein that regulates the pyramidal nerves. Mice brains and human brains are similar in this function. When the activity in a laboratory mouse's pyramidal neurons got too high, the mouse became passive, helpless, and would not try to escape electric shocks. Dr. Van Aelst conducted a series of experiments to identify the exact location where this brain activity occurred in mice. She identified the medial PFC. The ventromedial PFC is the lower half of the medial PFC. Bingo![4]

Someone with too much ventromedial activity would probably have their higher relational pathway (cingulate) running and trying hard to figure out what people were thinking. At the same time, they would be frozen and unable to move. This finding brought an especially sad and tragic case to Jim's mind. Penelope, a young girl molested by her father, exhibited the same mental and physical response. Her father would molest her in her parents' bed while her mother was in the room. Penelope told Jim how she would carefully study her mother's face, activity, and lack of reaction to what her father was obviously doing while she lay frozen, her mind racing.

Penelope married and had two daughters, but discovered that her husband was molesting their daughters. When she confronted her husband, he pistol-whipped her into silence. If she reported him to the law, she would lose her finances. She predicted that since they both worked for a religious organization, as soon as she separated from her husband, she would be fired and evicted from the organization's housing. That is exactly what happened. She could not find housing and her situation ended badly.

Penelope understood rather clearly what others were thinking (her cingulate cortex and higher pathway were running), but under intense emotions, her ventromedial PFC most likely got into a cramp that left her immobilized. However, attachment was a strong motivator, and her love for her daughters brought her enough power to find a way out. There was no doubt that Penelope could not speak up safely, but was her husband in stupid or intelligent enemy mode? Both are dangerous. We will examine the distinction between the two in the next chapter.

WHAT IS IN IT FOR ME TO GET OUT OF STUPID ENEMY MODE?

As we pointed out in chapter 3, we tend to think, "How do I *stay* out of enemy mode?" instead of "How do I *get* out of enemy mode?" The brain pathway into enemy mode is simply too fast for us to stop consciously. We can prepare consciously by recognizing risk factors for getting stupid. We can prepare ways to get out of enemy mode quickly before much harm is done.

What is in it for me to get out of stupid enemy mode quickly? Correcting stupid things we have said and done is not fun. Ray remembered when he lost it on a coworker and the years it took to rebuild trust with her.

While we are in enemy mode, we feel more alone, and we cannot tell who is attacking us or trying to help. Since, when we get stupid, the people around us are usually family, friends, and coworkers, it would be wise to already know who is on our side and keep them there.

Lisa Teaches Others

Lisa's compassionate response to Mason and his dad raised some interesting brain questions. She had said, "I had no formulated plan in my head when I stepped toward them," indicating that her conscious mind was not guiding her reactions. At the same time, she had a wide range of responses at her disposal without having to consciously think of them. This suggested to Jim that the faster-than-conscious processes in her right brain had some working models.

Lisa saw both the dad and Mason as people she could relate to and who needed help, evidence of an attachment response to the angry man and frightened child. When Lisa said, "I have been the kid, the parent, and the onlooker having no idea what to do! My dad was a violent raging man," we have a hint that Lisa could see a person behind the stupid enemy mode.

But to have some kind of response that could guide her mind, Lisa would need to have: 1) experienced a way out of stupid enemy mode, 2) positive examples in her mind, and 3) a confident hope that she could make a helpful difference.

Jim needed to see if that was true, so he asked her how she'd known what to do in the situation.

Lisa said she'd read and reread a story Chris Coursey related in the book, *Joy Starts Here*,[5] which he'd coauthored with Jim, Ed Khouri, and Shelia Sutton. Chris had seen a man losing his temper at the airport when his flight was canceled. Chris approached the man, connected with him, and got him out of enemy mode. "I studied how Chris did it," Lisa explained. "How did he emotionally attune to the person? What did he say? It gave me a model."

Lisa had practiced attuning to others by meeting her three daughters where they were and telling herself, "Now is not the time to give them a lecture." This practice helped her meet Mason's dad where he was and not where she wished he was. She achieved de-escalation and refriending.

Lisa went on to say that she had attended a conference in 2009 where Jim was teaching about relational brain skills. She remembered Jim using the analogy of throwing life preservers to where people actually were emotionally.

Jim had worked as a lifeguard in several Minnesota state parks, including Lake Itasca at the headwaters of the Mississippi River. Jim would practice throwing the life preservers to an exact spot in order to accurately reach drowning people. In a similar way, the higher pathway to refriending (through the cingulate) has to reach and accurately mirror how the other person is upset. Next, a mental test of strength begins. Either a "rescue" or a double "drowning" is ahead, depending on which brain is stronger. The helper brain might be pulled into enemy mode, or the helper brain might pull the other brain out of enemy mode.

"Did being Christian influence what you did?" Jim asked. Her answer again surprised him but made sense of Lisa's confidence. She told Jim of her healing journey where she encountered what she called the living Jesus, not beliefs or some plastic version of him.

Lisa became very serious, "God's great work of putting the world together extended to the way that Jesus put me together. That is my driving force to see the world put back together too."

Lisa started a six-week course at her Minneapolis church. It was hard for the church to let her teach practical relational skills and not make it a prayer class. To Lisa, the class was both. She led that class the night before the incident with Mason. Her first time de-escalating a live situation came the next morning.

Jim was really interested. "What did you teach?"

"We all need skills to settle ourselves and help settle others. If nothing else, we can stop and breathe and help others breathe. I explained how important breathing can be neurologically and physically." Lisa paused and made a little face. "Talking about breathing in church seems really wacky because we keep belief so disembodied. Breathing is how things started between people and God in the garden of Eden.

"I don't give too much information," Lisa continued, "but lots of breathing practice. I have them remember a good memory, then practice breathing. I tell the class, 'If all you can do is breathe, just breathe.'

If we see someone who is upset, we can say, 'Can we just take a minute to breathe?'"

Lisa had been successful in her interaction with the father and son for several reasons. She . . .

1. had an attachment to someone (her dad) who got into stupid enemy mode.
2. had seen in herself that stupid enemy mode was not an accurate reflection of her best self.
3. saw the need behind the stupid.
4. helped the man in stupid with his need.
5. saw herself and her people as "de-escalators."
6. practiced de-escalation internally.
7. had just taught others how to quiet themselves the night before (recent practice).

Lisa illustrated that it was possible but demanding to learn the way out of stupid enemy mode. She also provided evidence that her church had great difficulty seeing de-escalating as something learned at church. It is not that the church would oppose helping people out of stupid enemy mode; it was just that practical ways of forming a loving attachment to people in enemy mode was simply not in their existing toolkit.

MAKING THE CASE WITH LEADERS

When it came to stupid enemy mode, convincing Christian leaders from many fields that enemy mode *existed* was easy for Ray. Examples were plentiful, and it was obvious that something "flipped" inside the brain when people "lost it." While stupid enemy mode was easily observable, the question remained whether it was useful or even necessary at times. Was stupid enemy mode a weakness to be avoided or a strength to be used as needed? Ray talked to Kevin, the CEO of a publicly traded major manufacturing company on the East Coast of the United States. Ray also spoke to Jack Briggs at Springs Rescue Mission. Both Kevin and Jack regretted stupid enemy mode incidents in their careers.

Kevin served five years in the Army before working his way up in the manufacturing industry. Now with years of experience as a CEO and senior executive, Kevin recalled how enemy mode showed up in corporate settings and how the great leaders he had worked with responded. "The one thing I always saw about the best ones is that they very rarely lost their cool. They did not seem to get rattled. So, I try to keep that perspective."

Kevin sought advice from a mentor. "One day I was talking to my former boss who is still on our board. . . . When I would get upset about something, he would joke, 'I can see you're getting your Irish up.' He'd see me turn red, see that vein in my neck. He would know right away when I was upset. I would never challenge him in public. I would take a little bit to cool off. Then I'd go back up to his office, and say, 'Hey, can we talk?' I don't think there was a single instance where we didn't resolve it in private."

His boss didn't have an answer for how Kevin could avoid enemy mode; in the past, his boss even viewed it as a necessity. Kevin freely admitted that at times he "lost it" in stupid enemy mode and also felt that sometimes it seemed to work for him. During one meeting with a customer, Kevin became fed up with the customer's attempts to bait him. "Finally, I lost it, laid into him, and lectured him. Then I just shut up for the rest of the meeting."

Because his boss was present at the time, Kevin later apologized to him: "I didn't mean to lose my cool like that, but I obviously did. He pushed enough buttons where I finally lost it." His boss told him, "Wow, I've never seen you like that, but I think that other fella had it coming."

Does losing your cool in stupid enemy mode work? Yelling or threatening does seem to move the needle, make the sale, or force action, but the cost can be high. The relationship with Kevin's customer returned to cordial but was never the same. Might Kevin have been able to handle the situation without stupid enemy mode?

As Ray went over his case studies, he noticed the costs associated with stupid enemy mode. The cost was high regarding the impact on relational capital. Relationships were never the same after getting stupid. Results were unpredictable and often not good.

Ray turned to Jack Briggs, who flew fighter jets in the Air Force for thirty-one years, thus placing his life on the line. Briggs had the steely-eyed look of a hawk, a ready sense of humor, and a profound religious faith. He had seen enemy mode in the military and in non-profit organizations.

When he was a brigadier general in Afghanistan, stupid enemy mode burned a bridge with a peer. Briggs was requesting approval from a major general at headquarters for more fighter jets to provide close air support to ground troops. Briggs and his staff made what to them was a reasonable request. The general denied it immediately. The total number of troops on the ground was strictly limited. The higher headquarters had brought their band musicians.

Briggs said, "I got frustrated. I did. It was in total enemy mode. I went from a conversation with a peer from a different service to, 'You don't get this, do you?' And you know, my staff is listening."

"He came back to me, 'I get it totally.' I said, 'No, you don't! Why don't you send home the fifty band members?'"

Briggs immediately knew he shouldn't have made that stupid enemy mode comment. The four-star general in command of all US Forces in Afghanistan had to settle it. Briggs eventually got more fighter jets, but the relationship was harmed. He had set a bad example by falling into stupid enemy mode, and he regretted it. His bad example affected his staff, all of whom were younger and more junior in rank.

HELP WITH ESCAPING STUPID

Kerry Haynes was head chaplain at the VA Hospital in San Antonio, Texas. His specialty was PTSD and moral injury. Ray had known him for forty years and served with him as an Army chaplain.

Haynes spent his days helping veterans, some of whom needed legal advice or representation. San Antonio had set up a veterans court system in which judges and lawyers specialized in veterans legal issues and wore veterans' symbols on their robes and suits. Haynes told Ray: "The veterans court system in San Antonio is a beautiful thing. I was working with a young Afghan War veteran who was before Veterans Court for DUI. He was sure of going to prison because it was his second or even third offense. He was convinced nobody cared, and he was screaming at the judge.

"I said, 'Man, if you are screaming at the judge, nothing good is going to come after that. He's going to perceive you as the enemy and that you're not listening to him. He's not going to treat you as a victim but as the enemy.'" This was before Haynes knew about enemy mode.

Stupid enemy mode does not consider less damaging options, and yet, it is not the worst offender.

Haynes continued, "He didn't like me saying that, but it helped. He went back later and apologized to that judge. That takes guts for a guy with PTSD. He still had to do his pen-

ance, but it got easier after that. He learned that these guys in Veterans Court were for him, not against him. They're trying to help."

Ray's case studies had revealed that no refriending followed most episodes of stupid enemy mode. The damage to the group identity, teams, cooperative effort, and positive motivation appeared to be permanent and perhaps irreversible. Any discussion of the usefulness of enemy mode would need to include a cost to benefit consideration that included damage to relational capital.

The problem during stupid enemy mode is that the brain operates as though there is no relationship. Stupid enemy mode does not consider less damaging options, and yet, it is not the worst offender. Nowhere is the destruction of relational capital greater than during intelligent enemy mode, which we will consider in the next chapter.

INTELLIGENT ENEMY MODE

NOT ONLY HAD CEO KEVIN spotted stupid enemy mode at work, he had seen intelligent enemy mode there too. When Kevin learned about intelligent enemy mode from Ray, it struck him that a former executive was perpetually in enemy mode. "I didn't know it," Kevin said. "John seemed to be a great guy until you were pulling the knife out of your back. I just didn't realize at the time how manipulative he could be."

John used his intelligence to get rid of competition on the way to the top. He was going to be the winner. But before John reached the top, he had wasted his relational capital and derailed his personal life.

We celebrate winners. Many of those winners maneuver, scheme, and look out for number one while living in intelligent enemy mode. This is often seen in those holding authoritative roles (e.g., CEOs, pastors, or police officers). Intelligent enemy mode engages the predatory systems people and animals use to track and hunt their prey.

Ray mentioned intelligent enemy mode to corporate attorney Paul Glaser and was surprised by Paul's belief that intelligent enemy mode is institutionalized by contract law. Contracts, Glaser believed, pit two parties against one another. Normally the more powerful party dictates the terms from a place of strength that is not mutually beneficial.

Bob and Natalie used HOA rules against Joe and Sheila in the scenario in chapter 2. Driven by the need to win, people in intelligent enemy mode will deceive, bully, intimidate, and even throw close friends and colleagues "under the bus." Are these just rogue actors, or do we all act in this way at times?

While intelligent enemy mode can mimic the other two enemy mode styles, there are important differences. Unlike stupid enemy mode, when someone in intelligent enemy mode "blows up," they are not sorry afterward. Blowing up is useful for getting a "win."

When Coach Bobby Knight threw a chair across the basketball court during a televised game or kicked lockers and cursed reporters in a press conference, he didn't think he was acting stupid. He did not feel he needed to apologize. His behavior was justified by his supporters because he was a tough coach who got results. Knight was a winner.

WHATEVER IT TAKES TO WIN IS RIGHT

Intelligent enemy mode and the attitude "whatever it takes to win" go together. Coach Bobby Knight was the fourth most successful coach in college basketball history. His career began at West Point in the 1960s. Knight experienced extraordinary success despite frequent public displays of a volatile, combative nature. Early in his head coaching career, he lost his temper during a game, exposing volcanic anger below the surface. His behavior was justified as what tough coaches do to get results. After all, people said, Knight learned his coaching style at Army.

Because Knight was a winner, his character flaws were overlooked by college administrators for a long time. Institutions want to win, and they shield even predators who help them dominate. Knight was finally fired as head coach at Indiana University in 2000 after violating a "no-contact" policy with a student. Afterward, thousands of students protested and burned university president Myles Brand in effigy.

What did they believe justified the protest? Fans want their teams to win. Author John Feinstein talks about this in his book *A Season on the Brink* and closes with this chilling commentary:

> That is why, as I finish this, I am reminded of an incident that took place in January. After the Indiana-Illinois game during which Bob kicked and slammed a chair, and kicked a cheerleader's megaphone, Dave Kindred, the superb columnist for *The Atlanta Constitution*, wrote that he was disappointed to see Knight acting this way again. Kindred, a long-time friend of Knight's, ended the column by writing, "Once again I find myself wondering when it comes to Bob Knight if the end justifies the means."
>
> A few days later, Knight called Kindred. "You needed one more line for that [expletive] column," Knight said. "You should have finished by saying, 'And one more time, I realize that it does.'"
>
> Kindred thought for a moment and then said, "Bob, you're right."
> I agree.[1]

The last two lines should disturb us. Kindred thought Knight had done the right thing, and Feinstein agreed. The message is clear: Whatever it takes to win is right. Winning justifies bullying, intimidation, and predatory behavior. Intelligent enemy mode wins.

How Bobby Knight coached in the 1960s no longer worked in the 1990s. Ray discovered that Bobby Knight's protégé, Coach Mike Krzyzewski (Coach K), had some "Knight" coaching tendencies when he started but became more relational as a coach at Duke.

When Jim told Ray about some winning coaches for the Colorado School of Mines who were intentionally working to keep their coaching staff and players out of enemy mode, Ray was interested. Perhaps he could find some answers by interviewing them.

Ray asked Jack Briggs how he had seen intelligent enemy mode at the Rescue Mission. Briggs explained: "We have a women's addiction program. Men tend to own their individual issues while women own the group's issue. This relational dynamic frequently introduces intelligent enemy mode interactions between the women. Maybe a woman will accidentally push someone's buttons in a group setting. A spat between those two escalates. Then, a third person realizes she can elevate her own position by being the mediator."

Unlike simple enemy mode, people in intelligent enemy mode do not feel sorry for ignoring important relationships.

The third person is a faux-mediator in intelligent enemy mode looking for her own winning social status. Ray commented, "That's really devious, isn't it?" And Briggs agreed. Manipulating the conflict could gain them power and respect and a possible advantage with the authorities.

Everyday intelligent enemy mode is dangerous, but even more so when a leader wields it to protect their status and power. Unlike simple enemy mode, people in intelligent enemy mode do not feel sorry for ignoring important relationships. If you are hurt, it is not their fault. You are too sensitive about your feelings, or you are insensitive about how important they are.

STATUS AND WINNING WITHOUT COMPASSION

Pastor Mark Driscoll led Mars Hill Church of Seattle, Washington, from a small Bible study in 1996 to fifteen thousand weekend attenders by 2014.[2] Driscoll was a role model for thousands of pastors and millions of people who downloaded his sermons. The church's numerical growth and the lives changed were dramatic. Behind the scenes, relational and leadership conflict brewed for years.

Driscoll told emerging church leaders: "I am all about blessed subtraction. . . . There is a pile of dead bodies behind the Mars Hill bus and by God's grace it'll be a mountain by the time we're done. You either get on the bus or you get run over by the bus. Those are the options. But the bus ain't gonna stop."[3]

The elders of Mars Hill Church investigated in 2014 and determined that Driscoll had "been guilty of arrogance, responding to conflict with a quick temper and harsh speech, and leading the staff and elders in a domineering manner."[4] His behavior was what we call intelligent enemy mode. The elders wanted him to stay as senior pastor if he would work on his character issues. He resigned instead. The church imploded and virtually disappeared overnight. Ray and Jim lamented the Mars Hill story, but had heard many more stories of unknown Christian leaders in smaller churches and organizations operating in intelligent enemy mode. How can intelligent enemy mode be recognized?

Signs of Intelligent Enemy Mode

- Social status carefully guarded
  - Loyalty, vision, and mission do not value everyone equally.
  - Success depends on making top people look good.
  - Keeping Us and Them separate is valued.
  - People with lower status bear the blame.
  - People warn about the consequences of "crossing" the wrong person.
  - Stratification protects the powerful ones (pecking order).
- Control is more important than care or relationships
  - People are shamed and fired to "make an example" of what will happen if you . . .
  - We receive false assurances.

- Conformity is required (opinions, appearance, actions, beliefs, shared fears).
- Humiliation is used to control and intimidate resisters.

- **Image is carefully managed**
  - Propaganda and "spin doctoring" are active.
  - Discrediting others is a win for us.
  - We prize or broadcast our reputation.
  - We (or someone above us) must be seen as powerful and important.

- **Weakness is exploited**
  - Weaknesses are being watched, tracked, and used later to punish or control.
  - Everyone around me is trying to look strong or successful.
  - Someone is friendly to my face but critical when I am not around.
  - Someone seems too interested in what will cause me pain or shame.
  - We want to hide what we really think or feel because it doesn't feel safe.
  - We track what will cause pain or embarrassment.
  - People are afraid to reveal themselves.

- **Avoidable damages (lost relational capital)**
  - Competent people "disappear" without a voice.
  - We are rewarded even when the win has a high relational cost.
  - There are "people under the bus."
  - Damage to people or projects could have been avoided by listening.

- **Winning justifies actions**
  - Winning is the only real priority.
  - Failures are punished.
  - Relationships do not outlive a person's utility.
  - Vision, mission, and success justify human costs and losses.
  - There is an odd combination of ethical talk with unethical actions.

WHEN THE "BAD" BOSS IS A CHRISTIAN

The first examples of intelligent enemy mode to cross Ray's mind were the horror stories he'd heard of "bad" bosses. It seems everyone has had at least one Miranda Priestly, the iconic terror of a boss in the movie *The Devil Wears Prada*.

As Ray interviewed people for this book, he described the three styles of enemy mode and then asked, "Have you ever known somebody who stayed in enemy mode?"

Interviewee Emanuel immediately identified intelligent enemy mode in the worst boss he ever had.

Emanuel was born in Kenya. His family emigrated to Florida when he was a teenager. After college, Emanuel became a pastor and settled in a city in the western United States where he transitioned to business and community leadership.

His former boss, Pastor Tom, ran a megachurch in the Midwest where Emanuel was an associate pastor. Emanuel said, "Pastor Tom was a bully, an immense bully. He was very insecure."

In public, Pastor Tom was bold, brash, and creative. To his staff, however, he was a terror. Verbal abuse, including shouting at staff members in their face, was common. Tom exhibited traits of vanity and narcissism, and he was unwilling to receive input from his team.

Emanuel explained: "Tom's leadership was overtly about generosity. He tried to buy your love. He would be very generous if he wanted something. He expected undying loyalty to him and to his cause in exchange. Behind closed doors, Tom was a complete animal. He pushed his kids and family. He manipulated everyone. He screamed in people's faces over silly things.

"Tom was very different in public, a more temperate version, but he left people thinking, 'Is this guy for real?'" Emanuel went on to describe how building the church status and creating an edgy image got a winning response from the community. The community liked his creativity and edginess. The church became known for borderline offensive advertising that gained national recognition, created curiosity, and made it the largest church in the region. Status, image, and control obscured the avoidable damages and exploitation of weakness that went with intelligent enemy mode.

Emanuel remembered how focused the church had been on growth and showy, lavish events, including Easter egg hunts that involved dropping eggs from helicopters.

Emanuel remembers that as a staff member, "you had to be all about Pastor Tom."

"Do or say anything that sounded like you were not in support of him and you were out," Emanuel said. "He told people how to think. I mean literally from the stage, he would say things like, 'You are all sheep. You're all dumb.' I would be in the back, sinking down in my seat and say to my friends, 'How are we part of this church?'"

Yet, Emanuel was promoted to the executive team. When Pastor Tom laid out his vision for the church's future, Emanuel found the plan was dysfunctional. The vision made no provision for developing better character. Their future was growth, growth, growth, and whatever made Tom feel good. Emanuel didn't say much in that meeting because he feared being yelled at by the pastor.

After the meeting, Emanuel went to Tom's office. Emanuel acknowledged that growth was good, but he added that the church should care for and develop people. Every church should.

Pastor Tom listened, then replied, "Emanuel, this vision is only going to continue; you need to get with the program."

Emanuel went to his office and uncharacteristically fell to pieces. He immediately wrote his letter of resignation. Looking back, he says this loss was some of his greatest pain. On the positive side, that job loss served as the catalyst that sent him west. "If I didn't have that, I wouldn't be in this city and doing what I'm doing today," he added.

Emanuel ruefully added, "I worked for a sociopath who happened to be a pastor. He was probably the worst leader I've ever worked for."

The brain in intelligent enemy mode has no other value system to guide it except winning.[5] Since winning is created by imposing power on others, the measure of winning is often that the enemy loses. When using "you lose" as a guide, we do not calculate the least harmful solution. A police officer operating in intelligent enemy mode will not be concerned about the least harmful solution for a suspect. A deadly neck restraint, as was used on George Floyd, is better than restraining with handcuffs and jail because "you lose" happens faster. We want police, politicians, and even the military to calculate the least harmful solution with the force at their disposal. We cannot afford for them to be in any kind of enemy mode thinking in which the least harmful solution no longer computes.

IDENTIFYING THE SELF-JUSTIFIED WINNER

We previously met Dr. Naomi Paget, a seminary professor and professional chaplain who had worked with the FBI as well as police and fire departments. She had multiple disaster relief deployments worldwide, such as the Fukushima tsunami and nuclear reactor meltdown. She led disaster relief chaplaincy nationally for several organizations.

Paget identified a self-justified winner who exhibited intelligent enemy mode in her role as a leader of a nonprofit disaster relief organization. She explained that this leader would often get her way by criticizing others. "She looked for ways to make everybody else's ideas look wrong or not culturally acceptable," Paget said.

Paget regularly watched this leader imply that her opponents were biased or bigoted. "Everyone would back up so they wouldn't be labeled as prejudiced. No one wanted to look bad by disagreeing. She used those characterizations to manipulate people. Diversity issues are so sensitive that the minute she'd move to that topic, there was a political charge to it.

"I think that's intelligently predatory," Paget added, "because it's intentional. She calculated her attack so that she could get her way, her agenda. I called her on it a couple of times because, you know what, I've experienced enough prejudice to know what it really is." Paget, who is Japanese American, grew up in South Texas. "People can have an opinion, and it doesn't have to be a prejudice. It could be just an opinion."

Soon after talking to Paget, a report in the news alerted Ray to what appeared to be a case of predatory leadership. His friend, Kathy, confirmed that she had encountered intelligent enemy mode in the form of a boss who was a sexual predator.

Kathy was a CPA with a master's degree in finance and delighted to find a job with a nonprofit where she could live out her values. She believed strongly in the mission of this organization that cared for foster children. She had found her dream job! Kathy began as the bookkeeper and was eventually promoted to CFO.

Kathy said she heard rumors that the CEO was a sexual predator whose innuendos and behavior harassed his all-female workforce. On the last day of the year only the CEO and one other person were working as Kathy processed the mail and deposited year-end donations. The CEO walked around the counter so his arm was touching hers. She tried to tolerate her discomfort. His face was less than twelve inches from hers. Kathy moved away. He had invaded her personal space and made her feel unsafe.

If this was the only incident, Kathy might have overlooked it. Stories from other women kept coming. One young and highly respected coworker resigned. She would later state that the CEO had tried to seduce her multiple times. By the end, twenty women had told Kathy of similar experiences. Kathy found the work atmosphere intolerable and was forced to resign as well. A lawsuit and complaints to the state were filed. However, the organization's board of directors accepted the CEO's justifications and retained him.

As Ray continued interviewing Christian leaders, he uncovered case after case of self-justified and intelligent enemy mode in operation. But wait, didn't Jesus berate those who deployed moral justifications but ignored compassion and attachment love?

MORAL THINKING EASILY BECOMES SELF-JUSTIFICATION

One characteristic of intelligent enemy mode stands out in these examples from the faith community—the odd combination of ethical talk with unethical actions. Pastor Tom from the Midwest justified his abuse of Emanuel and the staff as producing church growth, even telling the staff that their pay was directly connected to the number of people coming on Sunday.

In enemy mode thinking, these people would conclude:

- My gaining status improves God's standing.
- Managing my image makes God look better.
- My control achieves what is good.
- Weakness makes goodness fail.
- The higher the human cost, the more noble the project.
- Winning achieves high moral purposes.

The brain is quite capable of operating without compassion in order to win. In fact, there is much in common between sociopathic, narcissistic, and intelligent enemy modes of thinking. During intelligent enemy mode, Christian and non-Christian leaders alike can use their ethical reasoning to justify their unethical tactics.

Can we expect moral thinking to control enemy mode? Most of the discussions among ethicists, social scientists, theologians, and university professors studying human behavior and the brain focus on moral thinking.

Spoiler alert! My brain justifies whatever I feel is right and then adds moral reasoning to persuade others. In short, ethical thinking does not reliably correct intelligent enemy mode and might make it even more dangerous. If I want to win, my brain justifies whatever gets me the win, provided it does not cost me too much. What it costs you only helps me win.

> **My brain justifies whatever I feel is right and then adds moral reasoning to persuade others.**

How the brain calculates costs depends on the state it is in. During relational states, relational costs count. During nonrelational states, like enemy mode, the costs focus on the win. The brain can generate moral sounding justifications for both.

Let's meet five professors who have a lot to say on the brain and moral reasoning.

Jonathan Haidt is a social psychologist whom we met earlier. He is fascinated by the differing moral values expressed and fiercely defended by conservatives and liberals. Using social psychology experiments and brain studies, Haidt set out to discover how moral values were formed. He concluded that moral values are not based on moral reasoning. Quite the opposite, "we reason to find the best possible reasons why *somebody else ought to join us* in our judgment."[6]

After arguing extensively that morality does not come from reason or the reasoning parts of the brain, he concludes, "If morality doesn't come primarily from reasoning, then that leaves some combination of innateness and social learning as the most likely candidates."[7] He continues, "We're born to be righteous, but we have to learn what, exactly, people like us should be righteous about."[8]

Haidt proposes a way to correct for the way feelings create self-justifications: "Rather, what I'm saying is that we must be very wary of any *individual's* ability to reason."[9] He then adds, "We should not expect individuals to produce good, open-minded, truth-seeking reasoning, particularly when self-interest or reputational concerns are in play."[10]

Haidt believes we have a genetic tendency, at least in some individuals, to value what is good for the group. Haidt looks for a solution to enemy mode through building moral capital in "hives." By his calculations, humans are 10 percent "bees" who work together and 90 percent chimps who don't.[11] Avoiding the abuses of self-justified moral reasoning can only be accomplished together in our hives. Haidt concludes, "We humans need access to healthy hives in order to thrive."[12]

Robert Sapolsky is a primate researcher and professor of biology and neurology at Stanford. Sapolsky can find an exception or contradiction for *nearly* every generalization about the nervous system. Jim was tempted to say *every* generalization, but Sapolsky would find an exception. Sapolsky points out that what we think about our morals and what we feel about our morals are both represented in the prefrontal cortex (PFC) but in different parts.[13] How we will feel if we do something is simulated in the ventromedial PFC (vmPFC) while what we will think is formulated in the dorsolateral PFC (dlPFC).[14]

It is commonly believed that what we feel and what we think are generally at odds. Sapolsky says, "A simplistic view is that the vmPFC and the dlPFC perpetually battle for domination by emotion versus cognition. But while emotion and cognition can be somewhat separable, they're rarely in opposition."[15] Emotions and cognitions align more closely as our experience becomes more intense,[16] such as when we are facing moral decisions about who should die and who should live. "[P]eople often haven't a clue why they've made some judgment, yet they fervently believe it's correct."[17]

How we learn moral reasoning leads Sapolsky to an extended discussion of culture and how compassion and empathy develop in the brain. For him, compassion and empathy become large factors in what kind of moral behavior we will exhibit. His solutions to what we are calling intelligent enemy mode would involve compassion and producing the right feelings, although he is not a bit clear about how we might "unlearn" a badly learned reaction like racism.

Ben Sasse earned his PhD in American history from Yale and became president of a Lutheran college before becoming a conservative politician and US senator. After looking over the evidence, Sasse concludes that people are lonely (not enough attachments) and easily gathered in "anti-tribes" where they justify being against some other anti-tribe. Sasse quotes a fourth-century BC proverb: "The enemy of my enemy is my friend."[18]

Sasse concludes that intellectuals and scientists of all traditions are always biased. "We all bring self-justifying biases to bear at the beginning of every day."[19] He uses moral reasoning to abandon moral reasoning as the way out of enemy mode. Since attacking others grows out of isolation, he sees the solution coming from group identities he calls tribes, where we belong for mutual care.

Iain McGilchrist is a medical doctor who teaches brain science in the United Kingdom. McGilchrist focuses on how the brain has shaped Western culture, education, and ethics. McGilchrist places the intelligent enemy mode process directly in the frontal lobes, as he explains here:

> The frontal lobes not only teach us to betray, but to trust. Through them we learn to take another's perspective and to control our own immediate needs and desires. . . . The evolution of the frontal lobes prepares us at the same time to be exploiters of the world and of one another, and to be citizens one with another and guardians of the world. If it has made us the most powerful and destructive of animals, it has also turned us, famously, into the "social animal", and into an animal with a spiritual dimension.[20]

McGilchrist, who is known to focus on the lateralization of the brain, places deliberate malice into the left prefrontal cortex, but compassion in the right prefrontal cortex.[21] Experience tells us that people will justify both. However, McGilchrist's theme is the primacy of the right hemisphere for identity and moral judgments, leaving the solution to intelligent enemy mode in the right PFC operations using the brain's "as if" simulator to predict how our bodies will feel if we do this or that.

Allan Schore taught at the UCLA School of Medicine where he combined many scientific disciplines that studied the brain from different angles. The main impact of Schore's work has been explaining the connection between identity, shared emotions, and the development of the brain.[22] Regulating emotions develops through attachments to significant others. Regulating emotions together with a more experienced brain develops identity and synchronicity in the right brain. Moral values, attachment, identity, and emotional control are lateralized to the right brain. The right brain is developed and trained relationally.

These five professors' writings agree that moral thinking is not our solution. We do not escape enemy mode through moral thoughts. Moral thoughts do not regulate emotions—attachments do. Without significant attachments that produce right brain synchronicity, the left brain is likely to justify anything.

We do not escape enemy mode through moral thoughts. Moral thoughts do not regulate emotions attachments do.

The five professors provide an intersection of ideas where we might find the solution to enemy mode. Haidt calls for a "hive."

Sapolsky looks for a culture of compassion and empathy. Sasse wants tribes of belonging instead of anti-tribes. McGilchrist places identity in the center. Schore finds that the combination of attachment and emotional regulation leads to an identity capable of moral actions.

Hives-tribes-culture-identity-compassion-attachment all add together into an identity group. To escape enemy mode with our enemies, we must belong to an identity group that attaches with compassion to our enemies.

Group Identity in the Brain after Age Thirteen

Schore points out that the brain goes through a sort of "molt" (known technically as apoptosis) at age thirteen. From that point on, the survival of *our people* (our identity group) becomes more important to the brain than our own survival. When few people traveled, media and news were scarce, and most people we met knew our grandparents, it was pretty clear who *our people* were. Global travel and access to multimedia, and access to the world via the internet since the industrial and the digital revolutions, have made defining *our people* much less clear for most of us. Still, our brains are wired to give more value to the survival of the group that defines us than we give to our own lives.

How we decide who *our people* are and what makes others *not our people* is a poorly studied area of brain science. Identifying *my people* acquires life and death power once we are older than thirteen. There is an obvious intuitive link between *not our people* and who the brain will regard as potential enemies.

Who our brains accept as *my people* may not match our consciously liberal, conservative, educated, or religious views. Enemy mode, hate, and ethnocentrism are connected somehow yet not the same. As we have seen already, the brain easily develops enemy mode with *our people*. It should be at least as easy to get into enemy mode with those who are *not our people*.

As the *Escaping Enemy Mode* project took shape, tracking down and sorting out the scarce and conflicting brain and social science was becoming a major challenge for the authors. Books were piling up on Jim's shelves much faster than he could read them. The literature provided very preliminary brain science. The conclusions were not compelling. Ray needed working solutions that Jim could not find. The reality was making them both nervous.

The social science writers had constructed theories about how hate developed and spread, but the brain science was sketchy. Could available brain science and social science produce refriending that would work?

Refriending appeals to us when our brain sees the other person as one of *our people* but achieves very little traction if the person is not. For many Christians, the rest of the world and their religions are *not my people*. When this is the case, the survival and welfare of "unbelievers" would not be prioritized in their brains.

Getting beyond simply talking about loving our enemies, as Christians claim to believe, required attachments. The brain was wired to build attachments when there is joy. Building relational joy with the rest of the world becomes essential for growing attachments that can escape enemy mode. Relational joy provides a theoretical bridge that converts strangers and enemies into *our people*. The more Ray and Jim talked, the more joy looked to be the main path to refriending. At least joy was a necessary element for escaping enemy mode. The first barrier would be persuading Christian leaders to implement the virtue of loving their enemies.

HOW INTELLIGENT ENEMY MODE WORKS IN THE BRAIN

One way to think of the three types of enemy mode is that they represent three levels of brain activation. Excessively low levels of activity lead to simple enemy mode. Excessively high activation contributes to stupid enemy mode. Schore pointed out that right-brain correction is particularly needed for both extremes of activation.[23]

We can intuit how our brain might need to "wake up" or "cool down" quite easily. What happens during intelligent enemy mode? Intelligent enemy mode runs right in the middle of optimum brain activity levels. We cannot say the brain isn't aware enough because intelligent enemy mode is very aware. We cannot say that it is too intense or upset because coldly calculated thinking is involved. We cannot say that intelligent enemy mode is too insensitive to others because the best predators are accurately aware of what their target is feeling, thinking, doing, and planning, and can spot any weaknesses. Con-artists and other socio-paths share this pattern. The part of the brain that computes these calculations is called the Theory of Mind (ToM) and is located near the junction of the temporal and parietal lobes but incorporated into motivation and action in the anterior cingulate.

To summarize, excessively low levels of brain activity lead to simple enemy mode. Excessively high activation accompanies stupid enemy mode. Both very high and very low arousal requires right-brain correction. Intelligent enemy mode, however, is a mid-level activation where the left brain is dominant.

LATERALIZATION AS A FUNCTION OF AROUSAL

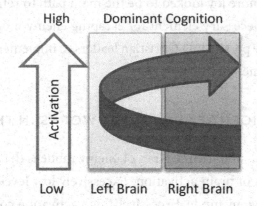

Based on Schore's relationship of primary and secondary processes and arousal.[24]

So, how is it that low, normal, and high levels of brain activation all result in enemy mode, albeit with different styles? What do the three styles have in common? What is missing in all enemy mode brain operations? The answer is the attachment signal. Attachment means that we will share what happens next with the "other" as though it happened to us. We can call the shared feeling compassion, but not without noticing that we can also have compassion for people we have never seen before. We can have compassion without attachment, but we cannot have attachment without compassion. We will consider how the brain experiences compassion in chapter 9.

Attachment, as evidenced by the presence of compassion, eliminates all three forms of enemy mode. Attachment responses will help us regulate extremes of brain arousal by raising under-activated levels (simple enemy mode) or lowering excessive levels (stupid enemy mode). Attachment adds compassion to the middle range (intelligent enemy mode). With attachment we can escape enemy mode.

If attachment was a choice, we could end the book with one more sentence. However, attachments are largely precortical in that they form before brain signals reach the cortex, and nonverbal in that they do not use words. These enduring psychological traits form differently at different ages, can be produced by fear or love, degrade when exposed to circulating glucocorticoids, can involve individuals or groups, and are heavily influenced by what the brain anticipates as an outcome.

Attachment, as evidenced by the presence of compassion, eliminates all three forms of enemy mode.

In general, the brain-related social psychology literature about hate, prejudice, violence, and enemies focuses on two factors: 1) Us versus Them, or 2) moral thinking and behavior. While authors and discussions acknowledge attachment systems in the brain, the role of attachment is underestimated. Attachment is often expected to produce conformity to Us with fear or disgust for Them. It will take some detailed discussion of attachment and group identity to see how attachment could provide a solution with enough power to help whole groups escape enemy mode. Then, we need to find groups who will test the solution.

Our brain quickly separates Us from Them before we are even conscious that we have seen a face, as has been described in detail by Sapolsky.[25] In general, people our brain identifies as Them alert the amygdala and energize the threat activation system to be ready for trouble.[26] This threat activation can be quickly corrected, even before conscious awareness, by the right prefrontal cortex.[27]

We know from everyday experience that we don't have attachments to all the Us people, and we can have compassion for some of the Them people. Every so often, two Thems form an attachment. So, attachment and compassion operate independently in the brain from Us and Them.

Jim met Father Ubald Rugirangoga of Rwanda, who is featured in the award-winning documentary "Forgiveness: The Secret of Peace." Both of Fr. Ubald's Tutsi parents were killed by Hutus. He himself escaped being killed on multiple occasions. The first such escape occurred in the 1960s when Ubald was a boy and his father was killed. The second series of escapes were during the 1994 Rwanda genocide. Fr. Ubald returned to Rwanda to build peace that would form lasting attachments between Hutus and Tutsis.

Straton Sinzabakwira was the Hutu who led the group that killed Fr. Ubald's mother. Straton was in intelligent enemy mode as he directed the murders. He was later imprisoned for his killings. Prison was where Fr. Ubald found him, forgave him, and began building an attachment. Fr. Ubald had compassion on Straton's son, who could not afford an education. Since Straton was in prison, Fr. Ubald paid the boy's tuition. The obvious attachment and compassion between Us and Them is evident across the documentary.[28]

Where attachments have their greatest influence is in the formation and operation of individual and group identities. The point here is that identity provides the predisposition to form attachments. If my group identity does not form attachments to blacks, whites, Jews, Mormons, Muslims, Japanese, liberals, supremacists, or people who are overweight or intellectual or gay or wear fur or hunt whales, then my brain is predisposed against attachment. Since the brain responds to anticipated outcomes by activating previously learned experience, I easily enter and stay in enemy mode with those with whom my group does not attach.

The lack of attachment or compassion is not because our brain sees others as a Them, but because it predicts that our identity group does not attach to that kind of Them. If we are people who attach to Them, an entirely different outcome is predicted. If Christians love Muslims and develop compassion for Them, Christian brains predict attachment to Them.

SOCIOPATHIC POWER AND "THE WIN"

Let us consider some of the reasons why current solutions to enemy mode do not work reliably. Two common solutions involve eliciting compassion and empowering others. Where these solutions run into trouble comes at the intersection of enemy mode and psychopathic brain operations. The simplest way to state the problem is that attempting to teach compassion to psychopaths simply makes them better psychopaths.[29] Therapy for a brain where attachment is "off" becomes a finishing school for predatory ToM (Theory of Mind) skills. Armed with a better understanding of how others feel and operate, intelligent enemy mode can manipulate, use others, and win more effectively.[30] Awareness training without attachment enables more intelligent enemy mode operations.

Social science experiments conclude that giving people power makes them more sociopathic even after warning them to anticipate and avoid the effects of power. Martha Stout of Harvard Medical School, author of *The Sociopath Next Door*, says, "Sociopaths love power. They love winning. If you take loving kindness out of the human brain, there's not much left except the will to win."[31] The prospect of eliminating enemy mode through empowering people fails to work reliably.

Simple and stupid enemy mode thinking fails to calculate the least harmful alternative due to a lack of prefrontal cortex activity. Intelligent enemy mode makes some calculations of the least harmful solution, but with two twists:

1. The "least painful for *me*" solution becomes the least harmful. Any painful damage to you (damaging exactly what you value) is your fault for not letting me win.
2. Causing you enough pain helps me win. The "least harmful solution" means the most pain for you so I will win.

It is not hard to see how bullies, torturers, terrorists, tyrants, and drug cartels calculate their wins. The same intelligent enemy mode plays out during divorce and business dealings. What is missing is attachment. There is no "*our* least harmful solution." Social and relational capital gets squandered during this relational blindness. Excessively harmful solutions become commonplace. Intelligent enemy mode is stupid in the bigger picture.

Lt. Colonel Dave Grossman established the field of "killology." He found that militaries worldwide have for centuries employed sociopaths who "have no remorse about the effects of their behavior on others."[32] Grossman is a retired infantry officer and former Army ranger who taught psychology at West Point. In his book *On Killing: The Psychological Cost of Learning to Kill in War and Society*, Grossman states that sociopaths make up a very small percentage of those in uniform, but sociopaths would not calculate the least harmful alternative. These become what Grossman calls wolves who prey on sheep.[33]

HOW DOES INTELLIGENT ENEMY MODE IMPACT ME?

Are we being played? Ray and Jim wanted to interview a professional who understood why a world in intelligent enemy mode might not be good for us. Ray knew Eric Bents, the executive director of Pinnacle Forum, a nonprofit organization for influential Christian leaders. Bents is a retired US Air Force intelligence colonel experienced in *influence operations*. Commonly called "propaganda," the military calls them influence operations to deceive enemies so they can't defend themselves effectively. Influence operations are professional intelligent enemy mode at work. With multiple deployments in Air Force intelligence, Bents was very experienced.

Ray and Jim agreed that Bents was the kind of leader who understood intelligent enemy mode thinking. But Bents had another thing going for him: he was a Christian leader who had both been a pastor and led a nonprofit organization. He was also the kind of person who might understand the value of escaping enemy mode—and he had influence.

Ray approached Bents, who immediately saw the similarity between intelligent enemy mode and influence operations. He saw intelligent enemy mode everywhere. He told Ray, "People do this stuff because it works. Influence operations work."

Bents had done military intelligence work during combat, so Ray asked, "Would you say that intelligent enemy mode is needed to do intelligence work?"

Bents admitted to the conventional wisdom: "That would be the consensus on the HUMINT [human intelligence] side; it's 'who's playing who.' Movies make a big thing of it, but I've watched this in real time."

He witnessed the battle of wits with detainees in Afghanistan, and he tried to warn his fellow officers. "One detainee in particular was extraordinarily intelligent," Bents recalled. "I would warn people. You think you're going to run the show when he comes in, but *he* is! You better be prepared. They wouldn't believe me, but I would be proven right."

Bents also saw influence operations in our culture in both traditional and social media. "They are trying to trigger outrage. Triggers are nonstop in social media and national media."

He explained: "I was doing a 24/7-type watch operation while deployed. The news was on all the time. I always turned the volume off. But, on the banner, one network used the word 'outrage' every fifteen minutes. That's clickbait displayed purposely because enemy mode drives clicks. That's a major systemic issue right now." US senator Ben Sasse makes a similar claim about the systemic issue of outrage and clickbait by both conservative and liberal media in his book *Them*.[34]

Ray asked Bents to expand on systemic issues: "So, marketers deliberately craft devious campaigns to play on people's fears and trip people into enemy mode?"

"Yes," Bents said. "A media group will say, 'Those liberals are going to do this and they're going to do that, or those conservatives are going to take away your abortion rights.' There's a seed of truth in it. Fear clicks people into enemy mode and opens their pocketbooks. That's the economy of the culture wars, unfortunately."

Once, when Bents was being interviewed to be an executive for a Christian public policy nonprofit, he told the interviewers up front, "I will not do fear-based fundraising. I just am not going to lead like that. We will lead by vision and not as a reactionary organization." They didn't hire him, and he was glad they didn't.

Ray remembered something former Congressman Geoff Davis had told him about raising money. Ray had interviewed Davis because of his high-profile career on Capitol Hill and as a corporate consultant. Davis had many stories of enemy mode from both politics and business.

Davis had a reputation as one of the most conservative members of the Republican Caucus during four terms in office; despite that, some conservative political action committees consistently raised money by calling Davis a RINO: Republican in Name Only. Enemy mode brought in the money.

Davis grew to despise these intelligent enemy mode calculations. He said it like this: "Create an enemy even though they're not my enemy."

He told Ray, "The real motive of these groups profiting from enemy mode is continually exposed when the target no longer adds value." Davis planned to retire when his younger children entered high school, and the day he announced his retirement, he said, "The noise disappeared."

Political activism, whether on the Left or the Right, uses the same tactics. Intelligent enemy mode is about the win.

WHAT IS IN IT FOR ME TO GET OUT OF INTELLIGENT ENEMY MODE?

Enemy mode used against us easily incites enemy mode in return. The basic feeling that encourages it is "he/she/they are not on my side." Many people are not on our side, but when we drop into enemy mode in response, we begin thinking about how to beat them instead of how to be our best selves. Our best selves treat each other as fellow humans.

When others are not on our side, it is easier to be bystanders who allow bullies their way. Click that thinking up a notch, and we exploit others. Click again, and fighting makes sense. Click again, and we see the reason to have Them as slaves. Click again, and ridding the world of Them starts making sense. Intelligent enemy mode thinking supports atrocities better than it protects us.

To put the value of getting out of intelligent enemy mode in financial terms, it destroys relational capital. Do we want to build, maintain, and leave behind a network of relationships where love, joy, peace, and understanding actively protect that network from predators? Then we had best not be running our brains in an intelligent enemy mode. Instead, we want to be in an intelligent relational mode.

There are two things that healthy brains value above simple winning: our identities and our attachment relationships. Ray thought about his ten-year-old self, crushing his little sister in a game. A reminder from his mom about who he was might have stopped him from gloating. But he had to win. His sister cried in frustration and flipped the game board! As we continue exploring this topic, we will discover that escaping enemy mode relies heavily on both. Our main incentive to avoid intelligent enemy mode is so that we can protect and grow our group identities.

The value of our identity is high enough that most people will die defending it. Our attachments will send us into a burning building. The survival of our identities and attachment relationships becomes more important than the survival of our bodies. Working answers to escaping enemy mode will be found in the company of our identities and attachments rather than in the company of moral thinking. I may think it is a good idea for children to have an education but am much more likely to spend money and time on education for my children or grandchildren.

One of the obvious problems with escaping enemy mode, or helping others escape enemy mode, is the need for relationships at the very moment when one or both sides feel like enemies. Our identity group must engage and embrace enemies when they still feel like threats. We saw Lisa make this type of bold engagement with the angry father. Most people will not.

There are groups who do engage people who are in enemy mode. Police and military leaders seek and engage enemies. Soldiers are formed through a process called "soldierization," designed to shape an identity group that engages rather than runs from enemies. Other military services do similar types of training. The training produces a group identity that could engage enemies along with some sharp distinctions between Us and Them. Since a huge number of veterans received soldierization-style training, it must leave a social impact.

Soldierization

Ray met Geoff Davis in the military, and Eric Bents served in the military. That connection got Jim and Ray thinking: What impact did soldierization have on their brains? On one hand, many aspects of soldierization build brave group identities that endure hardship and protect each other. On the other hand, the training was not created for escaping enemy mode.

Ray was trained at the United States Military Academy at West Point. Every cadet learned basic infantry tactics. The infantry's mission is to "close with and destroy the enemy." To transform a civilian into a warrior takes weeks, even years.

Soldierization forms groups of people who will obey orders, bond with their unit, and, when necessary, lay down their lives. Ray's West Point classmate Lieutenant General Sean MacFarland was the Deputy Commander of the Training and Doctrine Command, responsible for basic training. He described soldierization like this: "We assimilate people into the Army and teach them what it's like to be part of a cohesive whole."[35]

Ray wondered if military training increased his tendency toward enemy mode. Ray's training involved marching, martial arts, orders, bayonet drills, obstacle courses, and mountaineering. Boxing class as a plebe at West Point taught him to both take and give a punch. Bayonet training objectified the enemy. Training focused on finding the enemy, discovering his plans and intentions, and attacking. For Vietnam-era instructors, the enemy was "Charlie Cong" and his devious jungle tactics. After graduation from West Point, the enemy became "Ivan" and the Soviet horde.

Ray is convinced that the military enhanced his aggressiveness and ability to employ intelligent enemy mode without regret. Intelligent enemy mode worked for combat, but what about peacetime military life with his comrades at arms? Ray recalled, "In 1982, I was a junior Army officer in my first assignment in Germany. I was personally responsible for thirty soldiers in my command. For me, overcoming the enemy became winning the argument, proving my point, getting my way, and accomplishing my mission without failure.

"One of my soldiers was not getting paid properly, so I went with him to the Army pay office. I was angry and determined to make those 'lazy, incompetent' pay-specialist 'enemies' do their job and take care of my soldier.

"I arrived at the pay office in enemy mode, talking louder, restating my logic, and demanding service. I instantly justified my aggressiveness as moral behavior. My bullying manner would get the job done. Not once did I consider a less harmful alternative. All I cared about was getting the win. There wasn't even a faint interest in escaping enemy mode in my mind. My soldier's pay was corrected, but what damage had I done? What relationships had been strained?"

Maybe soldierization didn't affect every soldier the way Ray feels it affected him. Ray now sees that his use of enemy mode continued growing throughout his life. He approached people as tools to accomplish his agenda. The brain, you see, is a learning center. Teach it enemy mode, and it gets better at enemy mode. The brain is an explanation center. Deal in enemy mode, and it will justify enemy mode as intelligently as possible. But if we woke up the cognitive function of the dorsolateral portion of our prefrontal cortex (dlPFC) and took a look at ourselves, would Ray be the only one learning enemy mode, or have we developed enemy mode practices as well?

We have our own stories of being at the receiving end of intelligent enemy mode. We might be one of those pay clerks who experienced Lieutenant Woolridge in intelligent enemy mode in the 1980s. Yet we often justify our own aggression, raise our voices, insist on being understood, or feel others deserve how we treated them or saw them being treated.

We will see the impact of enemy mode in our next chapter. History provides a case study that should match the brain science of enemy mode. Family, school, work, church, race relations, war, crime, law enforcement, politics, and human history illustrate our need to escape enemy mode. Science and religion must intervene in this historical context to produce sustainable changes. Jim was finding limitations in brain science when it came to ways we escape enemy mode. Would history offer a solution?

ENEMY MODE IS ALL AROUND

LIMITING THE IMPACT OF ENEMY MODE is a large consideration for human cultures and institutions. Enemy mode poisons everything it touches. The bully lies in wait to steal a younger kid's lunch money. A corrupt politician receives bribes in exchange for favors. A nonprofit board overlooks egregious misconduct by a famous CEO. Jim and Ray grieved the suffering caused by the contagious nature of enemy mode and understood the need to limit the damage. Rather than suppress enemy mode, Jim and Ray were seeking ways to escape enemy mode, but they ran short of science, so they turned to history.

Governments protect us from people who are not on our side, while simultaneously generating enemy mode reactions. Go to a government office, the IRS for instance, and see if they seem to be on your side. Courts, and the law itself, are dominated by enemy mode. Lawyers are trained to operate in enemy mode. About 40 percent of Congress members are lawyers. Watch Congress and you will see people working to make the other side lose.

"To serve and protect" are the words displayed on the side of the police car that pulls you over. The feeling of being on the same side is usually missing as the officer approaches. Criminals operate in enemy mode. In response, jailors and prison systems return the treatment. These patterns appear to be global and ancient.

Various economic systems aim to control enemy mode exploitation. What will stop the bourgeoisie from exploiting the proletariat? Will money trickle down? Do industrialists exploit workers or do unions? Who the enemy is will vary. The actual impact of these economic systems always diverges from their rhetoric. Economics and governments at best restrain enemy mode. Capitalism, communism, socialism, imperialism, and totalitarianism, to name a few, have limited some exploitation only to empower other predators. Restraining enemy mode without escaping it is not our goal.

Educational systems touch the lives of almost every person in the Western world. Enemy mode is modeled, grown, and spread during the school years. Every level of education has amazing relational exceptions in teachers who recover their best selves, show compassion, attach, and care. Yet, stupid enemy mode has touched almost everyone on playgrounds, in hallways, and in classrooms. School boards, administrators, teachers, and students in all three types of enemy mode are commonplace. Intelligent enemy mode has become refined in parts of academia. Simple enemy mode is evident from top administrators to faculty. Medical schools and seminaries are not exempt, and high status schools may be worse. The obvious conclusion is that education has not produced a widely taught ability to escape enemy mode.

Armies and religions have touched almost every life in the Western world for millennia. Military training and combat experiences are prime suspects for building enemy mode. Religion and moral reasoning, particularly from Christianity in the West, are in the same shape as government, law, and education. By examining the historical records of culture, military experiences, and religion, we will see what doesn't work and may find hints for escaping enemy mode. But first let's explore why the science behind Jim and Ray's research has limits when it comes to enemy mode.

LIMITATIONS OF CURRENT SCIENCE

If Dr. Schore's need to spend years in the library uniting separate scientific fields tells us anything, it is that lots of data does not ensure coherence. The host of details about the brain staggers the mind. The sheer complexity leads the left hemisphere to ignore data points that don't fit its paradigm. Even when the data is good, the conclusions drawn by researchers are often questionable.

If we want to study the PFC and understand group identity, then we should only study people over thirty who have formed a group identity and have a mature PFC. Most of the scientific data about the brain comes from either college students with immature PFC development or people with localized brain damage. The population being sampled for brain studies is mostly what Haidt calls WEIRD (Western, Educated, Industrialized, Rich, Democratic) people.[1] This might be a good sample for examining woke brain operation.

Crimes of passion and great heroism are hard to study with college volunteers. The entire enemy mode problem is hard to reproduce in a lab. It is not so hard to see if cold or hot drinks will bias white college student reactions to pictures of black faces in the first two hundred milliseconds. Does that settle what happens on the Gaza Strip or Southside Chicago? Would the brain look the same for hungry refugees whose families just died or for the people that killed them? How do people in enemy mode torture and kill others? What is the impact on my enemy mode when someone I am attached to is tortured? What do generations of hostility do to the brain?

Wouldn't we expect more intense enemy mode reactions when attachments are involved? Jim could not find any studies of the effect attachment had on enemy mode. Most brain researchers pick random subjects and find experimental conditions that work for everyone. Attachments are individual and personal, so brain studies would need to consider the personal triggers for each research subject.

It is possible to select specific experimental subjects. Semir Zeki and John Paul Romaya from University College London found seventeen subjects (average age thirty-five) who would bring pictures of someone they hated to the lab. The subjects rated how strongly they hated the person in the picture and had their brain scanned while looking at the photo. When the researchers looked at the results, they found overlapping brain activity between people who hate and people in love.[2] The same spots in the brain could do either.

Interpreting Brain Scan Studies

Zeki and Romaya illustrate one well-known problem with interpreting brain scans: a single spot in the brain can do different things. Showing that the part of the brain that plays a role in object and face recognition (fusiform gyrus) actually *does* recognize a familiar face is simple. However, can we be sure that an active fusiform gyrus means someone is looking at faces? The answer is, not necessarily. The gyrus burns up sugar and oxygen for everything we watch with interest. Faces were simply studied first.

What a researcher in one field discovers may be completely unnoticed in a different field. Researcher A studies addictions; researcher B studies attachment. Both identify brain activity in the same spot. Zeki and Romaya encountered this very issue for activity in the insular cortex, as we will soon see.

The second problem with brain scans is that they show us where the brain is burning a lot of energy. That may not seem like a problem except that the brain uses a lot of energy doing what it does not do well. When the brain is doing what it is good at, scanning for where the brain is burning lots of fuel won't show any activity. Sapolsky illustrates this problem with brain scans taken of people lying or telling the truth. People who habitually told the truth showed no activation on the scans while telling the truth.[3]

If we scan the brain of someone who is adept at enemy mode, we might not pick up anything on the scan. If there were a person who had trouble doing enemy mode thinking, their brain activity would show up well. Scanning for places where the brain is using extra energy makes it difficult to know how enemy mode experts do what they do.

The third problem with brain scans is that the brain has different kinds of chemistry that can create activity. When a nerve is firing dopamine, epinephrine, norepinephrine, acetylcholine, serotonin, GABA, nicotine, or other chemicals, the nerve endings produce different outcomes but burn about the same amount of energy.

Most nerve chemistry operates in tiny spaces that are not visible to a scan. Since chemistry does not appear on scans, it must be inferred from regions that have more of a certain neurotransmitter. (Animal studies allow more invasive methods.)

Some neurochemical systems fire together using widely distributed nerve endings and have been called "value systems" by the Nobel Prize winner Gerald Edelman because they change the value of what the brain is doing at that moment.[4] However, these value system bursts are way too fast to be captured on brain scans.

A fourth problem with brain scans is how long they take. The brain can easily create new brain waves up to forty times per second. It takes a scan of at least five seconds of continued activity to have a reading. The brain scan cannot detect a brain wave or tell its frequency. Brain scans read where energy was burned over time.

Fast activity in the brain can be captured by electrical waves (EEG). What these brain wave studies supply in accuracy about speed they lose in accuracy about the source. A lot of nerves have to fire at once to make a wave so the source might be widely distributed. Then, the wave spreads out like the ripples on a pond. Outside the skull, we can see the ripples but need careful calculations to know more or less where they started.

The term "brain waves" is somewhat misleading. Yes, electrical waves are being recorded, but they represent rhythms and joint firing of many nerves. Think of an aspen tree with the wind blowing through the leaves. The faster the wind, the more the leaves flutter, creating "aspen leaf waves." If we record the sound of the leaves, we get waves. But the tree is not trying to produce waves; it is responding to wind.

In some ways, nerves and brain systems are more like vibrating guitar strings. Nerves fire at certain rates, unlike aspen leaves that don't do much quaking on their own. Warm a guitar string and it vibrates slower. Shorten a string and it vibrates faster. Loosen a string and it vibrates slower. Let it get older and it vibrates less. By noticing the changes in vibration, we learn about all sorts of factors, but only if we can tell them apart.

A fifth problem for both brain scan and brain wave studies involves activity that is too slow to show in the sampling period. Sue Othmer was the clinical director of the EEG Institute. Her background is in physics, neurobiology, and behavior from Cornell University and the UCLA Brain Research Institute. Othmer was one of the first to apply Allan Schore's brain model to neurofeedback. She told Jim that her interest arose because of a child in her family whose seizures were not adequately controlled, so she set out to find a solution. Othmer eventually broadened her focus from brain frequencies to include brain rhythms and states. These slower changes are harder to measure but easily observed outside the laboratory.

Despite the popularity of brain scans, much of what the brain does remains difficult to measure in the laboratory, but it is evident in the history of human behavior. Feeding, migrations, seasons, farming, education, and government are based on rhythms and cycles that are too slow to be called waves but are maintained in the brain. Consider the well-known circadian rhythm in the brain. The rhythm takes twenty-four hours to return to its originating level before repeating, so it can hardly be called a wave in electrical terms. But this slow rhythm is found in the nervous system and influences all kinds of things, including predatory and sleep behaviors. Attacking Bin Laden at night is one example. The special forces expected correctly that Bin Laden would be asleep at night due to his nervous system rhythms.

IS ENEMY MODE A PROBLEM
OR A NEEDED SOLUTION?

In the case of Bin Laden and the special forces, was enemy mode a problem or a solution? Both sides most likely considered their intelligent use of enemy mode as an asset. Since most of the human institutions suppressing enemy mode also operated in enemy mode a good deal of the time, the biggest challenge facing Ray's research was convincing himself and others that the harm from enemy mode outweighed the possible benefits. As Ray continued his interviews, multiple people told him that they didn't consider enemy mode a problem. Ray, on the other hand, was well aware of his own tendency toward enemy mode and could easily spot it all around him.

Business consultant Gary Wilkins related a story about Bill, a sales executive whose corporate sales manager used stupid enemy mode to motivate the team. If someone did not achieve their goals, the manager would verbally denigrate them in front of everyone. Bill said everybody would feel tensed up until it happened.

Gary observed, "It was obviously very destructive. The effect was that everybody on the team looked out for themselves and started competing, which of course drove the [sales] numbers to a degree but also made work a very toxic environment."

Bill too had begun to "flip his lid" with clients and his family, a clear sign of stupid enemy mode. We forget who we are, our PFC is off-line, and we act out of the back of our brain. When Bill "flipped his lid" with a client over a difficult problem, he was reverting to what he had seen modeled by his boss.

Eventually, Bill realized he was emulating his boss's behavior. He was in enemy mode even at home. He told Gary that he feared losing his family if he didn't change jobs. Although Bill loved sales, he left the company.

Gary described how enemy mode could be both a problem and a solution, but he could see the challenge of convincing leaders that enemy mode was counterproductive. They seem to feel that you can't be relational if you want results. He agreed the common mindset is: just get it done, and we'll clean up the mess afterward.

"Bill felt that this sales manager knew this 'angry boss' model would get momentum," Gary said. "After a meeting with someone new who was freaking out, the boss would put his arm around them and say, 'Hey, listen, you know, don't get too upset. That's just how we do things. You'll get comfortable with it.' The implication was 'This works, and this is what we are going to keep doing!'"

Ray replied, "Maybe managers justify enemy mode to themselves by taking employees to lunch and telling them, 'It's not personal. It's just business.'"

"Bill is an amazingly relational person," Gary continued. "You can just imagine what this was doing to his heart and soul. He's a Christian and really passionate about solving people's problems with his products. But he realized that this was just rotting him out from the inside."

Enemy mode thinking is prevalent; it's often how work is done and problems are solved. But at what cost?

THE HIGH COST OF
ENEMY MODE IN HUMAN HISTORY

Many questions remained unanswered. What happened in the brain when people went into enemy mode? What got them out? Why did some people stay in enemy mode? Ray and Jim decided that if science lacked tested solutions, they would look to history.

They looked back at the arrest and brutal beating of Rodney King in 1991. King, who was intoxicated and on parole for robbery, had been driving over the speed limit when Los Angeles deputies tried to pull him over. King led them on a high-speed chase for eight miles. High-speed chases are suspected of triggering stupid enemy mode in some officers. Once the chase ended, the officers pulled King from the car and beat him. The deputies were not calculating the least harmful alternative—a major characteristic of enemy mode—for what was widely viewed as racial reasons. A civilian recorded video of the beating that aired on television and the internet. The deputies were tried in a court procedure laced with racial overtones and signs of intelligent enemy mode. A year later, the officers who brutalized King were acquitted by a jury, and violent riots erupted. During the riots, King appealed for peace and pleaded, "Can't we all just get along?"

Doug Noll is a lawyer, peacemaker, and mediator specializing in difficult and intractable conflicts. Here's how he explains why we can't get along:

> The truth is that we are 98 percent emotional and about two percent rational. Thus, the assumptions underlying many disciplines and practices, especially peacemaking, need significant revisions. Much remains unknown, but the implications of the research so far demonstrate that we must be far more aware of neuropsychological factors of human conflict. These factors explain much about conflict behaviors. They also provide insights about new interventions in serious and intractable conflicts.[5]

Noll's percentages may be off, but we agree that human conflict arises from "neuropsychological factors," and new interventions are needed. We see that enemy mode is a key neuropsychological factor in why we can't "just get along." Our brains divide us. Finding the reason and how to escape is our purpose in this book.

The historical evidence for enemy mode abounds. Have we been watching the nightly news? Current news and human history are filled with examples of people who want "the enemy" to lose, can't tell when others are trying to help them, are gathering a following to attack the enemy, or are justifying their hatred. The phrase, "Kill them all: God knows his own!"[6] began during the Crusades at the massacre at Béziers. Variations still appear in the military, and even in cartoons and video games.

What might we learn from history about how our brains unite or divide us? Historical enemy mode examples are infinite in variety and depravity. Even a cursory review returned countless examples of enemy mode causing division. We considered the Nazis and the Ku Klux Klan; slaveholders and slave traders; South African apartheid; the Sand Creek Massacre; Wounded Knee; and conquerors like the Assyrians, Persians, Babylonians, Greeks, Romans, and Europeans, as well as how conquerors treated their victims.

Ray saw enemy mode in Bible accounts, such as Cain killing his brother Abel. Jesus' first followers were in enemy mode after he was arrested, which played out in one disciple's attack with a sword on a high priest's servant until Jesus stopped him. Ray discovered evidence for enemy mode's causation in this haunting quote from philosopher and theologian G. K. Chesterton: "Certain new theologians dispute original sin, which is the only part of Christian theology which can really be proved."[7]

ENEMY MODE IN RACISM AND WORK

Ray interviewed retired Army Major General Dana Pittard, an African American who grew up in the diverse culture of El Paso, Texas. He experienced racism in the 1980s Army. In that era, many football coaches too believed black men didn't have the "leadership qualities to be NFL quarterbacks."[8] That racist attitude lingered in parts of the Army as well.

Pittard would eventually become the second person of color to command a unit called an armored cavalry troop, but not before he had to overcome a racist commander. Pittard was an armor officer with four years of experience in tanks, but he would be required to bide his time.

Pittard was overlooked on his first day in that unit. While he waited in the squadron commander's reception area, his white classmate was invited in for a meet and greet. After thirty minutes, Pittard was neither invited into the commander's office, nor promised a command. But his classmate, who had no experience in tanks, was given a command. Instead, the commander told Pittard he'd be an understudy to a junior officer.

Pittard was taken aback and bluntly said to the commander, "Sir, isn't the current S4 a lieutenant?' [The commander] then quickly shot back, 'He's a [expletive] good lieutenant, you can learn a lot from him, Captain Pittard!' That was October 1985."[9]

Pittard discovered that the commander couldn't see past Pittard's skin color, and he watched a number of white captains get commands. Pittard later reflected in an interview to *Foreign Policy Magazine*:

> "It was clear that I was never going to get a command under this racist commander. It wasn't until well after he left command in 1986 that with a new squadron commander and regimental commander, Col. Thomas E. White, that I was slated to take command of an armored cavalry troop unit. I would end up commanding three straight company level commands with distinction."[10]

DO WE THINK THINGS ARE GETTING BETTER?

How is enemy mode operation trending? The philosopher Hobbes was pessimistic about human nature without a strong ruler. Rousseau had a rosy confidence in human nature and democracy. Both thought the right political and economic system could usher in peace, prosperity, and good will. All reform movements since the birth of Christianity—the rapid spread of Islam, the rise of the Enlightenment, and all revolutions including the French, American, and Bolshevik—have sought to make people get along and flourish.

If we had the right systems and if people made the right choices, things should be better, right? Where have five hundred years of political system tinkering and better decision-making gotten us? Since the Enlightenment, the idea that life would be better if people just made better choices has dominated Western solutions.

Moral reasoning and conscious choices come quite late in the brain's response sequence—way too late to change enemy mode. From our perspective, what will make a difference is not better political and economic systems or more information or better choices. We need to dig deeper into our brains to find lasting and transforming solutions for escaping of enemy mode.

There seems to be more evidence for Hobbes's pessimism than Rousseau's optimism. Sapolsky reviews scientific literature on why human beings war against one another. He quotes Harvard's Steven Pinker, who argues that "(a) violence and the worst horrors of inhumanity have been declining for the last half millennium, thanks to the constraining forces of civilization; and (b) the warfare and barbarity preceding that transition are as old as the human species."[11] Sapolsky puts Pinker squarely in the Hobbesian camp that human beings have always been this way toward one another.[12]

Human life has been getting better, but the story is complicated. Sapolsky reminds us, "At the dawn of the nineteenth century, slavery occurred worldwide, including in the colonies of a Europe basking in the Enlightenment."[13] Sapolsky then provides a list of how life is improving with examples of child labor laws, decline in homicides, and lower incidences of forced marriages, beating of schoolchildren, illiteracy, rape as a tool of conquering armies, and many other examples.[14] Things have been getting better, but they are still quite bad.

But has life always been bad because of enemy mode? We say yes. While we can't do brain scans of people in the past, we can examine their lives for signs.

Pittard and Ray lamented how divided the United States was during the pandemic regarding police brutality, Black Lives Matter protests, and the extreme discord over the results of the 2020 presidential election. Dana sadly observed, "We are more tribal than we think we are in our country. We just are. It's unfortunate."

Still, are things getting better? Dana compared today to fifty years ago. "I've heard people say our country has never been so divided. Did anybody remember we had a divided Army prior to 1947? Even the Army resisted integration until the Korean War. So, we had a divided society along racial lines for sure. I thought that was a lot worse than what we're going through now. I do think we're going to get through it."

"Hey, we've shown some of our true colors as a nation," Dana added. "I wish we could just educate the population on our history, just the facts, not even a slant. Let people make their own judgments and assessments but know our history. Then once you know the history, you realize what good and bad things we've done as a nation and what we don't want to do again."

After talking to Dana Pittard, Ray concluded that enemy mode was helping to fuel the racial divide.

ENEMY MODE AT CHURCH

Dr. Martin Luther King Jr. said long ago that Sunday morning at 11 a.m. was the most segregated hour of the week. Has this changed in the past sixty years? General Pittard told Ray another story that shows, at least in some cases, the answer is no.

Dana had recently retired from the Army and moved to the Midwest to become a vice president of a manufacturing company. He began worshiping at the nearest Lutheran church in his suburb. In this thousand-member church, he was the only black man. Dana's experience in Army chapels told him he would be welcome, but he discovered otherwise. When his sister came for a visit, they attended the church together, and she felt something and told him, "Dana, why do you even go here? These people don't even care for you." Dana found another church. Jim and Ray suspected this story was not uncommon.

The brain quickly separates Us and Them at a subcortical level. How we treat Them is cortical and learned. The brain learns at both cortical and subcortical levels. Can the brain learn a different sense of Us?

IN AN ENEMY MODE LONG, LONG AGO

In an effort to answer that question, Ray looked to a Christian emperor but found more enemy mode. In AD 772, Charlemagne, the Frankish king, considered Saxon pagans to be pests worthy of extermination. They resisted his empire, and his attitude toward them was in total enemy mode. Historian Tom Holland says of Charlemagne, "Like any king in the post-Roman world, he had been raised to view pagans primarily as a nuisance. The point of attacking barbarians was to keep them in order and plunder plenty of loot."[15]

Following years of rebellions, Charlemagne decreed in AD 776 that Saxons accept Christian baptism or die.[16] Five years later, the king met Northumbrian monk Alcuin and invited him to join his royal court. Charlemagne loved discussing theology, and eventually Alcuin convinced him that conversion was best sought by convincing, not compelling. "Faith arises from the will, not from compulsion," said Alcuin. Pagans should be persuaded, not forced to convert.[17] Great King Charles eventually changed the policy fifteen years later. This change was a clear improvement, but not an escape from enemy mode.

Next, Ray turned to ancient history. The more Ray learned about the Greeks, the Romans, and the Anglo-Saxons, the more evident enemy mode appeared to be ingrained in these societies.

Tom Holland specialized in the history of the Persians, Assyrians, Greeks, and Romans, and had always admired these cultures. But eventually, his fascination was replaced with antipathy. He writes,

Sparta and Rome, even when subjected to the minutest historical enquiry, retained their glamour as apex predators. They continued to stalk my imaginings as they had always done: like a great white shark, like a tiger, like a tyrannosaur. Yet giant carnivores, however wondrous, are by their nature terrifying. The more years I spent immersed in the study of classical antiquity, so the more alien I increasingly found it. The values of Leonidas, whose people had practices a peculiarly murderous form of eugenics and trained their young to kill uppity *Untermenschen* by night, were nothing that I recognised as my own; nor were those of Caesar, who was reported to have killed a million Gauls, and enslaved a million more. It was not just the extremes of callousness that unsettled me, but the complete lack of any sense that the poor or the weak might have the slightest intrinsic value.[18]

Spartan and Roman enemy mode practices are repulsive to us now, especially when it comes to sex. Holland said, "Sex was nothing if not an exercise of power. As captured cities were to the swords of the legions, so the bodies of those used sexually were to the Roman man."[19]

MODERN ENEMY MODE

It wasn't just the ancients who acted appallingly. We saw Jeffrey Epstein, his enabler Ghislaine Maxwell, Ravi Zacharias and his board of directors, CEOs, pastors, supervisors, Bill Clinton, and Harvey Weinstein, the Hollywood mogul pulled down by the #MeToo movement.

Weinstein lived the ethos of a Greek god or Roman Caesar. Eighty women accused Weinstein of sexual harassment, assault, or rape. Holland says of men like Weinstein:

Except that the freedom to [sexual expletive] when and as one liked had tended to be, in antiquity, the perk of a very exclusive subsection of society: powerful men. Zeus, Apollo, Dionysus: all had been habitual rapists. So too, in the Rome to which Paul had travelled with his unsettling message of sexual continence, had been many a head of household.[20]

Weinstein's behavior was intelligent enemy mode—no different from many great men of Rome and Greece.

President Bill Clinton was also a professing Christian, yet predatory toward intern Monica Lewinsky. When asked in 2004 by *CBS News* anchor Dan Rather why he had done this, Clinton said,

I think I did something for the worst possible reason—just because I could. I think that's the most, just about the most morally indefensible reason that anybody could have for doing anything. When you do something just because you could.[21]

Disgraced Christian speaker and apologist Ravi Zacharias is another egregious example of intelligent enemy mode. Zacharias was credibly accused of sexual misconduct by numerous women.[22] His ministry and prominent allies initially defended him aggressively. His accusers were sued, and his victims felt crushed. An internal investigation later found him to be a serial sexual predator.[23]

As Ray and Jim continued their research, examples of enemy mode by Christian leaders kept appearing. Intelligent enemy mode uses the predatory system used for hunting to track others and exploit weakness for a win. We are familiar with sexual predators, but other predators are hunting for power, money, status, control, and fame.

President Richard Nixon was a Christian who viewed his opponents as enemies and kept a list. His paranoia and enemy mode maneuvering are well documented, particularly by his own recordings.

As mentioned earlier, we've seen Pastor Driscoll's drive to win spring from enemy mode. In a 2006 sermon he said, "I want everything—because I want to win. I don't want to just be where I'm at. I don't want anything to be where it's at. And so for me it is success and drivenness and it is productivity and it is victory that drives me constantly."[24]

Andrew Carnegie provides a good example from American economic history. He became one of the richest men in the world of his time, and then gave it all away. His business practices were Gilded Age enemy mode, and he became a model for generations of business leaders. Holland describes Carnegie's predatory business practices:

> An immigrant from Scotland who had gone from labouring in a cotton mill to monopolising the production of American steel, his entire career had been what the ancient Greeks might have called an *agon*. Rivals were there to be crushed, unions to be broken, the resources of capital to be concentrated in his own grasping and restless hands. Farmers, artisans, shop-keepers: all had to be broken to what his critics termed wage-slavery.[25]

ENEMY MODE IN HISTORY: DID ANYONE ESCAPE?

Throughout history, the damage caused and justified by enemy mode runs parallel with the mistakes made trying to appease a top predator in enemy mode. We have not detailed these accounts because they offer no escape from enemy mode. Massive death tolls and suffering follow when people back my enemy-mode-champion-predator who can beat up your enemy-mode-champion-predator. Yet, aside from building bigger forces, more intimidation, and more moral reasoning, no cure for enemy mode thinking has been found. Protests against the horrors caused by our enemies breed new enemies to target.

While individual reformers stood out in history, movements seeking to end enemy mode proved hard to find. The list of groups willing to build and redirect enemy mode seemed endless. Police tactics, politics, wall building along borders, mandatory vaccinations, election integrity, global warming, oil drilling, and an endless list of topics could trigger enemy mode. Conservatives and liberals, college professors and truckers, activists for all kinds of rights, and social media pundits choose an enemy rather than escaping enemy mode. Educating, mobilizing, exposing, empowering, recruiting, and justifying their actions activates enemy mode thinking.

Regardless of the ideology, moral reasoning does not change the way the brain processes enemy mode. At best, moral thought restrains our reactions. At worst, moral thought justifies the new targets. It is *liberté égalité fraternité décapiter.*

NEW DISCOVERY GIVES JIM HOPE

Jim returned a call from his neuropsychologist friend Suzanne Day from Québec. Suzanne was board certified in neurofeedback. She constantly pushed the limits of therapeutic methods through training and certification in new technologies like infra-low brain wave biofeedback, quantitative EEGs, and brain mapping. Her understanding of neurodevelopment had led her to use movement, sound, brainstem activation, and neurofeedback interventions. Whenever Suzanne discovered something new, she told Jim. The news this time involved her training with Dr. David Kaiser of Kaiser Neuromap Institute in Los Angeles.

Suzanne soon had Jim on the phone with Kaiser. Kaiser was finding very different characteristics at the same brain location when the frequency changed. A very active cingulate cortex predicted criminal behavior at a slow speed (4–7 Hz), but not at the higher speed (10–11 Hz) that was normal for adults.[26]

Kaiser reported that as different regions of the brain increasingly fired together, the frequency of cingulate activity slowed. The brain was responding less and less to anything but itself. Kaiser found this **excessive synchronization** within the brain produced relational blindness.

He called this pattern "relational" because brain activity in one part of the brain was closely related to other regions that are usually independent. What Kaiser meant by relational was that the brain was firing in relationship to itself. It is very self-absorbed and egocentric, where everything is "about me"—my feelings, my reality, and my desires.

Kaiser's use of the term "relational" can be confusing because people with this pattern are very unrelational with other people. Kaiser found these self-absorbed patterns in offenders like murderers, rapists, habitual criminals, and people who lie when they will obviously be caught. The brain's internal reality obscured its perception of what other minds were thinking. Oh, there might still be enough observation to track a target in intelligent enemy mode but not enough to share what the target is feeling. The cingulate became a tracking system that didn't feel what others felt. The brain was now dominated by its own feelings, including its own pleasure in the hunt.

When different sections of the brain operate with some independence in relating to the external world, the independent function improves shared reality with other minds. Normal adults average a 10 Hz frequency in the cingulate with their eyes closed. With eyes open, that speeds up a bit to allow right-brain to right-brain communication. At this frequency, understanding and mutual mind states form between adults using the cingulate cortex.

The nineteen electrodes Kaiser placed around the head allowed him to use software to calculate average frequencies for general locations. It occurred to Jim that he had never seen a study that combined the frequency information with the activity levels on a brain scan. Brain scan activation in a region did not record the frequency. But, if an activated cingulate at 5 Hz predicted criminal behavior risk while the same activation at 10 Hz did not, it would make a big difference in understanding enemy mode.

Why don't researchers study the MRI image and the EEG brain frequencies together? Because the machines cannot work side by side!

The MRI makes huge electromagnetic waves, and the EEG records tiny ones. It would be like trying to record the sound of a butterfly's wings during a tornado. Even the wires from the EEG would degrade the MRI while the MRI blew out the EEG.

The brain region, level of activity, and activity speed all become part of what the brain was doing. Jim wondered how much a slowed and self-focused brain state contributed to simple enemy mode. Excessive synchronization might contribute to stupid enemy mode as well. However, all this synchronization information was missing from the brain scan studies.

HOW DOES THE HISTORY OF A WORLD IN ENEMY MODE IMPACT ME?

Escaping the impact of wars, crime, family conflicts, hostile classmates, religious conflicts, or prejudice on our families is impossible. Brains in enemy mode are drawn to fighting when there is a threat. We feel the tension when people are ready to fight. We are usually clear when we have been treated like enemies. Enemy mode, however, is a two-way street. Our ancestors received, but also dished out, enemy mode treatment.

We have already seen that our moral reasoning preferentially tracks and justifies how we have been treated unfairly, while justifying the way we and our ancestors treated others. It becomes almost impossible to take a fair inventory of how our enemy mode has impacted others; our brain jumps to justify us and push us back into enemy mode once again.

While this might give rise to some compassion, it could as easily give rise to hate. Dialogues between people in enemy mode are rather unproductive and degrade into endless arguments. Arguments ensue about trivia—like the shape of the table at the Paris Peace talks.

Perhaps the biggest impacts of past enemy mode have been:

1. Hopelessness
2. Fear-based relationships of all kinds
3. Hurt and distrust
4. The drive to be super-powered/superpowers

Most of the consequences of enemy mode have been unintentional. However, not only are terrorism, domestic violence, genocide, organized crime, slavery, and human trafficking deliberately intended to subdue others, but governments and institutions, deliberately or unwittingly, cultivate enemy mode. Perhaps one of the best studied is the process of soldierization. Ray and Jim were determined to look at how the military built an identity group that supported enemy mode and learn what they could about building identity groups that helped people escape enemy mode. Perhaps the secrets they were seeking would be found in the very fires of Mordor where they were forged.

Enemy Mode and Soldierization

Every branch of the military in developed countries does some form of recruit training. There have been forty-one million service members in the US since 1776, with sixteen million in WWII alone. According to the US Department of Veterans Affairs, in 2020 there were 19.5 million living veterans.[27] Every veteran's family has been impacted, but how have these military experiences impacted our relational, human brains?

Could we learn something from training for war that would help us escape enemy mode as groups? At the very least, we needed to be able to address the problems caused by soldierization, because every family in the world had been impacted.

What does soldierization do to young brains that are still forming? Could it make enemy mode operations more likely? What impact could it have on fear, pain, and attachment to others? Ray had some observations that started with bayonet training, a key part of Ray's soldierization process.

A bayonet is a foot-long knife mounted on the end of a rifle with two purposes: 1) to intimidate; 2) when necessary, to kill. Ray explained, "We grasped rifles with bayonets. Our sergeants showed us how and led us in war cries like, 'The spirit of the bayonet is to kill!' and 'Blood, blood, blood makes the grass grow!'" Ray was a Christian during bayonet training. He shudders at the memory, but conversely, he loved the group nature of fifty soldiers making the same bayonet fighting moves together.

Training culminated in the bayonet assault course. Simulated figures were the enemy, and soldiers were unleashed to stab as many as they could. The Army discontinued this in 2010, but Marines still do so in basic training. The goal was to learn to channel aggression in a combat situation.

We met Lieutenant Colonel Grossman and his book *On Killing* in chapter 5. Grossman believed 1960s Army bayonet training led to dehumanizing the enemy. He quoted veteran Tim O'Brien: "To understand what happens to the GI among the mine fields of My Lai, you must know something about what happens in America. . . . You must understand a thing called basic training."[28]

O'Brien remembered his Vietnam-era drill sergeant disparaging the enemy (Vietcong): "If you want their guts, you gotta go low. Crouch and dig! . . . The road to My Lai was paved, first and foremost, by the dehumanization of the Vietnamese . . . which declared that killing a Vietnamese civilian did not really count."[29] The Us-Them divide widened and enemy mode intensified.

Grossman discovered that human beings have an extreme aversion to taking another life, and the strongest aversion is seen in hand-to-hand combat like bayonet fighting.[30] Taking a life with a bayonet is very rare as a result, and the normal human response to being threatened with a bayonet is to run. Soldierization of 1960s-era soldiers widened the Us-Them divide and enabled intelligent enemy mode, in which anything was possible. That created the conditions that led to massacres like My Lai. Ray and his West Point friends were trained by men who fought in Vietnam.

Enemy Mode Traumatizes Warriors

Ray and Jim made their own analysis of soldierization. A young person was conditioned to bond to a new attachment within a military culture, operate as a group, forge a new identity as a soldier, and not respond when the amygdala said something was scary. One summary of the process would be that soldierization forms a group identity that doesn't frighten easily. The group identity effect appeared quite clearly during combat. One would think that in combat, accomplishing the mission was most important. Ray and countless veterans said that when life was on the line, the most important thing was caring for your fellow soldiers, and, when necessary, laying down your life to protect your buddies.

Combat could have more damaging effects than soldierization. Chaplain Haynes (who we met earlier in the book) told Ray of one soldier who entered a supposedly empty bunker. He was shocked to discover an Iraqi soldier and killed him reflexively. A decade later, that veteran was haunted and traumatized by what he did in an instant. For an estimated 10 to 15 percent, combat will produce PTSD, which, like enemy mode, involves disruption of the experience processing pathway by intense feelings. During a PTSD reaction the brain is energized to face an enemy that is no longer present and shuts down the relational circuits.

One dramatic case of the impact of combat service on a soldier involves Frank Sheeran, who had served as a Roman Catholic altar boy before WWII. After the war, he became a hitman for the mob and confessed to killing Teamster president Jimmy Hoffa. During his time in the service, Sheeran had served 411 days in direct combat with the 45th Division. Charles Brandt interviewed Sheeran in his book *I Heard You Paint Houses* and concluded: "It was during his prolonged and unremitting combat duty that Frank Sheeran learned to kill in cold blood."[31]

Soldierization helped override an amygdala in overdrive. Ray used to think the process "toughened" people up, but what if it also causes collateral damage to the brain's ability to stay relational? Soldierization could deaden the relational self and result in nasty side effects. Soldierization might make compassion and shared pain unreachable anytime someone felt like an enemy, even in everyday life. Escaping enemy mode required compassionate feelings toward enemies and even sharing their pain.

Recovering from Soldierization

Decades ago, when Ray was a hospital chaplain, he visited an eighty-year-old patient. The man was proud of his WWII wartime service, but through tears, asked, "Will God ever forgive me?"

The man had been assigned to a coastal defense unit in Virginia. One day, the US Navy sank a German ship off the coast. As his unit launched boats to take prisoners, their commander ordered, "No prisoners." The vet had executed a German sailor in the water and suffered alone for decades as a result.

Ray and Kerry Haynes both entered the US Military Academy in the same era and would later become Army chaplains. Both men have spent a lifetime reflecting on what they learned in the Army.

Chaplain Haynes led moral injury recovery groups. Moral injuries can occur when soldiers do something in the line of duty that violates their moral values. Haynes told Ray about a Vietnam veteran who had served as a "tunnel rat." The man had volunteered to lead the way underground, armed only with a pistol, a knife, and a flashlight. The rules of engagement stated anyone in the area, including civilians, was an enemy and could be captured or killed. That day, he was not alone in the tunnel, with devastating consequences.

Haynes continued, "[He] is a very sweet Hispanic man who has hated himself all of his life. He's in one of our faith-based groups. He told the group, 'They called us child killers. Well, that's because I am.'"

The vet continued, "I was coming around the corner in one of those tunnels and I opened fire, and it turned out to be a woman and her children, and I killed them all before I knew who it was."

Haynes said, "We helped him to unpack his intent. His intent was not to kill noncombatants, but there was not supposed to be anybody in those tunnels. He was trained to be in enemy mode. He killed noncombatants, and that has messed with him for forty, fifty years.

"His wife was in that group with him. We encourage adult family members to come with them if they can. She came up to me afterward and said, 'He has never told me that story.' We were so moved. Telling us made all the difference for him."

The group showed him compassion and provided a way for him to find healing. How was this soldier's brain different from Frank Sheeran's brain? Why does it matter in a book on enemy mode? It matters because how we help folks out of enemy mode has lifelong impact.

LESSONS LEARNED FROM SOLDIERIZATION

The main effects of soldierization emerge as the ability to engage a threat, protect one's identity group, comply quickly, and, at least initially, dehumanize the enemy. Soldierization provides identity, status, and a sense of attachment to a group of comrades in arms while reducing the attachment, status, compassion, and identity of the enemy.

Could soldierization bring out our best self? That depends upon our culture's view of the best self and the value assigned to predators. For the Greco-Roman soldier, being the best self meant owning slaves and raping at will. Cultures who value winning predators see a best self as an apex-predator with limitless enemy mode operation. But for a relational brain, this cannot be the best self.

A best-soldier-self was still an incomplete best-human-self. Soldierization produced the ability to engage a threat, protect "my" group, and destroy the enemy. Destroying the enemy did not help soldiers escape enemy mode. Soldierization could develop protectiveness and group loyalty, but was not designed to produce best selves that escaped enemy mode. Two out of three wasn't bad.

Even though soldierization was intended to produce combatants, any conclusions about the soldierization process on enemy mode need to stay separate from the effects of combat. Most PTSD or moral injuries happen as a result of combat conditions. Killing or inflicting great pain can severely impair attachment, identity, and compassion. These are some of the contributors to enemy mode, as well as the effects of life, human suffering, and death caused by enemy mode.

A further point is that soldierization was not the complete military experience. The primary mission of West Point was to build leaders of character. Character develops by following role models.

Ray talked with General Bob Brown, one of the Army's most senior retired leaders. As a four-star general, his last command was of the United States Army Pacific. At the time of the interview, General Brown had just become CEO of the Association of the United States Army.

Brown labored to correct toxic leadership and, when necessary, remove toxic leaders. (General Becky Halstead, who we'll meet in chapter 7, did the same.) While Brown was not familiar with enemy mode, he knew a leader of character when he saw one. He told Ray, "If you are not relational, you are not leading well." Brown called such unrelational individuals toxic leaders; Ray considers them leaders in enemy mode.

Brown elaborated, "You can have transactional leaders that get stuff done, in some cases better than the relational, inspirational leader who truly shows they care. But the routine tasks aren't the challenge."

Transactional leaders in enemy mode might be better at easily measured tasks, but relational leaders build a strong group identity of trust and attachment in their team and gain something more.

Brown explained, "When you're facing a complex situation, be it dealing with COVID assistance or in combat against an adversary trying to outsmart you, you need to be a relational leader who builds trust and empowers an effective organization."

He added, "When transactional leaders are confronted with these complex situations that require trust built as teams, they don't do as well. They also just won't perform as well in the complex world we have today.

"I guess every generation thinks their time is the most complex. The 'fog of war' used to be *not enough* information. Back then you could be more transactional and demanding because you had all the info yourself and nobody was going to second guess you. Now the 'fog of war' is *too much* information. Now if you don't empower junior folks and implement best practices from the cutting edge where troops are closest to the problem, you won't be successful."

FEAR AND REMEMBERING WHO YOU ARE

The amygdala and related circuits further energize our body and nervous system at the first sign of potential threats. The adrenaline reaction starts before we are even consciously aware, as we saw in chapter 4. The tradeoff for quick and dirty speed is accuracy. The amygdala learns what might be a threat and sets off an alarm when anything similar triggers it, even if that's in a place or situation unassociated with the original location and event.

Blue shirts (because terrorists wore them) could trigger terror in former hostages even after their crisis was over. Boots (because they were worn by Nazi Holocaust officers) have made death camp survivors in Chicago soil themselves. Dogs (because of dog bites) alarmed Jim even when they were harmless. After living through the Argentine dictatorship (where people disappeared forever after police raids), a young lady felt terror when police in uniform passed by her in Colorado. The amygdala is fast but stays forever frozen in time.

The PFC operates in real time—in the present moment. About two hundred milliseconds (a fifth of a second) after the amygdala signals alarm, the PFC can shut it off, provided the alarm is not relevant in the present moment. *He has a gun! No, it's a cellphone.*

When social scientists use brain activity for their research, some interpret the results of amygdala activation as "what the person really feels" and the PFC as "suppressing what I really feel to be socially desirable." Sapolsky agrees with this interpretation.[32]

The alternative explanation is that the PFC corrects a mistake by the amygdala. Let's see how this plays out. Imagine an ex-hostage in Kansas sees someone wearing a blue shirt. The amygdala triggers, and the PFC shuts off the alarm. Does the ex-hostage have a hidden prejudice against blue shirts or does the ex-hostage realize that Kansas is safe at the moment? We can ask the same about boots in Chicago, friendly dogs, and police uniforms in Colorado. People's amygdala reactions mean they were once frightened by the trigger and little else.

The amygdala provides the energy, and the PFC will identify the mistake and shut off the energy or direct the energy into action according to how our identity group sees the activation. The values of my identity group can override or support my fear-based experiences. We saw in chapter 5 that after the apoptotic period at age thirteen, the PFC makes the survival of my identity group more important than my own survival.

Ray pondered how his friends from high school turned out. Some went into the Army to become soldiers, and others studied poetry at liberal arts colleges. Soldierization and liberal arts education build toward very different group identities. Soldierization trained PFC responses that favored a fast overriding of fear without soul-searching. Liberal arts education supported very different PFC responses because the group identities were very different. Were the soldiers now more prone to enemy mode?

What Is in It for Me to Escape Enemy Mode?

People in enemy mode are out to win at the expense of others. In fact, expense to others is just what they like. But, what of the people closest to us? Do we want to be sure they always lose?

Isn't refriending likely to earn the gratitude of our children and their children? Consider the historical impact of enemy mode on you and your family, work, friends, mate, and education. Is there damage? Would you rather leave less of that damage behind you? Did a divorce have you in enemy mode? Would you rather escape that enemy mode, or remain enemies for all time? Would one less driver in enemy mode improve your commute? If everyone escaped enemy mode, the reduction of harmful actions and their consequences would be tremendous.

The impact of enemy mode drove Jim and Ray's research. What could be gained if Christian leaders led an escape from enemy mode? What if even one in five people could get out of enemy mode? They'd only need to create an enemy-free zone with four other people in order to help spread refriending across the globe.

HOW DOES ENEMY MODE WORK?

As noted earlier in this chapter, activity in a specific part of the brain could mean several things. Thanks to Dr. Kaiser, Jim discovered that different frequencies in the same spot produced very different outcomes. Jim also noted that the different speeds at which the brain processes stimuli might result in different interpretations by the amygdala or the PFC. Jim and Ray wondered if the brain was correcting itself for jumping to conclusions or covering up what it really felt.

When Zeki and Romaya did their brain scans of people looking at the picture of someone they hated, the researchers observed that the degree of hate activated the same systems as the degree that people were in love.[33] Were these the hate systems or the love systems? Let's break down the possible answers. The fronto-medial PFC was actively picturing the person's encounter with the hated individual. The premotor cortex was actively considering what the person would like to do to the hated one. People looking at a picture of their beloved would also be imagining the encounter and what they would like to do with the one with whom they are in love.

155

The third reaction came from the insular cortex. What is going on with the insula? An examination yields conflicting research conclusions. When Haidt[34] or Sapolsky[35] mention activity in the insula, they interpret the activity as disgust. Disgust has certainly been mapped to the insula. Disgust could fit with hate but not with feeling in love. In addition, the insula is implicated in nicotine cravings.[36] If we damage or block the insula, the desire to smoke goes away.[37] Disgust does not fit with what makes smokers crave another smoke. The insula is active in all three conditions: craving a smoke, being in love, and being "in hate."

The insula is implicated in reactions to other people's race, belief, and values. Haidt and Sapolsky assume this activity means disgust. Racism, sexism, and a wide range of aggressive antipathies are presumed to be generated by the desire to throw up whenever insula activity is detected on a scan. If this conclusion is right, then we may overcome intelligent enemy mode with any anti-nausea treatments.

Rather than energize, disgust de-energizes the body. Schore says that disgust reduces the heart rate, suppresses breathing, lowers blood pressure, immediately suppresses visual attention, and begins sensory rejection, thus, "initiating a state . . . of passive coping."[38] Disgust leads to avoiding whatever is not life-giving. Perhaps this "not life-giving" disgust feeling explains how love can turn to disgust after a betrayal.

Visit a bad accident scene, severely sick friend, or emergency room, and we find people feeling disgust but helping others with compassion. Disgust might keep us away from the town waste treatment facility or out of a dumpster, but the de-energizing reaction of disgust cannot be the main element in enemy mode.

So, what is the insula activity telling us? Schore says the right anterior insula "integrates somatosensory and autonomic functions in order to generate visceral awareness of subjective emotional states."[39] He lists these states as "attachment, fear, sexuality, aggression, disgust, etc." We could say that the insula helps us feel our emotions in our bodies. Any emotional state that leads to a body reaction, for better or worse, uses the insula. Gut-wrenching compassion, the butterflies of being in love, the intense desire to smoke, or the urge to punch a hated enemy all join the urge to throw up and activate the insula.

What would the brain need to do for intelligent enemy mode to operate? The brain would block the insula from getting involved. The insula produces compassion. Intelligent and predatory enemy mode would need to operate in "as if" mode most of the time. Does this match what we know?

"As if" thinking is found in the medial-frontal segment of the PFC. The top section (dorsal) that forms part of the dorsal attention network (DAN) is not tied to the insula, so it can imagine without having to feel the pain. This is the area where Kaiser found slowed brain activity in the subjects who killed, raped, and set people on fire.

The Holocaust provided a historical record of people who torture and kill other humans. One remarkable observation was that Nazi doctors were more effective killers than Nazi soldiers. In fact, psychiatrists researched Nazi eugenics methods by experimenting on and even killing psychiatric patients. At the end of WWII, Allied psychiatrists tried to uncover how death camp operators could torture and kill all day and then go home and be normal family men. The investigation by Dr. Robert Lifton concluded that those who ran death camps and gas chambers were particularly good at "as if" thinking.[40]

Lifton's alternative to developing a genocidal personality is what he called an "embodied self." He described the body awareness that we have traced to the insula when he calls for "a self that includes a measure of unity and awareness of body and person in regard to oneself and others."[41]

The lower (ventral) section of the medial-frontal cortex is involved in the ventral attention network (VAN) and feeling our feelings in our bodies. This vmPFC region connects our identity with our body. When we are home and the lights are on, the vmPFC and insula are in harmony. We are aware of our body and feel compassion for others.

Intelligent enemy mode must block this harmonious activity.

If the ventromedial PFC gets involved and the insula begins feeling in our body what someone else is feeling, intelligent enemy mode will not work. We might be able to block that activation. Nicotine numbs it. Disgust would drain energy and probably block attachment feelings. But to kill and torture, people need hate or anger energy flooding the body and blocking the awareness of everything else. If we block those right hemisphere feelings, our left brain goes for the win. Winning confers status to the "as if" self. We all want to be winners when we don't feel the pain of others.

Escaping enemy mode demands large amounts of compassion, attachment, and identity. Once again, Lifton is informative: "It must be emphasized that the problem is never merely, or even primarily, one of individual psychology."[42] What he calls "collective currents," and what we might call group identity, constitute the greater force.

People who have good attachments seem motivated to escape enemy mode through compassion and attachment love.

Despite the gaps in the brain science of enemy mode and differing interpretation by scientists, two general directions emerge. First, people who have good attachments seem motivated to escape enemy mode through compassion and attachment love. Second, people whose group identity (like EMTs and ER staff) is to be life-giving will escape enemy mode (despite disgust and other feelings) to care for people they have never met. This group will even save their enemies.

A look at human history suggests that people have united to suppress enemy mode in others but have justified themselves. The very institutions that limit enemy mode become infected and operate in enemy mode. Every family in Western civilization has been impacted by government-sponsored enemy mode training through soldieriza-tion of a family member or the impact of war.

Like the ethicists, chaplains, and military commanders who felt the weight of "what we have wrought" when we turned civilians into sol-diers, Ray was troubled. While soldierization might produce protective-ness and group loyalty, it didn't produce best selves that escaped enemy mode. However, since escaping enemy mode required engaging others while they felt like enemies and forming a strong identity group, soldier-ization might teach us something.

It is now time to take the first step out of enemy mode. In our next chapter, we will track our personal enemy mode operations and observe them carefully. We can only escape enemy mode and sustain our gains if we find new solutions that work better than our current ones.

7

RECOGNIZING ENEMY MODE IN MYSELF

THERE ARE THREE MAIN REASONS why it's important to notice when we are in enemy mode. First, during enemy mode, we are not being our best selves. Second, we damage relational resources during enemy mode. Third, noticing our enemy mode gives us a chance to get out. Enemy mode is a form of impaired brain function that does not announce its presence or ask if we want it.

Enemy mode causes a sort of tunnel-vision focus on the "win." Introducing the topic of escaping enemy mode to a brain in enemy mode produces the reaction, "Why would I want to lose? I have important objectives. I don't have time for that. Why should I back down?" As for relational costs, stupid and intelligent enemy mode thinking insist that we are dealing with an enemy, so any losses are just what those people have coming.

Retired Army General Becky Halstead was one of the first women to graduate from West Point. She was also the first female graduate to be promoted to Brigadier General. Halstead commanded in Germany in the early 2000s, and then deployed to Iraq to lead twenty thousand soldiers in hundreds of Army units across the battlefield.

Before her combat deployment to Iraq, Halstead had served under a toxic boss. Her challenge was to stay out of enemy mode when dealing with him. She said, "I always tell people, you know it's bad in Germany when you can't wait to get to Iraq."

She offered numerous examples of bullying, domination, one-sided conversations, and what she felt was a lack of character and good judgment.

Halstead was in a pressure cooker, working for this toxic boss and preparing to deploy to combat. What helped her stay out of enemy mode?

Halstead said she knew she was never alone, even when she felt discouraged and the situation was intolerable. Her daily rhythm kept her grounded and focused on keeping three tanks full: physical, emotional, and spiritual. Her attachment to God as a Christian made a huge difference. She read the Scriptures. She had added a favorite Scripture verse to her Army dog tags, reminding her to stay relational with God and people. Her other reading included books by leadership expert John Maxwell.

Halstead built a personal board of directors (BOD) composed of her chief of staff, deputy commander, her senior enlisted adviser (the sergeant major), a lieutenant colonel on staff, and her chaplain. She totally trusted them; they kept her thoughts in confidence.

Ray asked, "Let's say you're discussing a scenario with your board of directors, and you are about to flip your lid and go into stupid enemy mode. How did they help you?"

They helped her avoid enemy mode first by letting her say whatever she was thinking. "Normally I have to choose my words really wisely. You know, they just let me be emotional with them and then not be emotional with other people. I recognize that it's very important to lead with emotion, but it's very dangerous to be an emotional leader because then you create walls, people get defensive, and they misunderstand."

They then helped her to reframe that thinking. "The beauty of my personal BOD was they knew the situation was affecting me personally, whereas it was not affecting them that way. They helped me reframe by asking questions like, 'Why does that bother you so much?'"

Even during disagreements, the discussions with this group allowed Halstead to clarify her values and identity. Sometimes they would say, "You just gotta let that go, ma'am. You can't let that bother you."

Halstead's chief of staff was a colonel who later became an Episcopal priest. She would challenge Halstead with, "You care too much." Halstead responded, "I can't believe I'm hearing that from you! Is that possible? Can I care too much?" But, in doing so, Halstead believes her chief of staff helped her keep perspective.

"I let them say things to me that they knew I would disagree with, but that would result in an even deeper conversation. It was good food for thought for me to know how to proceed. Maybe I could let it go and not address it externally, but I still knew I needed to address it internally. I knew that it wasn't going to do me any good to go up to my boss and try to have a conversation with him."

Halstead stayed relational in her own brain and with others where relationships were possible. She maintained her relationships with God and with grounded, steadfast, and values-based people.

RECOGNIZING ENEMY MODE BEGINS WITH NOTICING

The way the brain adapts to the environment involves *state-dependent learning*. We learn what works under certain conditions. If our cellphone does not work, we do not search for our keys. If the microwave won't cook, we don't look for termites. In any state of mind, we look for what is relevant to that state.

Enemy mode is a state of mind. We cannot correct enemy mode by avoiding it. We must recognize enemy mode during enemy mode. We learn how to escape enemy mode when we are in enemy mode. Otherwise, we only notice enemy mode after the fact and do not improve our ability to refriend under pressure.

People who practically live in enemy mode have the most exposure but also the hardest time detecting enemy mode thinking. Enemy mode becomes just how things are. Using the relational circuits (RC) test in chapter 3 helps us recognize our usual symptoms of relational blindness. If our RCs are off, we are in some sort of enemy mode.

We learn how to escape enemy mode when we are in enemy mode. Otherwise, we only notice enemy mode after the fact and do not improve our ability to refriend under pressure.

People who frequently go into enemy mode with us will also show symptoms. Pointing out how their RCs are off won't be appreciated.

One night, Deborah and Ray were talking with some friends. Ray disagreed with some of the things Deborah was saying, and he considered interjecting his opinion. Ray recognized he was in enemy mode.

Ray had recently finished extensive relational brain training. He noticed that his relational peace was missing and his heart rate was elevated. Ray had shifted from enjoying a happy, interactive conversation with friends to experiencing the strong desire to "fix" his wife. Has this ever happened to you? That is simple enemy mode at its worst.

Ray immediately began to do some deep breathing. By quieting himself, he returned to relational mode. No one else seemed to notice, but Ray had a small victory.

Since the opposite of enemy mode is relational mode, we improve our recognition speed by practicing relational mode. Relational mode is characterized by feeling attached to long-term relationships where we can rest and be quiet, experience joy regularly when together, and feel present in our bodies. We saw some of these characteristics in the training that Lisa was providing in chapter 4 that enabled her to connect with the screaming father and find his better self. (Chapter 9 will help us escape enemy mode starting with noticing when we are in it.)

Ray was becoming a changed man and commented to Jim, "Working to stay relational with people has the highest payoff. I can't imagine working without my full brain engaged."

THE SIGNS OF ENEMY MODE

Obviously, using the checklists for the three different types of enemy mode in chapters 3, 4, and 5 will help spot enemy mode thinking. If our reaction to using the checklists is "bah humbug," we are probably in enemy mode. If we have a Dickensian Jacob Marley character in our lives, we can ask him or her to go over the checklists and tell us—if we have a tendency toward one of the three enemy modes. Once we identify our classic signs of enemy mode, we can escape faster.

A good sign we are in enemy mode is that no one wants to tell us—to put the bell on the cat, so to speak. If we really want a choice of getting out of enemy mode, we do need our own Jacob Marley. Marley might have the same problems we do, but he is a good enough friend to tell us ours. We generally need to give our friend permission to speak because such friends are not that common. We thank our friends when they do point out our enemy mode. Shooting the messenger a few times adds to the relational costs of enemy mode.

"I don't have any enemies" was an almost universal response when Jim spoke with American Christians about enemy mode. Most had been Christians for some time and were leaders. These nice Christian people resisted naming enemy mode. "We should forgive," "We should just overlook it," or "I just turn it over to God," were reasons to drop the topic. Once they were shown the checklists of enemy mode thinking, everyone recognized the patterns.

Professor Richard tended toward simple enemy mode, oblivious to how people felt. Plant manager Diane tended toward stupid enemy mode and letting anyone who made mistakes know how stupid they were. Pastor Will tended toward intelligent enemy mode to deal with staff, parishioners, and his wife.

The real discussion starter with Christians was noting that Jesus expected his followers would spontaneously respond with attachment love for their enemies. "How do you do that?" was the amazed response from people Ray and Jim talked to. It was like asking them to fly, and yet it's impossible to miss what Jesus commanded. One young leader missed the point and asked Ray, "What if they are actual enemies?"

Taking an enemy mode inventory at the end of each day is a good way to spot recent enemy mode. St. Ignatius was a fairly narcissistic sociopath as a young man, but by practicing daily self-examinations (now known as the Ignatian Examen),[1] he began to stay out of enemy mode. Christians in Europe at the time were focused on being right in their beliefs. During those days of the religious wars between Protestants and Catholics, Ignatius taught his followers to avoid fights by practicing the Ignatian Examen.

HOW CAN I KNOW IF I AM IN ENEMY MODE?

It bears repeating that state-dependent learning requires us to notice enemy mode while we are in enemy mode in order to escape. Thinking during enemy mode needs to engage our values and identity in the PFC. Here are some questions we can stop to ask while in enemy mode that will help activate our PFC:

Is this relationship important? The right brain in enemy mode (PFC off) answers, "It doesn't feel like an important relationship." The left brain might still answer, "Yes, this is my husband or head of sales or mother-in-law, etc.," but we feel indifferent or annoyed. With the PFC back on, we feel protective of the person and relationship.

Do we have each other's backs? Answering no leads to asking if we *want* or *need* to have each other's backs. Enemy mode will not get us there.

Is this a moment to be proud I'm human? Somewhere near the core, enemy mode means we are not attributing valued status to another human. We are also not mentally ready to produce one of human-kind's better moments.

We might also notice a lack of compassion. Since the PFC is run-ning during intelligent enemy mode, we need to ask a few more ques-tions about ourselves. Intelligent enemy mode always justifies itself, so we can expect more difficulty answering the next three questions.

Am I offering justifications to protect my image? Answering yes to this question increases the odds we are supporting an "as if" identity rather than strong attachments with others. Not only can an "as if" per-sonality be dangerous, as we saw with the Nazi doctors, but it also in-validates attachments. We know when people like our image but don't know us.

Are production, success, winning, and control my only values? Even if we answer no, feeling annoyed at the question indicates a prob-lem. When others' values don't seem important at the moment, they are also not being protected. We can incur large relational damages.

Is serving the vision my justification for relational losses? With no studies to prove it, the chances seem high that idealistic people find themselves being used and burned out while supporting some reform, revolution, ideology, or religious vision. Career advancement can do the same. We have already seen how pastors can use vision to justify throwing people under the bus.

Ray shook his head in disbelief and said, "I have just listened to the last episode of Christianity Today's *Rise and Fall of Mars Hill* podcast. I am furious that Driscoll could build a church; lead it in an abusive, high-handed, and controlling way; and leave a trail of victims to serve his vision."

Ray added, "What makes me angrier is that his supporters bought his vision-based self-justification. Five days after he resigned in 2014, he was invited to attend a conference with hundreds of pastors in Texas. Robert Morris, a megachurch pastor in Dallas, implied in his comments that Mark Driscoll was a victim."[2]

Ray was still fuming that a prominent pastor's enemy mode lifestyle was overlooked and widely supported. Apparently, so were the editors of *Christianity Today*. Leaders in intelligent enemy mode defended a man many now view as an alpha predator.

A LITTLE HELP FROM MY FRIENDS

Since the brain considers the welfare of my identity group to be more important than my own after the apoptotic period at age thirteen, enlisting our peers in our effort to get out of enemy mode is a very powerful influence. We saw General Halstead put this into practice earlier in this chapter. People watching us for signs of enemy mode are likely to notice it first. What our peers notice has immediate importance to brains older than thirteen.

To enlist peers, we will need to tell them what enemy mode looks like. What are the signs? Explaining to others is a good way to make things clearer in our own minds. By telling people around us what enemy mode looks like, we improve detection. We might even preempt some enemy mode attacks from them. Discussing enemy mode beforehand reduces damage and shortens episodes.

Receiving a 360-Degree Review

When people in power ask for evaluations, particularly if they have exhibited enemy mode in the past, not everyone wants to speak up because old wounds inflicted by predators using intelligent enemy mode set off amygdala alarms. But 360-degree evaluations administered by an external investigator increase participation and objectivity about a leader's emotional intelligence. Three-sixties evaluate relational effectiveness with others, whatever their position.

Greg Hiebert found profound professional value in the 360 as a tool to increase self-awareness. As a leadership coach and professional business consultant with senior executives in the healthcare field, he had used this tool for himself and at least two thousand times with clients. Hiebert is also the author of *You Can't Give What You Don't Have* and coauthor of *Changing Altitude: How to Soar in Your New Leadership Role*, Ray's West Point classmate and fellow Army officer, and a graduate of the Harvard Business School.

"One of my highest scoring areas was rigidity," he explained. "If you look underneath, rigidity is stubbornness and the need to be right. I went to one of my colleagues. I knew she'd be honest. I said, 'Can you give me some feedback? Because my score is in the 37th percentile, but I don't see it.'

"She said, 'When you get fixated that you're right, you get an idea, fight for it, and it comes across to me as combat. I have to have a lot of energy and feel really strong to do battle with you.'"

For Hiebert, that was life changing. "I began to see a pattern that characterized a good portion of my life—being right."

When Greg was trying to convince others, he could actually be attacking, a sign of enemy mode. Now he can more quickly recognize it. "I can stop most of the time. But there are moments where I slip. It's not pretty. I usually have to apologize profusely."

Hiebert was learning rapid recognition. His apology was his escape from enemy mode.

General Bob Brown and the Value of 360s

We met General Bob Brown in chapter 6. Ray was pleased to learn Brown was a strong believer in the value of 360-degree evaluations.

As a four-star, he worked to reduce toxic leadership in units he commanded. Often the only way to stop toxic leaders in the military was to fire them. Brown had done that a few times. But he told Ray that a 360-evaluation created awareness and the chance to change. He even asked his subordinates to give him a 360, which the Army didn't require for four-star generals. The Army discontinued the evaluations for a while, but Brown lobbied to get them going again.

"I argued that the 360-evaluation was one of the most important things the Army did to avoid toxic leaders," he told Ray. "I'm a huge fan of the 360, and I took one as a four-star. I did it at every rank." He added, "[It was] kind of unusual for a four-star to do it, but I welcomed the feedback."

RECOGNIZING SIMPLE ENEMY MODE IN MYSELF

Simple enemy mode takes over insidiously in a tired, distracted, overly focused, or disinterested brain. Simple enemy mode is the lack of relational arousal. The absence of a "something" is much harder to notice than the presence of a something. We notice a furious dog in the car but might forget something in our purse until we need it.

Dormant relational circuits produce enemy mode thinking. Testing my RC function (covered in chapter 3) should be done at least twice a day if we have a tendency toward simple enemy mode. If our brain was an app, we would see if the link to "that fellow human" has been grayed out. Their human presence does not activate anything in me right now.

One of Ray's first attempts to explain enemy mode was to a CEO with C-suite roles in major corporations. The CEO saw enemy mode as "an interesting concept," but he couldn't think of any specific instances other than the 2020 presidential election.

Others, like Greg Hiebert, responded positively to Ray's explanation. "The concept is incredibly insightful. If I can keep the construct of enemy mode front and center, I can also work to avoid its detrimental effects when it arises. I can even prevent it from sabotaging an important relationship in my life over something as innocuous as the TV remote."

What Makes Me Want to Stay in Simple Enemy Mode?

Once we feel the sting of being ignored, forgotten, overlooked, disliked, or demoted, an incentive for simple enemy mode is formed. If we don't try to connect, we might not get hurt—it's a little like holding your breath so you don't smell the skunk.

Simple enemy mode had been Ray's best work tool, even as a pastor, since it helped him not get distracted by relationships. Then Ray worked with Alan Briggs. Alan is a relationally gifted supervisor, leadership consultant, coach, and author of *Staying is the New Going*, *Guardrails*, and *Everyone's a Genius*.

Ray asked Alan for feedback. Alan saw Ray as focused, intense, and faithful to the task, but without knowing how to bring that same focus to the relational side of his work. Alan felt Ray's focus on tasks may have developed in the military where what gets done gets rewarded. Ray agreed. Enemy mode felt like a strength and the only way to get work done.

Did Ray's performance drop by giving up enemy mode? Not at all. He said, "If anything, my performance is much higher. My performance improved because my team is more effective. Working relationally and more effectively are actually the same thing. I learned a lot when I took a 360 last summer and received good feedback from my team and my boss."

How Is Simple Enemy Mode a Weakness?

Major General Dana Pittard, who we already met, and Ray talked about how enemy mode harmed individuals and teams. After first being met by racism, Pittard led three successful commands and received special recognition as the best company commander in the US Army in Europe. General John Shalikashvili pinned on his medal and asked then-Captain Pittard to address the Army leadership in Europe, including many generals and colonels.

"I talked about not getting beyond what I call kind of a bubble, which is your own fears of people," Pittard said. "I told the story of having been in a unit—and I didn't name any names—where my commander couldn't get beyond my color. And it's too bad. I'm sure there are others that he didn't use because of his own prejudices. We could have been a better team if he used all the players on the team. That's what enemy mode does." After his address, Pittard received a standing ovation.

Simple enemy mode keeps us in what Pittard called "our fears and comfort zone," relationally blind to allies and their potential. Pittard believes that no one would have ever heard General Colin Powell's name if Jimmy Carter's Secretary of the Army Clifford Alexander had not forced the Army to revise promotion policies in the 1970s. Powell would have been a retired colonel, not a world-famous four-star general.

In enemy mode we miss opportunities and exclude people. And the people we hurt are exactly the ones we want close to us.

RECOGNIZING STUPID ENEMY MODE IN MYSELF

Feeling chagrined and thinking, "Why did I . . . ?" identifies when I feel stupid because I didn't express my best self. James felt that way.

James, a friend from Ray's Army days, retired as a colonel. He was a passionate Christian whose smile could light up a room. His proudest moment in the Army was commanding an Army brigade in combat in Iraq in 2005–06. After retirement, James went to work for a major defense contractor in Washington, DC. James's example of stupid enemy mode came from business and was very detrimental to his career.

James's company was sponsoring an ideas fair, so he entered the competition using his Army experience with soldiers who had traumatic brain injury (TBI) and PTSD from Iraq. "I felt horrible about how we had treated these walking wounded. After I started working for the defense contractor, I remembered this Army problem, and I studied it."

Together with a medical doctor, James worked to develop his concept, and his idea was selected. James told Ray, "A senior associate was given my idea to take to market. She wanted me to go away. She felt I had no reason to be involved. I absolutely went into enemy mode, and I stayed in enemy mode. She was an enemy, and so I was going to fight fire with fire."

"When her VP contacted me directly, I stayed in enemy mode, thinking he was also the enemy. He was just trying to talk to the guy who created the idea and figure out what to do with it," James recalled. "This VP was trying to help me. I didn't know that."

Enemy mode assumes bad motives and goes on the attack. After attacking and saying something stupid, we may get focused on how we embarrassed ourselves and miss why the other person felt like an enemy. We make more progress by discovering why our brains went into enemy mode. Where do we feel vulnerable? Examining what went on before we did or said something stupid helps prevent a repeat performance.

What Makes Me Want to Stay in Stupid Enemy Mode?

Stupid enemy mode can become the way we "motivate" people. Stupid enemy mode creates movement but also creates fear. Stupid enemy mode may work short-term, but the damage is long-term because we have not considered the least harmful alternative.

We aren't talking about emergencies. There is a time and place to shout and use strong language, like when the house is on fire. In an emergency, that is the least harmful alternative and not stupid enemy mode.

How Is Stupid Enemy Mode a Weakness?

How much damage do we want to do to those we love? Stupid enemy mode harms people, creates passive team members, breeds fear-based motivation, and causes unnecessary stress.

Ray talked with General Halstead about their life as cadets and the constant barrage of yelling from upper-class cadets. Yelling produced results. "So many people think that yelling and screaming at people works," said Halstead. "I didn't run faster because I got yelled at. I ran, but I don't think I ran faster or better. I just did it out of fear. I have written about people that I have worked with who were in positions of leadership but not respected as leaders because they operated that way."

Halstead found leaders who led in stupid enemy mode were not productive. She observed, "It was their leadership style, but it wasn't leadership. What happens is you don't retain people." She didn't lead that way and didn't allow that leadership style in her units.

General Halstead was faced with a toxic sergeant major. A command sergeant major is the senior role model for all the sergeants in the unit. She corrected him for his profanity, yelling, and screaming, telling him, "This is so unprofessional." Becky's sergeant major thought he was being effective. For him, the yelling was a good, intelligent plan, but Becky didn't see it that way.

He responded, "Well, ma'am, I made it this far and nobody ever seemed to have this problem with me before."

General Halstead responded, "Sergeant Major, nobody else ever dealt with it. I'm dealing with it because my role and responsibility as a leader is to develop more leaders, not followers. All your yelling and screaming is developing followers. I'm into developing leaders. There is a big difference." She fired him. The sergeant major could not see his own weakness.

RECOGNIZING INTELLIGENT ENEMY MODE IN MYSELF

Intelligent enemy mode thinking looks for a weakness to exploit. Computer hackers think this way. Intelligent enemy mode users are usually in conflict with someone close to them. Cheating partners think that way. People who operate in intelligent enemy mode are usually proud of their wins.

Ray was surprised to learn how common intelligent enemy mode is in everyday life and in families. Once Ray explained how intelligent enemy mode worked, his interviewees had many stories. Kathy encountered the manipulative nonprofit CEO who was a sexual predator. CEO Kevin had the scheming, back-stabbing colleague.

Dealing intelligently with a threat is not enemy mode when we seek the least harmful alternative. Joe served in special operations involving cross-cultural issues and threats in the Middle East and Africa. Joe explained that 99 percent of success was good situational awareness and knowing how to minimize collateral damage. Joe believed that if you must act, you must do it with overwhelming power to disable your adversary.

Joe felt his faith made him a better soldier. He had not been in a personal fight since his early twenties but had encountered other threats as a professional. He had also seen needless loss of life from enemy-mode-fueled emotional and personal offense. Joe provided a good contrasting example for facing a threat intelligently but without enemy mode blinders.

Joe was married to Sarah, whose brother Tim lived in enemy mode. Tim was angry, controlling, and verbally abusive with anyone he felt he could dominate. Tim divorced his first wife for a younger woman, often had issues with his employers, and changed jobs every couple of years. Over time, Joe and Sarah concluded it would be best for their family to have minimal contact with Tim. One evening, at a family gathering, Tim could not be avoided, and he tore into Sarah.

Joe explained that his brother-in-law had been drinking a lot when the words erupted. Joe was in another room when he heard the exchange. "If Tim had caught himself and apologized for his outburst, it would have ended, but in his mind, apologies showed weakness.

"I went to protect my wife in case something happened. Tim had just assumed an aggressive physical posture and told the family he would never back down. That's when I entered the room. The group at the table became eerily quiet. I decided that to defuse the situation, I had to get my wife out. If you perceive a threat, egress is often the best course unless you are cornered and forced to fight."

Joe was calculating the least harmful course of action to defend Sarah. When you can still calculate the least harmful alternative, you are not in intelligent enemy mode; you are a protector. Joe wanted to de-escalate, but there seemed few alternatives.

Joe stated: "There were weapons in the house, and Tim usually carried a handgun. I had my back to the front door and the entire group was jammed into a dining room with no other realistic exits. I stood six feet from the table, silently looking at his forehead while scanning the room. If things got hot, others would likely be injured if a weapon came out.

"I knew what I could do, and I was prepared to hurt him. I had not been that angry in twenty years. I was later told that my outward demeanor changed. I went cold and emotion disappeared from my face."

Joe was not in intelligent enemy mode at this moment. He kept his relational circuits running and was able to calculate least harmful alternatives. Remembering his attachment to his wife prevented him from going lethal in his response.

Joe froze Tim in his tracks: "Be careful! You have no idea who you are dealing with."

Tim only knew Joe as the introverted brother-in-law who seemed weak because he never joined the arguments that often dominated family gatherings. Tim was in stupid enemy mode, and, as we saw in chapter 4, stupid enemy mode freezes when it senses a threat from a superior force.

"I was surprised by the reversion to lethality that I considered as my military training kicked in," Joe said. "The family had never seen that side of me. I saw Tim as a physical and emotional threat to my wife."

Joe backed out of the room and got his wife out of the house. "I was told later it scared Tim because he actually thought that I or one of the special operations guys that worked with me was going to come up and kill him. What a weak man. I hate bullies."

Ray was beginning to ponder his own need to win. He also was aware how that felt when he used that now-dreaded tool of intelligent enemy mode. He felt compassion for others more often. He was also encouraged when he heard from Emanuel that Pastor Tom was changing. Though he'd used intelligent enemy mode as he led the church in the Midwest, Tom was now on a journey to stay relational. Tom had connected relationally in recent years with Emanuel and demonstrated evidence of life change.

What Makes Me Want to Stay in Intelligent Enemy Mode?

Intelligent enemy mode keeps looking for the "win" and a weakness to exploit. Threats at one end of the spectrum and winning at the other provide much of the reason to keep intelligent enemy mode operational. But what are the threats? Social status challenges are a frequent cause for enemy mode reactions as we will see in our next chapter. Often what we react to as a threat is looking bad to others and having our social status lowered. We often label this as rejection, being misunderstood, criticism, prejudice, and unfairness. We want to be intelligent around "those idiots." Open discussions of enemy mode toxicity and positive group identities can reduce this activating effect of feeling subordinated.

How Is Intelligent Enemy Mode a Weakness?

Don't we always want to win? Ray continued to hear and feel uncertainty about intelligent enemy mode being a weakness. Intelligent enemy mode had long functioned as a strength that won important victories. Was it not, at least, an ugly necessity, a kind of toilet paper for that end of the world?

Ed Khouri remembered a sergeant from his police days whom he described as a "cowboy"—an unprofessional police officer. Ed said the sergeant was also a predator who always had a deal for someone and would take advantage of situations when he thought he could get away with it.

Khouri said, "There's a fine line between aggressive police work and stupid police work. I like to be aggressive but not stupid. Some examples come to mind. I was at a disturbance call late one night. My sergeant and I and two others showed up at the property. The resident was drunk and being loud and stupid. But you can't arrest somebody for disorderly conduct on their own property. You can be an idiot on your own property.

"The man was aggressive to the sergeant and got up close in the sergeant's face and yelled at him," Ed observed. "Sarge was being 'cowboy.' He didn't like this guy in his face. Nobody likes a guy in their face, but I had learned people are allowed to scream at you and it's not a big deal. Sarge didn't like it. So, he shoved the guy and escalated the situation. I ended up in the ER."

Khouri agreed that the sergeant was in intelligent enemy mode at the time.

The main weakness of intelligent enemy mode is the inability for the brain to tell (while in it) if others are for us or against us. The very capacities needed to test for attachment and shared compassion are being suppressed. The brain that would exploit trust for a win will not trust others. Treating our allies with distance, deception, and distrust proves to be a major flaw. When a team member is always in intelligent enemy mode, it is not good for the team. The team faces the uncertainty about whether they are being played or manipulated or exploited.

HOW DOES MY ENEMY MODE IMPACT ME?

It isn't a stretch to say the biggest impact of enemy mode is going to be my lost relationships. Even simple enemy mode, where you or I don't feel like we are in this together, creates quite a chill over time. Once I get into enemy mode of any kind, my brain stops thinking win-win and begins planning a you-lose. The shift from people being in love to getting a divorce makes the point. Divorce is avoided by people who refriend and escape enemy mode easily. Divorces are costly and painful for those who cannot escape. It doesn't take much investigation to discover that the biggest losses business owners encounter are caused by enemy mode—often their own divorces.

What will coming home in simple enemy mode every night for decades cost us? The authors have witnessed the cost up close. A Christian leader divorced his wife of thirty years on the grounds she would no longer sleep with him. Closer analysis revealed a husband in enemy mode who only cared about his own dreams and ambitions, with no sense of "us." He had been extraordinarily successful in his career. However, the combination of simple enemy mode, his strong drive to succeed, and weak attachment as a couple produced predictable and heart-breaking results.

Divorce, separation, breaking up, quitting work, and unfriending almost universally produce enemy mode on both sides. Family members[3] and friends blame each other for the alienation[4] over things like COVID-19 mandates, vaccines, politicized views on Black Lives Matter, immigration, politics,[5] global warming, ecology, and rights for any group of people.

HOW DOES ENEMY MODE WORK?

"We implicitly divide the world into Us and Them, and prefer the former. We are easily manipulated, even subliminally and within seconds, as to who counts as each," Sapolsky concluded.[6] Thems are much more likely to generate an alarm signal from the amygdala, at least for WEIRD subjects. An unknown Them can trigger some fear, distrust, curiosity, ambivalence, or other reactions based upon the impressions the amygdala pulls in from the hippocampus.

The difference between Us and Them is not enough to automatically create enemy mode. Amygdala reactions to Them are not the same as enemy mode. We can quite easily be in enemy mode with Us people. A well-known Us can incite stupid enemy mode in a flash.

In the relative absence of attachments—that is, when we are dealing with strangers—there are two mechanisms in the brain to consider: 1) memory impressions versus real time (present moment) updates, and 2) real time operations versus identity group response patterns.

Memory impressions versus real time updates. In a relational brain (one with the RCs on), the PFC will update amygdala reactions created by past memory impressions in real time.

> *Yes, that is a blue shirt.*
> *No, we are not in a building with terrorists.*
> *No, the police officer is just protecting pedestrians.*

The alarm signal has been checked and will be turned off.

With the relational circuits impaired by factors such as weak or missing attachments, alarm signals are not checked reliably. The alarm signal continues to go off, and people try to make the feeling stop. The amygdala reacts to being ignored the way a child reacts if parents won't check under the bed to see what made that noise. The alarm stays on.

Suppose my amygdala reacts with fear to someone wearing a hooded sweatshirt. Perhaps it even reacts to anyone mentioning a hoodie. The killing of seventeen-year-old Trayvon Martin in 2012 on his way to buy Skittles while wearing a hoodie has cemented the garment as an icon of race relations. Fear and distrust anticipate where this will go. A reaction to the hoodie does not make a hoodie-wearing person into a Them. Some African Americans are frightened to go out wearing one. If the alarm stays on, enemy mode will follow for whether the person in the hoodie is an Us or a Them.

If we have relational brain operation, we will check and see if we are acting like humans should (no one will be attacked for wearing a hoodie) and then turn off the false alarm from the amygdala using the

PFC. This takes about two hundred milliseconds—the amount of time I need to have a conscious thought. By that time, I am conscious of the process; my alarm is gone.

Is the "real me" my amygdala reaction or the PFC that shuts off the false alarm? My brain thinks the PFC is the real me. If I have an irrational fear alarm (like a fear of flying), it will irritate the real me.

Real time operations versus identity group response patterns. The PFC has subdivisions. Once the PFC takes over real time operations, the real questions about Us and Them begin. The ventromedial PFC (vmPFC) determines how I see and feel in real time. The dorsolateral PFC (dlPFC) informs me how my identity group sees and handles this bit of real time. Hoodies may be Us or hoodies may be Them or hoodies may be insignificant. The dlPFC supplies how our people treat this situation. If our people see people in hoodies as enemies, our brain moves toward enemy mode—unless our people see in enemies a chance to attach, share mutual mind, and share pain when needed. We stay relational.

Enemy mode seems essential at the moment we are in it. *I defend my rights and opinion.* Alternatives disappear as the enemy mode brain stops creating ways to work together, believing you are not on my side. With our curiosity and creativity gone, the brain is no longer calculating the least harmful alternatives. Instead, the left brain seeks control and a win. As far as thinking and creative problem-solving are concerned, enemy mode is a failure and a weakness.

Ray said he thinks he had put Bobby Knight in an enemy category. We met General Bob Brown earlier. As a West Point cadet, Brown played NCAA Division I basketball for Knight's protégé, Coach Mike Krzyzewski, and had also gotten to know Coach Knight personally. Brown told Ray a more nuanced story that helped Ray not consider Knight an enemy. Knight could at times show great compassion and generosity to former players.

Coach Bobby Knight regretted how he treated future NBA superstar Larry Bird, who was on Knight's Indiana team as a freshman, but transferred as a sophomore. Seth Davis, a sportswriter, says, "Knight would later regret treating Bird so coldly. 'Larry Bird is one of my great mistakes,' [Knight] said. 'I was negligent in realizing what Bird needed at that time in his life.'"[7]

What Is in It for Me to Get Out of Enemy Mode?

Jim's wife, Kitty, became seriously ill. As she was dying, she looked back on her life. Kitty said that she most regretted her enemy mode moments, attitudes, and reactions. Kitty's own injuries were forgotten. Her enemy mode moments were what she wished she could undo.

By refriending my way out of enemy mode, I *minimize the damage to the people I love.* My brain in enemy mode inevitably reads enemy mode into the motives of others. I will fight and injure my friends, not seeing that I have misconstrued their intentions. Wanting to escape my enemy mode flows from this reality.

Living a life I am proud of provides another motivation for escaping enemy mode. Being surrounded by people who love me means spending little time as enemies. Refriending after the inevitable enemy mode moments with my friends and family is only possible when I get out of enemy mode. I will rest, digest, sleep, heal, and play much better surrounded by friends instead of enemies.[8]

My choices lead to either a predator-free zone or becoming the predator. I create an environment around me that is safe from predators when I am not in enemy mode. Job, a well-known biblical character, lived before there was Judaism, Christianity, or Islam. He is revered as a holy man by all three religions. Job is revered for living an exemplary life in his community. For Job, the centerpiece of his life was creating a predator-free zone for those near him.[9] Job helped widows, orphans, and vulnerable people in their time of need while sheltering them from attack.

Now that we have examined how to identify enemy mode in ourselves, we face the next hurdle: admitting to others we are in enemy mode. Our identity group might not want to hear it. We will encounter people with three-star toxicity and others who will gladly be our personal board of directors. Chapter 8 will show us how we navigate getting real.

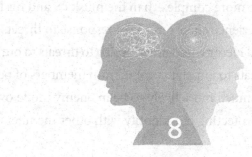

8

ADMITTING
ENEMY MODE

THE LARGE MALE MUSK OX NUZZLED UP behind the female and the narrator of the nature documentary asserted that the male would know when the female ox was receptive. Right on cue, the narrator announced, "Another large male arrives . . ." and enemy mode was on.

We have seen how enemy mode operates; it is time to look at the why and when of enemy mode. Enemy mode is a response to a perceived threat. When we think of threats, we might picture scenes from a popular crime show. However, the threats behind enemy mode are much more like the threat faced by the amorous male musk ox—maintaining status.

> Humans generally experience enemy mode in response to threats to our status, attachments, and identity, and not so much to threats to our safety.

Human societies are more complex than the musk ox and his harem. Humans generally experience enemy mode in response to threats to our status, attachments, and identity, and not so much to threats to our safety. The most frequent threats to our status come from members of our own identity group. We are much more likely to be in enemy mode over status, attachments, and protecting our identity with other members of Us.

STATUS PROTECTING

Chickens have pecking orders. Cows have hierarchies and will punish farmers who milk them out of order by knocking over milk buckets with a well-aimed kick. Monkeys have social orders that persist for generations. The mother will teach its baby where it stands socially and will enforce standings between other females with violence. In much of the mammalian world, including primates, challenging social status is likely to get females, males, and sometimes infants hurt or killed.

An indicator of how important something is to the brain is the speed at which that particular characteristic is processed. For reference, it takes about two hundred milliseconds to become consciously aware. Sapolsky points out that determining the gender of a person by their facial features is processed in one hundred and fifty milliseconds. He goes on to point out that people will accurately distinguish a high status person from a low status one in forty milliseconds.[1] He states, "Social dominance looks the same across cultures—direct gaze, open posture (e.g., leaning back with arms behind the head), while subordination is signaled with averted gaze, arms sheltering the torso."[2] Sending these signals to others is managed by the PFC, but uncertainty and violations immediately set off the amygdala alarm. The brain readies enemy mode operation very quickly at the first sign of a challenge to my social status.

During a breakfast gathering, Marius told Jim a story about visiting his ancestral home and dining in a restaurant that once had been their ancestral castle. His daughter looked around and said to him, "Our peasants are doing well." We laughed. It seemed positively medieval to think we want to have social status. How we view having and defending our social status will impact how well we will admit to enemy mode and what we are willing to do to escape and refriend.

Meanwhile, Belinda and Trudy were sitting a bit further down the table trying to figure out what was going wrong between them. Belinda damaged her PFC going through the windshield of a car and could not read or give social status messages correctly. She interrupted higher status people while they were speaking, looked directly at a person when she should look away, and leaned in and raised her voice in ways that, unintended by her, conveyed, "I am challenging your social status right here in front of everyone." But Trudy and all the nice people in the room didn't believe they would enforce social status by reacting. All the same, Belinda had had a history of triggering enemy mode reactions from women ever since her car accident.

Of those gathered around the table, Trudy had acquired her social signal style from living in New Jersey. Cathy had her social style from the South. Julia had learned her status and style in Argentina. Jim displayed a general indifference to social status signals, which, counter-intuitively, signal high status. While some signs of social status are universal, each identity group adds styles to more universal signals. Violate these unspoken rules, and the brain senses a challenger to my status. Enemy mode is not far away.

People with very high status can ignore rules, overlook other's feelings, and have the best, the prettiest, the tastiest, and the rarest. We are aware of status symbols, such as cars, designer shoes, home location, jewelry, clothing labels, makeup, and elite seating, but these are rarely the direct source of triggering enemy mode. We are more interested in how the rest of the pecking order sorts out. Have someone cut in line or in traffic, and our status is offended. Who is second violin, wears sunglasses inside at night, sports the motorcycle gang colors, doesn't wear a belt, has plastic surgery, wears lots of clothes or almost none, has white teeth or a gap between their upper front teeth, walks in first or third, has a gardener or is the gardener with his own truck, or secures the choice spot in line on the freeway off-ramp? Who walks in, who waits to be called, who can be late, and who does the firing? It is a safe guess that enemy mode has shaped this status from top to bottom. Anything that appears to lower my status, particularly within my identity group, is asking for enemy mode responses. Did you feel a response to any of these symbols? Were you mystified by others?

The symbols of status are complex and constantly changing. Sometimes expensive jeans lend a person status, and other times holes in the jeans do. On the red carpet, revealing clothing may be a sign of status, while it may lower status on a street corner. In areas of the world of widespread malnutrition, being fat can signal high status. Where food is plentiful, status may look like being slender. Reactive, anti-status groups may flip these characteristics for their group status.

Whole identity groups have relative social status. Group status is very dangerous to violate. Any group members who are lowering group status can be ostracized, expelled, humiliated, or even killed. These are considered honor killings. Violence has been used extensively to lower the status of racial and ethnic groups in the United States and elsewhere.

ENEMY MODE, STATUS, AND HATE

Jim stopped at a coffee shop (although the real reason he and other customers were there was for scones). He heard the owner calling other store owners in the building to complain about the landlord overcharging them—it was Us versus Them. The barista was talking intensely to his lawyer about a nasty fight over his right to see his preschool-aged daughter.

Jim was sitting with Ben,[3] a retired builder, whose mother had been part of Hitler's Youth—something he rarely disclosed. Linda, whose father was Jewish—something she rarely mentioned—joined them. After the lawyer left, the barista looked their way and said emphatically, "I hate that guy, but I guess I need him so I can see my girl." The story about his ex-wife followed.

Enemy mode was in the air, and the similarities between hate and love that show up in brain scans crossed Jim's mind.

A woman walked in and began talking to the owner. Linda recognized Cindy as a local artist whose works were on display near the scones. Cindy's voice was loud and artificially friendly. As Cindy started walking back out, Jim waved her over and offered to buy her a coffee. She was surprised but sat down when she saw Linda.

"People here never invite me to sit with them," she said.

Linda was surprised and asked why.

"Because I am Native American. We are not wanted up here."

Cindy could count on being rammed with a grocery cart at least once each time she went to the local grocery store. No one said, "Excuse me." Some people glared at her to assert their higher status. Others acted like they had not seen Cindy to lower her status. Some shoppers, Cindy said, reached into her grocery cart and removed items they wanted and went on as though it was their right to pillage other shoppers.

A brain in enemy mode easily justifies hating and lowering the status of others. Hate is an enemy mode process in the brain. Sometimes hate can be hot, stupid, and obvious. More often, hate is cold and intelligently calculating. Hate can even be devious and hide under pleasant conversation and false cordiality. Native Americans have encountered this careful and intentional deception, but we see it in every movie about high society or spies. This intelligent form of enemy mode is by far the most destructive.

Cindy's coffee arrived, but she declined a scone. As everyone talked, Cindy's voice came down from that tense and artificial tone to one of relaxed friendliness. Jim's take was that Cindy had entered the shop expecting an enemy mode reception. The strain showed in her voice because she had tried to sound friendly to avoid an attack. Simply eating together will reduce fear and lower the potential for enemy mode reactions.

Hate is not limited to ex-spouses, lawyers, and targets of racial injustice. Hate and enemy mode are often triggered by opinions. People who hate have opinions, but hate is not an opinion. Opinions, however, are often meant to lower the status of someone. Enemy mode usually follows opinions about status-sensitive topics.

Jim gave an example. "I received messages for months after making a one-sentence comment about white privilege. Without even knowing what I said about white privilege, people were in enemy mode because I used the term." Any opinion about white privilege means status is under discussion. If this was a nature show, the narrator would say, "A challenger appears."

Hate is very understudied by neuroscience, considering the enormous impact that hate has on people and history. Opinions can quicken or reduce the spread of hate, but opinions are merely tools. Hate is a state of mind toward enemies. Unfortunately, the shoppers banging into Cindy with their carts never asked themselves if Cindy was really their enemy. Her simple presence in the grocery store was seen as a challenge to their sense of higher status.

Jim had been observing the interplay between status enforcement and violence for decades. Years before, Jim and a small group visited Dr. John Perkins in Mississippi for a few days. Dr. Perkins, a well-known author, speaker, and teacher on issues of racial reconciliation, told a story about growing up in Mississippi and having to stop talking when walking past houses of white people. Any black person who didn't "know their place" was likely to pay dearly for the perceived status challenge.

While the group was at lunch, Dr. Perkins went on talking for a while and started repeating a story he had told earlier. Jim considered interrupting him but decided he didn't have a strong enough attachment with Dr. Perkins to keep an interruption from feeling like a status challenge, so he listened to the story a second time.

A couple of years later, Jim was at the Christian Community Development Association (CCDA) convention to speak, along with Dr. Perkins and one of his dearest friends, Wayne "Coach" Gordon. Dr. Perkins took to preaching and walking the stage all the way out of the reach of the lights and TV camera range. Coach went over to him and pointed out where to stand so Dr. Perkins would be on camera. This produced a good-humored but intense response from his friend: "I'm tired of you white folk telling me where I can go!" Dr. Perkins was likely intuiting what the African American audience would see as a social status challenge from a white man to a black man and putting it into words.

Perceptions of status and challenges are integral to another topic that can produce instant enemy mode. Cultures that build cities almost universally accept sun exposure as a sign of low status. Red necks or darker skin indicate who has been in the fields, out in the rice paddies, on ships, herding cattle, and working hard in the outdoors. Sun avoidant cultures associate lighter skin with high status groups with enough wealth to be well-clothed and living in buildings. Cultures in which those of low status work in factories and mines associate sun exposure with leisure time spent above ground and outdoors. Here a tan gives status. Other status indicators include height, leisure time, and money to look beautiful. Height, lighter skin, and more clothes are widely associated with higher status. Differences are often felt as unequal status. When interpreted as a status challenge, enemy mode usually follows. Can you feel any of these words alarming your amygdala or think of someone who would be in enemy mode by now?

Seo-Jun Lee was from a higher status group in Korea. Her face was not round, and her skin was quite white. She covered herself carefully to avoid the sun. After university, she found work in Hawaii. On the island, anyone with leisure time went to the beach and enjoyed the sun. Seo-Jun adopted island ways, which resulted in a light tan. On a visit to Korea, she was severely criticized by the women who had been her friends. They did not want to be friends with someone with sun exposure who would lower the status of their entire friendship group.

Lowering the status of the entire identity group is not the only concern such groups have about their members. Attacks by powerful high status groups who feel their status is challenged are a huge threat. We have already seen how non-compliance with "knowing your place" can bring an attack. Members of a low status identity group often enforce low status compliance to avoid attacks.

In many cultures women are seen as lower in status. Women in groups with low status often enforce compliance on other women. Even "protective" enforcement of low status can become enemy mode quite easily. Protecting a low status identity group from savage attacks by high status groups can produce self-policing status reductions among women but also may reduce attacks from predators.

I Take What I Want

High status individuals are often quite predatory, i.e., "I take whatever I want." Enemy mode can demand sexual access, claim the best views, get rich off the workers in sweat shops, or consume what others grow even when those who labored grow hungry. Whether decreed as *jus primae noctis*[4] of medieval legends or simply through social power, beauty could make women (peasants, maids, slaves, or indigenous) vulnerable to attack. Very rarely were great expectations realized for low status groups and especially for women.

Even four-star generals can assert themselves on three-star generals in a predatory way. This status exerting, "nature documentary" chest-thumping behavior can be active or passive. Ray observed more than one three-star general sidelined and ignored by their immediate four-star supervisor. Status was asserted by who gets to decide.

General Halstead was preparing her unit to deploy to combat in Iraq. We've heard about her boss, the general in intelligent enemy mode. Meet his boss, a general who had his own reputation for being a negative leader and displaying enemy mode behavior. Halstead was required to brief him on her upcoming mission in the Middle East.

However, her supervisor directed her to *not* brief the general on her full mission. That put Halstead in a bind. She replied, "Sir, excuse me, but this briefing is so that every one of the commanders deploying can brief him on our full mission set." This also presented a status conflict for Halstead. More stars mean more status, and she had one star.

Her boss erupted, "I don't care. I don't believe in the full mission set that you've been given. So, you will not brief it." Becky responded by saying, "But, sir, when I'm deployed, I have this mission, and I'm going to be answering to another commanding general."

He shut her down and ordered her not to do it. Halstead struggled with the right action to take. She eventually decided to brief the whole mission anyway, and her boss was furious.

Halstead wondered if she would be fired before she even deployed. "The good news was, as toxic as some believed the top general could be, at least he really respected me, and he appreciated my team. He wasn't going to let my boss fire me for briefing my full mission set, which is what he'd ordered."

We see status conflicts where "Karens" use their status to get their way with restaurant wait staff or store clerks. When their status demands are not granted, they immediately insist on speaking to a manager. Ray's daughter Kathleen worked in a coffee shop where a "Karen" treated her rudely and demanded someone else prepare her beverage. Ray asked, "Do these 'Karens' have a profile?" She said, "Yea, they are typically middle-aged white women driving SUVs!"

Status conflicts can arise when soldiers are in conflict with local police, especially when race is involved. Lieutenant Caron Nazario was an African American/Latino officer in the Army Reserve. When a police officer signaled for him to pull over on a dark highway at night near Windsor, Virginia, Nazario did what his parents taught him and drove to a lighted gas station near other people. Two minutes later, he was politely asking why he had been pulled over when an officer pepper-sprayed him.

Lieutenant Nazario, in his Army uniform and blinded with pepper spray, got out of the car, was forced to the ground, and was handcuffed. The VA Attorney General sued the town for discriminatory policing.[5]

Black soldiers, who served with distinction during WWII, returned home to face similar racism. After defeating Nazi and Japanese "bullies," they came home to face racist bullies who saw them as status challengers. Back home, they suffered savage, crippling, and deadly attacks, which a brain in intelligent enemy mode will justify.

A milder form of enemy mode can be seen in nonprofit organizations. Ray observed Jeff, who had a falling out with the leader of a nonprofit where Jeff volunteered. A difference of opinion became a status fight. The leadership asked Jeff to leave; Jeff felt hurt. Months later, Jeff encountered the leader at a gathering and erupted in stupid enemy mode anger. He apologized the next day, but relational damage was done.

Ray asked Jeff where his intensity came from, and Jeff answered, "I was really angry. I think it came from early childhood stuff. I had no standing with my parents." Jeff grew up in a home where children had no status or voice, were seen and not heard. He now used anger to demand a higher status.

Even among medical doctors, status enforcement kills and degrades. Abusive treatment of hospital residents by higher status medical staff leaves a trail of suicides, particularly among international doctors doing their residency.[6] Female physicians average lower pay.[7]

If challenging a person or group's status precipitated enemy mode, was it possible that giving status to others could help escape enemy mode? As Ray and Jim considered their target group, they wondered if raising the status of others would fit a Christian group identity. Certainly, honoring others and choosing the lower place for oneself was a central teaching of Jesus. Jesus disregarded his status and honored others—particularly women, outcasts, and the poor. Honoring wasn't going to happen if Christians were in enemy mode.

> *Anytime I feel entitled to my status or that my status is being pushed down, it will be hard to admit enemy mode. It will be easiest to admit my enemy mode to someone of equal social status.*

ATTACHMENT PAIN

Loss, grief, abandonment, loneliness, jealousy, hurt, and rejection are just a few of the words we use to describe attachment pain. Enemy mode seems to offer some "protection" from attachment pain by blocking attachment. Each style of enemy mode shows some lack of function regarding attachment. Simple enemy mode does not have the RCs sufficiently activated. Stupid enemy mode has the RCs overloaded from excessive arousal. Intelligent enemy mode blocks attachment by living an "as if" life, as we saw in chapter 6. When the "as if" circuit is running, we are disconnecting from our bodies when attachment is needed.

What all three modes accomplish by avoiding attachment is the pain that comes from attachment gone wrong. When boosting social status, a disconnection from attachment allows status climbers to dispose of lower status friends, partners, and families without pain to themselves.

Attachment pain usually makes the news because it precedes many acts of violence, taking enemy mode to a criminal level. Hurt someone's mother, sister, child, or pet and attachment pain is activated. Revenge killing, murdering a cheating partner, "revenge porn" against a former mate, and jealous fights start with a loss that causes attachment pain. Enemy mode *with* attachment pain is the basic plot for every crime show and most human violence on the news. When there is a workplace shooting, a family found killed in their home, or a serial killer reported, we expect the motive to involve attachment pain. Was there an ex-wife or girlfriend? Was someone cheating? Were the parents cold and abusive?

> *Anywhere I feel attachment pain or that attachments are threatened, it will be hard to admit enemy mode. It will be easiest to admit my enemy mode reactions to someone who has a strong and fearless attachment to me.*

LAYING MY LIFE DOWN FOR MY IDENTITY

People will kill and be willing to die themselves to defend their identities. Since our identities grow from attachments to family and identity groups, the insults to our identities that lead to enemy mode often lower the status of our mothers or ethnicity. Our identities are strongly associated with the PFC and its functions. Personal identity uses a great number of vmPFC functions, which, if impaired, contribute to enemy mode. Our "as if" identity featured during intelligent enemy mode uses mPFC functions. Our group identity after age thirteen (as it involves the regulation of enemy mode) uses the dlPFC in relation to the vmPFC. Escaping enemy mode is going to require both individual and group identity functions in the brain to be operational.

Some people are willing to lay down their lives for others. These heroes have an identity of honor, an honor that protects other people at the risk of their own lives. Ray liked reading Congressional Medal of Honor citations for heroism in combat. NYC firefighters who ran in full bunker gear toward the World Trade Center buildings on 9/11 went in to protect and save because it was who they were.

Protective leaders defend their teams. General Halstead would suffer for her team. Her identity meant she was willing to endure harsh reprimands from a superior when necessary. That was the kind of general she was. "The team understood I would get beat up, but I was going to be a buffer to keep them from being beat up. If that cost me my second star, cost me my job, so be it. But my responsibility was to protect and care for them," Halstead said. "It's kind of like being a mom, right? I have to do that; I will be that buffer. I'm not afraid of it. Hey, no problem if this is where my career ends. I can look at myself in the mirror, knowing that it ended with my character intact."

How did she become a person who'd be willing to "take a beating"?

Halstead has looked to two examples, one from history and one from her faith tradition.

"Rosa Parks was an ordinary woman who took public transportation. One day, she is just tired of being treated unfairly, and she says to herself, 'I have to stop this or at least try,' and so she refuses to take her seat in the back of the bus. She didn't know when she took that action that she was going to become a national icon. She just did it because it was the right thing to do. She was being treated wrongly. She had no idea of the historical impact that would unfold. I tell people, 'Don't lose your Rosa Parks moment in history.'"

Halstead continued, "Nobody had it worse than Jesus. We're not perfect. He was perfect. He helped everybody; we don't help everybody. He got it all right. And yet he suffered the most tragic death, humiliation, and pain—one that none of us could have endured. And he did it for us."

> *Anytime I feel my individual or group identities are being distorted or misrepresented, it will be hard to admit enemy mode. It will be easiest to admit my enemy mode to someone who encourages my best identity.*

HOW DOES LEARNING ENEMY MODE IMPACT ME?

The brain is a learning machine. Enemy mode creates its own state-dependent learning patterns to improve its ability to attack, defeat, and destroy the enemy. We become more effective the more time we spend in enemy mode. Given that the brain in enemy mode cannot tell that someone else is not in enemy mode, our improved abilities are most likely to harm the people closest to us.

It will be easier to see the extent of my enemy mode if I start with the understanding that it is something I have learned; it has been useful to me at times and my brain has found ways to get better at it. While I may be ashamed of some things I have done and said or proud of other ways I have imposed myself, I can see how enemy mode created a pattern. I need to know how that pattern worked for me before I can consider changes.

Ray told Jim how enemy mode worked for him. For a decade, Ray quoted a saying to himself about his possibility of promotion: "They are going to promote someone. They may as well promote me." At the time, Ray considered this motivation to be his best. Looking back, he now saw it as the justification for whatever put him in the best position for promotion. This justification for his enemy mode cost Ray twenty years working two jobs and five straight years constantly away on Army duty. He would say he was called to it, but was this his best self? How did he justify it? Each time his attachment pain triggered simple enemy mode, Ray's state-dependent learning built his new normal. Ray was learning to be physically present but emotionally distant. Problem-solving in his head replaced connecting with the people at his table.

Ray was honored to have served at senior levels and thankful for opportunities that promotions provided. He did not notice at the time what those years cost him. He was now carrying the sadness and regret of missed relational connection because he was living in enemy mode. For Ray, escaping enemy mode has not been without the pain of past losses.

Jim asked Ray if he liked himself now. Ray answered, "I do. I am beginning to feel things that I have not felt in some time, like hope and tenderness. I am noticing relational signals more often, even though I can still miss them. I still miss nonverbals during video conference calls. But I am less frozen when other people have big emotions around me. That said, I am not content. I have a long way to go in my journey to escaping enemy mode spontaneously. I didn't get here overnight, and I won't get out overnight."

To fully explore what we have learned during enemy mode, we should not attack ourselves. Self-attack is enemy mode turned

Self-attack is enemy mode turned inward, and it will find a way to stop our exploration and therefore block our change.

inward, and it will find a way to stop our exploration and therefore block our change. We change more effectively through compassion for ourselves and sharing the pain we created for others.

The good news is that if we start learning how to refriend while we are in enemy mode, this also engages the brain's capacity to learn. Calculating the least harmful alternative is native to the brain, as are secure attachments. Our brain has a bias in favor of learning its way out of enemy mode once we know we can.

Any time I am in enemy mode with myself, my shame will make it hard to admit enemy mode. When I look at myself while I am in enemy mode, I am going to attack myself. It will be easiest to admit my enemy mode if I consider how it may have served me or even saved my life.

WHAT IS IN IT FOR ME TO GET OUT OF ENEMY MODE?

My brain is never fully functioning while I am in enemy mode. A brain in enemy mode is fundamentally unstable. Trauma and neglect, in all their forms, tend to produce enemy mode operations for this very reason. Sections of the brain may be running too slowly. As we also learned from Dr. Kaiser, the brain may be too lock-stepped to see other perspectives. Amygdala excitation can cause us to lose synchronization. Low PFC activity can make us miss noticing what we value, do something stupid, or become overly focused. A major incentive for getting out of enemy mode is to establish full brain operation.

> Anytime I feel my brain is unstable, it will be hard to admit enemy mode. It will be easiest to admit enemy mode when I am quietly connected with myself, my body, and my identity group.

HOW DOES ENEMY MODE WORK?

Intelligent enemy mode operation appears to be guided by a kind of empathy but without compassion. As when tracking a wounded animal, a predator notes the signs of distress in its prey but doesn't feel them. The tracking can be very accurate, as professional fighters know, but leads to the "kill." The medial-frontal PFC system has a simulation function that is somewhat separated from personal experience and allows us to pre-test outcomes but also to create "as if" identities. "As if" identities are well-suited for getting results and seeking status but poorly suited for compassion.

The PFC also has a personally connected mode of functioning where we feel in our bodies what someone else is experiencing. These functions involve the vmPFC and the insula. Once the insula becomes involved, we begin feeling compassion.

Jim and Ray strongly suspected that many religious people lived from their "as if" circuit. There was no proof of this. The model could explain how people who thought they were spiritual lacked compassion, but the science to prove the theory was not there yet. Ray felt that many military leaders also lived from their "as if" circuit.

What is the incentive to grow an "as if" identity instead of a relational one? The immediate benefit for us as individuals is feeling less vulnerable. After all, in an "as if" identity, nothing hurts as much. The downside is that I don't feel totally like the real me. I act one way but feel that if you knew the real me you might not like me. In other words, I perform but isolate my real self. I have status without substance. I have a lonely but highly praised existence. I have a defense against toxic shame.[8] I have a resistance to any healthy shame that might help me become my best self. I can even track and kill without compassion.

Escaping "as if" leads straight to vulnerability. Brené Brown built a strong case for the value of vulnerability. Her TED talk on the power of vulnerability has garnered over fifteen million views and has been translated into over fifty languages. Millions of people were interested in escaping their "as if" existence. Vulnerability provided a path. Brown's social psychology studies provide one of the clearest guides for developing group identities free of toxic shame.[9] Vulnerability leads to discovering our best selves.

> *The longer and harder I have worked to grow an "as if" self, the harder it will be to admit enemy mode. It will take me some time to discover and admit my enemy mode. But I am in more danger than I know. If someone upsets me by telling me the truth, I should buy them lunch. I look for people who are not afraid to help me find my better self.*

STEPS TO ADMITTING ENEMY MODE

Let's just be clear. If you live with regular fighting, drug abuse, drinking, domestic violence, illegal activities, child abuse, and other hostilities (hooligans and Raiders fans?), there is going to be a lot of enemy mode going on. You may have to go somewhere safer to be able to admit the danger, even to yourself. If you are actively holding your own in a conflict, you know that trying to get out will be dangerous. Intelligent enemy mode makes it very hard to find a safe place.

Here are some practices that help us see and admit to any kind of enemy mode.

1. Quieting: Find a quiet and safe place to rest so your mind will not need to be in enemy mode. Notice and give a word to how your body feels.

2. Appreciation: Take time to appreciate at least three meaningful experiences you have had so that you stabilize your brain chemistry (three minutes minimum).

3. Relational mode activation: Remember and make a list of three or more good and cozy relational moments in your life. Notice and give a word to how your body feels.

4. Make a list of the times in the last day (or week if needed) that it felt like someone else was not on your side. Notice how your body feels and give it a word.

5. If your brain becomes "hot, cold, or upset," go back over steps 1–3 before continuing.

6. Starting as far back as you remember, make a list of enemy mode situations or relationships you have experienced. Notice how your body feels and your mind reacts. If any of the memories reload old feelings too intensely, give that event

a name and put it on a list for later consideration. Repeat steps
1–3 as needed if you notice you are staying upset.
7. Make a short list of how you usually feel and react during
   enemy mode.
8. Put the list aside for a few days, and then review and update
   what you have written.
9. Explain enemy mode to someone you trust. Have them
   tell you when they have seen you in enemy mode—you felt
   someone was not on your side.

When our usual style is simple enemy mode, it may be difficult to
get into relational mode or notice when we are not. Doing the first
three steps, or perhaps the whole list, with someone we feel attached
to can help. Asking all people close to us to say something when they
notice we are in simple enemy mode will raise our awareness.

When our usual style is stupid enemy mode, we are likely to be carrying toxic shame. A 12-step recovery program will help us take a fearless
moral inventory. It is very helpful to notice what happens just before the
stupid enemy mode episodes and find what we can change. Taking responsibility will help us find something we can do differently next time.

When our usual style is status-based intelligent enemy mode, we can
make note of our fantasies of power, control, respect, justice, or revenge.
These fantasies can give important clues to how our status has been
damaged and what prevents our mind from escaping enemy mode.

One additional idea is to imagine hosting and feeding an "enemy"
or someone we usually like when we are in enemy mode with them.
This use of our "as if" circuit adds clarity and detail that will help us
become aware of our enemy mode reactions.

Winners, Status, and Pushback

Ray began this research and book writing project as a retired Briga-dier General and a former pastor. He had a significant voice in the Army that he lost as a retiree. As a pastor, Ray influenced pastors, but getting a church, denomination, or movement to recognize enemy mode was a challenge for a lower status "former." Many Christians resisted or failed to understand the need for their fifth of the world's population to ac-tively refriend. Sometimes the pushback was along the lines of, "Why are you so focused on the brain? Isn't Scripture and creed enough?" Other times the pushback was in the form of indifference. Ray found that his most resistant audience was, unfortunately, pastors.

Ray's lack of status felt like the poor man in our dedication quote, "No one listened to him because he was a poor man." When, or if, high status megachurch pastors embraced the brain science about escaping enemy mode, their influence would spread the ideas to the many status-conscious churches. That day had not yet arrived.

Ray and Ed Khouri conferred about why pastors might be resistant to brain science. Khouri's theory was that pastors didn't have education about the brain or even counseling. Brain science is relatively recent in human history, approximately the last thirty years. Academic insti-tutions are conservative and generally slow to adopt new innovations. Theological seminaries and Bible colleges are even more so. Pastoral training is directed to theology, Bible, history, and pastoral preparation.

Ray wholeheartedly agreed with Khouri. Ray's master's degree in the-ology was more than 75 percent about how to understand, study, and preach good sermons about the Bible. To his chagrin, Ray had not taken a single counseling class. Yet, pastors had direct responsibility for de-veloping people who actively refriend their enemies. It was frustrating!

For decades, Ray, like many North American pastors, had modeled his work after megachurch pastors like Rick Warren and Bill Hybels. The phenomenon of the megachurch began in the twentieth century and was not slowing down. Megachurch status begins when a church gathers more than one thousand in attendance per weekend. There are thousands of such churches worldwide, yet they still are only 1 to 2 percent of the total churches. When an organization scales up, distance is created between leader and followers. The leaders are typically entrepreneurial men (they have almost exclusively been men) who are comfortable with distance from people. Would status-seeking pastors be the role models for change?

Ray talked to one senior pastor who showed little interest in the brain science behind how people learn or get stuck relationally and emotionally. He paid no attention to how or if the people in his church developed. In fact, he and the leaders around him resisted any suggested changes that developed people.

Pastor Frank experienced the same resistance inside the church that Ray received from outside it. Frank was an associate pastor in one of America's most prominent evangelical churches. Pre-pandemic, the church was one of the country's largest. The staff culture had become fear-driven with large amounts of narcissism. Frank lacked the status to influence the whole church or its many campus locations. He could influence his team and the people they served, but that was about all.

Ray and Jim commiserated about the cost of challenging enemy mode practices in churches. They both had many friends who had been driven off as status challengers. Churches were like businesses where status trumped human costs. Former Facebook insider Frances Haugen said she wanted the company to practice their values of creating community instead of fueling division. She insisted that Facebook had developed an algorithm promoting the most divisive or angry posts. Doesn't that sound like enemy mode clickbait? Haugen contended that Facebook knew harm was being caused but put profits over people.[10] She was calling for leadership to bring out their best selves.

Haugen lacked the status to force change. No one listened, so she uploaded thousands of internal corporate documents to the internet, quit her job, and testified all over the world about her concerns. The Facebook Corporation immediately denied her accusations. It seems fair to say that they did not see Haugen as on their side. Any attachments failed.

We have found that attachments provide both our most important status and best chances of escaping enemy mode. In our next chapter, we will use all that we have learned to prepare our escape from enemy mode.

PREPARING TO ESCAPE ENEMY MODE

THE COLORADO SCHOOL OF MINES has had a successful NCAA Division II women's volleyball program for the past fifteen years under Head Coach Jamie Magalei and Assistant Coach Heather Roberts. The program was consistently winning and making consecutive appearances in the NCAA tournament, but the coaching staff was looking for an added piece to the puzzle.

Ray spoke with both coaches to learn how they were adopting a relational approach to coaching. He found them preparing to get out of enemy mode.

Frequent signs of enemy mode can be seen in sports, so how these coaches led an escape might work anywhere.

Roberts had grown curious about how she was interacting with the team. "I think we were both feeling it. We wanted to fully enjoy what we were doing. We wanted new tools that would bring joy to our careers for another fifteen years."

Magalei and Roberts were looking for a better way to coach. They led a winning program and wanted to be sure they continued to love their work. What were they missing? They asked their friend, leadership coach Lori Mateer, for help. Mateer specialized in relationships, attachment, and coaching. She helped Magalei and Roberts see that they had been operating in and out of enemy mode. They instead wanted to improve on staying relational, so Mateer suggested that they prepare to help the team out of enemy mode by beginning with themselves.

Roberts's dad had coached her in high school. He had been a very relational coach, but she had developed an opposite coaching style when she got to Mines in her early twenties. Roberts felt she had to use enemy mode to motivate the players, and she disliked how that felt. Operating in enemy mode showed her best intentions without reflecting her best self.

Magalei's mom coached her in high school and had a task-oriented and determined style of coaching. Magalei also wanted to add relational skills to her coaching tool belt so she could show up as her best self.

For Roberts, each game was about how to draw a win out of her players. But even winning didn't bring her satisfaction. "I'd come home after a win and should have been feeling great," Roberts said, "but instead the relational joy piece of coaching was missing."

The players "just didn't see" the relational side of coaching, according to Roberts, but she said, "We wanted our players to know us and understand we cared for them. We needed guidance in learning how to make that happen."

The coaches are also best friends and wanted to grow what they'd been building. "We've done this for so long together, and our lives are intertwined," Heather said, emphasizing the importance and strength of relationships.

Previously, Magalei and Roberts had focused most of their energy on on-the-court strategies. Coaching the whole person would require staying relational with their team. With Mateer's guidance, both coaches began to invent their own relational way of coaching.

Some of the changes they made included:

- Engaging a leadership coach and giving Mateer permission to observe and ask them pointed questions to help them stay out of enemy mode and keep things relational with the team.
- Recognizing and admitting enemy mode within themselves.
- Building attachment with their players.
  - Taking the team on an outing to a national park while at an away game.
  - Involving the players in their personal lives, such as when Heather invited the whole team to her baby's gender reveal party.
- Smiling and joking with the players more often.

These simple changes had a big payoff over time by building attachment and group identity. In chapter 12, we will return to see what happened for Magalei and Roberts.

PREPARING CHRISTIANS TO ESCAPE ENEMY MODE

Ray had begun preparing with his own escape from enemy mode at work. Serving under a difficult supervisor, Ray had practiced identifying his emotions by noticing what his body was doing, and by calming himself with deep breathing, especially during painful disagreements. One day, Ray was verbally attacked and cursed at because of a decision he had made. He felt panic in his chest and narrowing of his vision, so as soon as possible, he left the room. This type of mistreatment had kept Ray in intelligent enemy mode for weeks in the past. This time, Ray knew a better way. He immediately took a walk. While walking, he did deep breathing. He felt his body calming down. After a few minutes, he was able to feel compassion for the man who had cursed at him. Later that week, Ray engaged the man in a curious conversation about what had caused the verbal attack. They would never be friends, but Ray was able to mainly stay out of enemy mode with him for as long as they worked together.

Ray looked for other models of preparing to escape and thought of Emanuel. We met Emanuel in chapter 5, a Christian leader who transitioned from a pastor to a new role in city government. When a senior city official unexpectedly demanded a meeting with him, Emanuel became worried and sought advice from a mentor. Emanuel said, "My mentor advised me to go into the meeting curious."

Emanuel quieted himself before going into what he feared would be a contentious conversation. Quieting helps keep our relational circuits engaged so we stay relational. Staying curious in a difficult conversation indicates that we are not in enemy mode.

Unfortunately, the conversation went downhill fast. "From the minute I entered, it was obvious to me this was going to be a one-way conversation," said Emanuel. "He didn't know me but certainly had lots of opinions about my character. When I realized he didn't want to know me, was not going to be relational, and this was not going to be a conversation, I remembered that I had been coached to stay curious, so I began asking questions."

The meeting was painful and exhausting, so Emanuel quieted himself again. He went back to his mentor who "talked him off the ledge" by helping Emanuel remember his best self and neutralize toxic shame. In a few days, Emanuel's best self began feeling sadness and compassion for the city official.

A similar incident happened to Chaplain Haynes, who we met in chapter 4. After Ray explained the enemy mode to him, Haynes immediately recognized enemy mode in himself and admitted that he needed to make changes at home and at work.

Just like General Halstead had her personal board of directors, Haynes consulted with Ray about a challenge in his department. For two years in a row, another chaplain and ethnic minority had been turned down for additional training. He was beginning to wonder if the reason was discrimination on Chaplain Haynes's part. The training was funded by the VA, and completing it was required for advancement.

Haynes felt unfairly accused and went into enemy mode.

When Ray asked what Haynes was going to do about the situation, he said, "I am going to send him an email and not meet with him."

Ray wanted to encourage the chaplain's best self and challenged him. "What is the most relational way to respond to him?" Ray would have been ill-equipped to ask such a question years before. He would have advised overwhelming the man with explanation and justification, not realizing this is an enemy mode solution that would have put the man in enemy mode.

Haynes pondered, "He wanted to meet with me, but I don't know if I have time." The question got Haynes thinking and his best self scheduled the meeting.

He later told Ray that he felt compassion for the man's sadness and disappointment. We know that compassion prevents intelligent enemy mode. Meeting face-to-face builds attachment and keeps us out of simple enemy mode. So, rather than just sending an impersonal email, Haynes met with him face-to-face and began helping the chaplain prepare his application for the next training. Ray was learning the steps to prepare to escape enemy mode and could share them with Haynes.

CAN'T WE JUST DECIDE TO ESCAPE?

No. Enemy mode has enough difficulties and real risks that we should prepare for our escape. At this point in the book, we will presume that most readers are interested in doing that. But like all mental skills, escaping enemy mode is learned. Like all state-dependent learning, escaping enemy mode is learned *during* enemy mode. However, there are some skills we can learn in *advance* that will help.

All three types of enemy mode involve less than ideal mental function.[1] Escaping enemy mode involves activating brain functions that are missing or shut down at the moment. During enemy mode thinking, our motivation for escaping is low, and we might not have any experience knowing our way out. If most of us were to suddenly decide to explain quantum physics or organic chemistry to a class, we would have the same problem—no learned experience in this topic. What would most of us do? We would quit or never try.

Learning new things involves expecting some failures. The preparations for escaping enemy mode help us have fewer, briefer, and less frustrating failures, which provide something that even enemy mode understands: the hope for a win.

WHY AREN'T WE TRYING TO AVOID ENEMY MODE?

Life will routinely test our ability to stay out of enemy mode. If we are not prepared, we will fall into it rapidly. One day, as Ray was helping Deborah unload groceries from the car, a heavy object fell out of the bag and shattered on the ground with a loud crack, like a gunshot. Oily liquid ran everywhere. Ray had just dropped and shattered a bottle of olive oil. The intense sound shut down Ray's anterior cingulate.

Ray jumped and began shouting angrily at Deborah. It wasn't the mess that upset him but the anticipation of Deborah's disapproval. He felt ashamed because he had not carried the bag the way Deborah had always advised.

Something happens *just before* a stupid enemy mode incident that causes the anterior cingulate to overload and block the PFC's autonoetic function. Autonoetic means "knowing I was there." Autonoetic memory would have shown Ray his contribution to dropping the bottle. Once his anterior cingulate overloaded, Ray's brain was acting like

Ray was not there and not responsible for anything.

Without his PFC to help, Ray was emotionally on edge. His mind was racing, his pulse was up, and he could not think straight for several minutes. While Ray's brain blocked seeing his part in the mess, his amygdala anticipated Deborah's disapproval. Ray's autonoetic memory could find no record of Ray being part of the problem at all. A vicious enemy, said his amygdala, was about to attack him.

The fast-track operations deep in the brain go into action before conscious thought has a chance, and when these fast operations make a mistake, we are in enemy mode before we are conscious of how we got there. Self-rescue means learning how to get out of enemy mode.

When Jim learned to scuba dive, he also learned self-rescue techniques. Self-rescue was also an important part of learning to back-pack in the High Sierra. The more practice the better when it comes to self-rescue. We are working to speed our recovery time. Spending one day in enemy mode beats staying there a week. When we start self-rescue, within minutes or seconds, the amount of damage we sustain for our best self becomes minimal.

Stupid enemy mode is one place where avoiding enemy mode can help. The losses associated with doing and saying something stupid are worth preventing, if possible. We still need to learn how to get out of enemy mode with the practices that follow. We can learn to predict almost all stupid enemy mode before it happens. The conditions that set it up are not hard to guess. We are looking to find a less harmful alternative we can use before we get stupid.

Certain people (e.g., an ex-wife), certain situations (rush hour), certain locations (work), certain times (payday), certain topics (my rights), or certain conditions (too long without eating or sleeping) set the stage for stupid enemy mode events. These are common, and negative interactions with them would be fairly avoidable if we got creative.

The one option that rarely works is trying to "stuff it" and go on. A much better work-around involves what psychotherapist and social worker Wendy Maltz called "playing with the trigger."[2] What she means is that we should find the trigger that sets us off and start coming up with creative, even ludicrous, ways we could react instead of what we usually do. Being creative ahead of time helps the PFC engage to find the least harmful alternative. The next time the toilet seat is left up, I can imagine standing on the toilet and playing the trumpet loudly. Trying to make noise on a trumpet is just as ineffective as what we already do, but thinking about alternatives restarts the brain. Talking the triggers through with others is usually more successful than trying to solve the problem in our heads alone.

If I don't want to be stupid, I have to be present. If I am not here, there is nothing I can do, and you are the problem. There is nothing I can actually change before I go stupid. As a result, I attack you. Once my brain realizes I *am* here, I have options. We want to focus on that moment of real opportunity just before we go stupid and play with the trigger.

After shattering the oil, Ray felt his heart rate spiking, his vision narrowing, and his breathing becoming shallow. In combat, Navy SEALs who feel that way have trained themselves to practice box breathing: four seconds in, four seconds hold, four seconds out, four second pause. Making box breathing a practice could prevent going stupid after a trigger. Berating ourselves for how stupid we have been is asking for a repeat performance.

Returning to peace took Ray a long time. Meanwhile, Deborah quietly and calmly began to clean up the mess, and that helped Ray. Eventually Ray's anterior cingulate got uncramped, and he was able to see what really happened. Ray apologized for his stupid enemy mode. Apologies also help us learn.

TWELVE SKILL PRACTICES FOR ESCAPING ENEMY MODE

This is not the place to try and teach, build, or even explain emotional and relational intelligence. Instead, here is a list of skills that help us get out of the distress of enemy mode. As we pointed out in chapter 1, no one enjoys being in enemy mode. It is an unsatisfying and even miserable experience.

Anything we can do on demand makes us feel more confident. For example, if I can lower my blood pressure on demand or improve my singing tone on demand, it gives me a great sense of ability. A major part of being skilled comes from what we can do on demand. Hoping we can pull something off if the conditions are right and the wind is behind us feels rather risky.

Checking the list of practices below that help us escape enemy mode can help us identify weaknesses in our plan to escape and which areas need attention. We will unpack six of these later in the chapter.

Practice self-quieting

It is obvious that self-quieting will help us avoid doing something stupid, but good self-quieting is also the strongest predictor of mental health. An important part of self-quieting is reaching a place of being present and in touch with how our body feels. This ensures that our PFC and insula are operating. Emanuel did deep breathing and stayed curious before and after his contentious meeting with the city official.

Know where to land

Practice being relational and what it is like to have your RCs on. Knowing if we are out of enemy mode without being familiar with our relational brain state is difficult. Noticing when our RCs are off and deliberately getting them back on is fundamental.

Avoid toxic shame

Being angry or critical of our mistakes gets a quick response, but is not sustainable as a motive for change. Instead of changing, our brain will look for ways to avoid thinking about anything that brings toxic shame. Toxic shame focuses on what we have done wrong. Toxic shame is always destructive to our identity. Focusing on what we did wrong inspired Daniel Wegner of Harvard to write *How to Think, Say, or Do Precisely the Worst Thing for Any Occasion*.[3] A healthy shame message shows us our mistake but reminds us of our identity. Healthy shame helps us focus on becoming our best self in the situation.

Write a description of my best self

It is pretty hard to focus on my best self without first having a clear idea of who I am proud to be. After an episode he was not proud of, one man had the word *Authentic* tattooed on his chest as a reminder of his best self. We may need help with this one. We can ask those who are attached to us to help us literally write out this description.

Feed an attachment

All three styles of enemy mode include lost awareness of attachment. Reminding ourselves of meaningful attachments is one key to escaping enemy mode. Gaining voluntary control over reviving attachments is helped by deliberately making someone's eyes light up. Pick a meaningful attachment in your life and get some smiles. Enjoy the sparkle in their eyes when they see you.

Practice intentional compassion

Compassion comes easiest when someone hurts someone we love. We can start there by letting our cingulate cortex share what our loved one feels and notice how that feels in our bodies (insula). The harder (but more useful) practice is sharing the hurt we have produced, either accidentally (hard) or during enemy mode (harder). Feeling the hurt we produced (without justifying ourselves) is an effective way to reduce future damaging actions on our part. Practicing intentional compassion begins with noticing the hurt, especially the hurt we have caused. Compassion grows when we allow ourselves to sit in the pain with the person we have hurt without trying to fix it.

Sitting with them validates the pain, and we will find our ability to feel compassion growing.

Explain to others what I plan to do

Our chances of success escaping enemy mode with people we know well is going to improve if they know what we are trying to do. Explaining how enemy mode works for us and what we plan to do to get out of it also helps the procedural left brain to clearly remember what we plan to do. Explaining our plans relationally also helps our state-dependent learning notice who we plan to refriend. In time, we might even get reminders from others about what our best self really wants. General Halstead's board of directors helped her do this.

Locate and enlist an encourager or coach

Dr. Ken Canfield, who was at the time at the National Center for Fathering, told Jim that men who became the best fathers were generally not the ones who had great fathers. Canfield described the best fathers as "overcomer" fathers who, based on their own difficult life experience, set out to become the best. Canfield said these overcomers needed two things: healthy examples and an encouraging partner. If we want to achieve what seems out of reach, we need encouragement.

Practice discussions about finding the least harmful solution

Enemy mode thinking fails to consider the least harmful alternative. Enemy mode wants to nuke the idiot opposing me or whatever the target might be. Since escaping enemy mode is being learned, we can be sure that our brain will not be crisp and clear about the least harmful solution. Practicing figuring out the least harmful solution while we are calm and with people we are attached to will help both sides know what we need when the time comes.

Start off easy with someone you generally like

Find your "bunny hill" person. Practice with someone who is easy to refriend.

Get to know your usual enemy mode patterns

All of us have been in and out of enemy mode already. We might not have known what it was at the time or noticed how we got out.

> ## Observing the patterns we already have established helps us notice the start of enemy mode faster.

Observing the patterns we already have established helps us notice the start of enemy mode faster. Noticing how we escaped enemy mode previously builds hope that it can be done even if our methods could stand some serious improvement.

Pick a start time when you are rested and less stressed

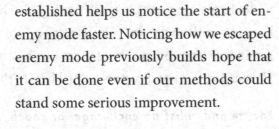

Observing what we usually do is helpful, so we should maximize our chances of successfully refriending our way out of enemy mode by picking a good time to try. If we are tired, hungry, and stressed, our success will usually be much better after some sleep and a meal. We will only keep trying for a while as those little calculators in our basal ganglia will eventually tell us this won't work and we give up.

SIX CASE STUDIES PROVE
THE CONCEPT OF ESCAPING WORKS

Ray and Jim discovered six case studies that arose from their research and lives.

Writing a description of my best self: At the beginning of this quest, Ray realized he wasn't sure about his best self. After study and reflection, group discussion with his work team, and conversations with Deborah, he wrote a description of his best self, which he calls his positive identity. He began to read this to himself and his wife often. His description includes both positive and negative expressions:

- I am a person who recognizes when my relational circuits are dimming and takes steps to keep them online. I am not a person who takes out my frustration on others.
- I attune kindly with sadness and share the pain when someone is sad. I am not uncomfortable when someone is sad.
- I am someone who is gentle with weakness and is happy to take second place. I am not a person who takes advantage of others' weaknesses.
- I notice when I am overwhelmed, and I take a break for quieting. I don't overwhelm others.

Avoiding toxic shame: Ray's fellow West Point alum and author Greg Hiebert told Ray about Father Linus, a Franciscan priest who was good at helping others avoid toxic shame by remembering their best self when they were forgetting who they were. He never used toxic shame to confront people. Fr. Linus and Hiebert served together in Catholic youth ministry in Atlanta, Georgia, for years. Hiebert said the priest lived out the essence of Saint Francis—being in tune with the world around him, lowering emotional negativity, and increasing emotional positivity.

"He could sense when people were getting off kilter, and he would say, 'Let's step back,' and then he would ask, 'Is this who we are? And is this what we're called to be?'" Greg fondly remembered how Fr. Linus closed every conversation with "peace in all good things . . . peace in all good."

Locating and enlisting an encourager or coach: Coach Magalei and Coach Roberts were firm believers in getting their own coach. Magalei said, "Until Lori was in our life, coaching to me was how I was coached. What Lori brought in was an area completely untapped within our program and within us as coaches." Roberts added, "When we started to invest relationally in the players, we realized we didn't know how, but we wanted to remain relational with the players and help them. How do we do that? We needed someone who was way more knowledgeable. That was Lori." Lori Mateer helped these coaches know themselves better and escape enemy mode with their players.

Practicing intentional compassion: Ray felt compassion for Jeff, who had been fired from his volunteer position (as we saw in chapter 8). Ray asked Jeff, "Where did your intensity come from?" Jeff revealed his anger was from deep pain in early childhood. To help Jeff tap into his compassion for others, Ray asked him a question the next time they met: "Where can you feel compassion for the woman you disagreed with? What did you lose by getting angry with her?" Jeff had no immediate answer but began to consider how the woman might have felt, and it built his compassion toward her.

Feeding an attachment: Pastor Frank began studying and applying relational brain principles that helped him stay more relational and stay out of enemy mode. The most important shift was to feed attachment. Frank deepened his emotional attachment with his fourteen-year-old son. Frank said, "Even last night, we had a little disagreement, and then this morning I just looked at him face-to-face because I was trying to activate those relational circuits. I said, 'It's good to see you back. This is who you are.'" He is more deeply connected now to his family and to his team at work.

Frank leads his team differently. The first thirty to forty-five minutes of each team meeting are spent answering this question: "What is bringing you joy today?" Sharing joy feeds their attachment to one another. The team has also learned to recognize the absence of relational attachment on other teams and with other leaders. Frank went on to say, "We have a team that's full of relational joy with each other." That's attachment at work!

Getting to know your usual enemy mode patterns: By the time Jim and Kitty had been married a few years, they could predict a fight every time they put up the Christmas tree. The tree would be crooked, water would get spilled, a decoration would need to get moved, but there was always something to spark enemy mode. The upset lasted all day until they sat down together to admire the tree, which somehow spontaneously took them out of enemy mode.

The couple easily recognized the enemy mode fight pattern, but it took them a lot longer to realize that stopping to appreciate the moment would help them escape enemy mode.

HOW DOES STAYING IN ENEMY MODE IMPACT ME?

During enemy mode, we don't enjoy relationships, so the longer we stay enemies with people we love, the less opportunity we have to enjoy being together. Losing the love we have been able to find impacts both of us if either of us stays in enemy mode too long. Every night we go to sleep in a stressful enemy mode state, our bodies pump glucocorticoids—stress hormones. As we mentioned in chapter 5, these chemicals block attachment formation. That is a great idea if we don't want to start a relationship but not so good if our brain is blocking us from seeing that someone else is really not against us.

Ray remembered a birthday dinner for his daughter Kathleen when he was distracted. Ray told Jim, "I was thinking about deadlines to prepare the budget, board members who didn't seem to trust me or the team, a fall marketing campaign to carry out, and the lack of progress on our enemy mode book. Kathleen and Deborah said I felt distant. I was. I had slipped into simple enemy mode."

Ray realized that while he was mentally "multitasking" (which, by the way, is impossible), he missed many delightful family moments. Seeing the tears of his disappointed daughter Kathleen was the worst part. By the next day, Deborah and Kathleen had helped Ray return to being fully present and enjoy the time celebrating with them both. Ray was feeling the cost of enemy mode and learning to be relational and present.

WHAT IS IN IT FOR ME TO GET OUT OF ENEMY MODE QUICKLY?

Lasting friendships are what we gain when we get out of enemy mode quickly. The Beatles were great friends, and their musical talent and personalities changed the world. The members of Crosby, Stills, and Nash were in line to be the next big band, but the evidence suggests that they did not get out of enemy mode well. We need a little help from our friends so we do not waste time on the way out of enemy mode.

Good friends help one another out of enemy mode. Let's say, hypothetically, that Rich, George, and Paul are friends. If George gets into enemy mode with Paul but neither is in enemy mode with Rich, George forms a bridge out of enemy mode. Good attachments with a third person help us learn to refriend others while we are still in enemy mode. Rich provides a non-enemy mode perspective that his pals can share in order to help them refriend.

During the pandemic, three women met regularly via online conferencing. The purpose of their group was to practice staying relational with each other, but they got off to a rough start and ended up in enemy mode. Hulda was deeply distracted whenever Sarah was driving during a group meeting. Hulda remembered that her friend's son had been killed while texting and driving. Sarah calling from her car triggered fear in Hulda. Rather than speaking to Sarah, Hulda decided to drop out of the group.

Kathy saw what was happening and became a rescue attachment by appealing to Hulda and reaching out to Sarah. Sarah became defensive and reactive, which is an enemy mode response, but she also heard Kathy's words and recalled the love Kathy had shown in the past. She thought, "They truly want to be with me!" thus rekindling her joy and attachment feelings toward the group. Eventually, the three talked openly about their feelings, Sarah changed her schedule, Hulda rejoined meetings, and the group experienced the joy of deepened growth and connection. Because Kathy recognized enemy mode and had prepared herself, she influenced their group to escape enemy mode even though the journey was not easy.

Our identity group models for our right PFC how we deal with people who feel like enemies at the moment. What do we do when one of our people does not seem to be on our side? What do we do when someone who is not one of our people feels like an enemy? When re-friending is part of our group identity, it will help us keep our friends and maybe make some new ones.

HOW DOES A BRAIN IN ENEMY MODE LEARN?

The brain in enemy mode is a learning machine. Some of what it learns is state-dependent—again, learning what to do under specific conditions. During enemy mode, the brain can either be learning how to be a stronger enemy or how to refriend others. We can learn from our personal experience but also through media, history, or even fiction.

History provides many examples of people learning to improve their enemy mode skills. When taking a course on crime scene investigation, Jim observed that serial killers develop their style and technique with practice. Charles Manson learned how to influence people and increase his control over others.

"What fires together wires together" is how neuroscientists describe a brain learning to do certain things. Looking back in history, Ray and Jim found many examples of people who got better at enemy mode, and very few who escaped it.

Politics: Former Marine, Harvard graduate, and lawyer Chuck Colson, who became President Richard Nixon's "hatchet man," said of himself, "If I was valuable to the President . . . it was because I was willing at times to blink at certain ethical standards, to be ruthless in getting things done."[4] A colleague said, "Colson would walk over his own grandmother if he had to" to get Nixon reelected. After a stint in prison, Colton was a changed man because of a religious conversion and led efforts for criminal justice reform.

Crime: We already met mob hitman Frank Sheeran, who learned to kill without remorse in combat in WWII, and then said, "By this time, I thought nothing of doing what I had to do."[5]

The Rich and Famous: We may never find out how many young women Jeffrey Epstein abused. He developed a system to get better at his predatory sexual practices. His money and enablers helped him expand operations.

Business: We already met Andrew Carnegie, one of the robber barons. His career shows a man getting better at crushing the opposition and cutting workers' pay. He didn't care that his steel mill manager was going to cut his workers' pay when a union agreement ended in 1892.

Sports: Mike Tyson was an alpha predator looking for a win in the boxing ring. He found a way and got better at staying in enemy mode by harnessing his own fear as fuel to dominate his opponents: "Fear is my friend. I love fear. Fear allows me to reach my highest potential. . . . Fear pushes us."[6] Tyson's enemy mode was learning aggression from his trainer, Cus D'Amato.

Church: Ray learned to focus on work in enemy mode, while it became easier and easier to neglect his wife and children. To this day, Ray deeply regrets having learned that so well. His brain would feel torn between connecting with his wife and children versus getting back to work. There was always a sermon to write, a phone call to make, a meeting to prepare for. The people needed him! Eventually enemy mode became dominant because learning and repetition turned gray matter into white matter, the deeper tissue of the brain.

Even stupid enemy mode is learning: first, the brain learns to anticipate threats and becomes stupid faster; and second, it learns how to reduce consequences after the fact. If our group identity includes fights or violence when we get together, we will prepare for those. This learning makes it easier and faster to get into enemy mode and avoid paying consequences later.

On the other hand, if our group identity aspires to less predatory ways, raising rather than lowering the social standing of others, protection of identities, and lasting attachments, then we can help one another learn how to escape enemy mode while we are still in it. It takes someone staying interested in helping us during our enemy mode moments. Once some skill is acquired, we continue learning and improving our speed. This takes as much practice time as learning to play volleyball well.

KNOWING WHEN TO START

We should certainly begin finding ways to prevent stupid enemy mode as soon as possible, but, as we will see in the next chapter, all the practice of getting out of enemy mode is still helpful and needed. In real time, we begin recognizing enemy mode more quickly and getting out before we really get stupid and regret it. There is something to be proud of!

By now, Ray knew that being in his sixties had not stopped him from developing new neural pathways. Neuroplasticity allowed him to grow but not do so alone. He had a wife, family, and colleagues with him on this journey.

Given that enemy mode contains the motivation to win, we are ready to start when escaping enemy mode begins to feel like escaping will be a win for us, our friends, and our best self. We have been practicing a few skills, and now our "as if" circuit is telling us that this could work. We have at least one person to encourage us without toxic shame. If these were ski lessons, we would be ready to head to the top of the bunny hill. Soon we will be on the slopes.

Escaping enemy mode ultimately depends on living a life that is relational, at least most of the time. The three central elements of relational life are: building joy, bringing out the best in others, and recovering quickly when enemy mode starts. The next three chapters will examine how this is done.

ESCAPING ENEMY MODE

10

ESCAPING ENEMY MODE ultimately depends on living a life that is relational, at least most of the time. Living relationally means a life of daily joy as we recognize and bring out what is special and best in ourselves and others. In Christian language, being regarded as special is called "grace."[1] Escape from enemy mode follows helping each other bring out our best selves.

Jim and Ray were encountering some resistance to the idea that we have a best self. Without delving too far into it, conflicts about the inherent good in people contributed strongly to the historical Catholic-Protestant split between Christians and sparked many European wars.

Jim grew up hearing that beliefs, right choices, and a strong will were his responsibility for living a righteous life. God would provide the rest. Of course, the impact of beliefs and choices happened far too late in the brain processes to change Jim's character or prevent enemy mode. Chronic appearances by his less-than-best self left him with a sort of quiet desperation. Right beliefs and trying harder produced a chronic, overcontrolled, simple enemy mode life. Growing up with Christians who used toxic shame for control led Jim to chronic low joy. Worse yet, Jim was developing an "as if" self that, unnoticed by him, was becoming more professional and less compassionate with time.

Jim's mom grew up under the American circuit-rider Christianity that followed the Second Great Awakening between 1795 and 1835. The Second Great Awakening was the era of revivalism, abolition of slavery, and the temperance movement, which eventually collided with the Roaring Twenties and resulted in prohibition. What Jim's mom had experienced with alcoholics and stupid enemy mode made her a temperance activist. Advocating for women and children took her to South America during WWII as a missionary teaching literacy in Colombia.

Revivals in the old West and South often shamed sinners as a fulcrum for persuasion. The faster people repented and made the right choice the better. The fear of hell added motivation on the sawdust trail and in tent revivals. But, while emotional decisions on hot summer nights could turn lives around, shame and fear often lingered. Some bad habits stopped, others became hidden. Deeper transformation evaded many. Fear and shame did not help people escape their old "as if" self or chronic enemy mode.

Jim's dad, Earl, grew up and into a neighborhood gang in Buffalo, New York, where Jim's grandfather lived in intelligent enemy mode with most of his relatives. Grandpa Wilder sold moonshine during prohibition. Grandpa had been a blacksmith, steamfitter, and bike racer, so he was strong enough to get away with stupid enemy mode in fights. Grandpa hated toxic religious people like his own Protestant mother and his wife's Catholic parents. Those Protestant and Catholic families were enemies with each other.

Jim's dad knew nothing of religion but wanted out of gang life and away from who he was becoming. Friendly people at a neighborhood Christmas party in a local Baptist church took him off the streets to follow Jesus. Earl, finding less change than expected, went to a Keswick meeting in upstate New York. People in Keswick, England—who, like Earl, had made good choices and espoused right beliefs but were still disappointed with their shameful ways—developed a solution in 1875 that was later brought to the United States. The movement involved a second choice to firmly reject one's unholy self. This abolition of self and pride should lead to God living through the gap left behind. Earl made the decision to rid himself of his bad, prideful self.

Keswick did not provide a basis for Earl to bring out a better or new self.[2] The result was an accumulation of toxic shame to suppress his old self. For his entire life, Earl was careful not to say anything good about himself or his sons that would give them "a big head." The abolition of an enemy mode gangster self is not all we need to grow our best self.

After serving as a medic and chaplain's assistant in an otherwise Jewish army unit under General Patton during WWII, Earl went to Colombia and married. He stepped from the frying pan into the fire as a Protestant missionary in that Catholic country. Catholics, usually led by the local priest, were arresting Protestants, and sometimes burning down their churches with the members inside.

Colombia was in a time of civil war and violence. Enemy mode, hatred, politics, and religion erupted in simple, stupid, and intelligent enemy mode expressions, including murder, torture, and terrorism. Killing neighbors resembled the genocide in Rwanda but on a smaller scale. Estimates of murders in Colombia vary but were about a quarter of the million in Rwanda.

Politics and religion fueled a dangerous mix. The liberal party had a red flag; the conservative party had a blue flag. In liberal towns, the houses all had a red stripe while houses in conservative towns had a blue stripe. Protestants were tolerated in liberal, red-striped towns but might be killed by conservatives upon entering a blue-striped town. Anybody might be killed during a nighttime raid. The first decision Jim's father had to make was whether to place Jim's crib where it would be safer from gunfire or from bombs.

Several years before Jim was born (during WWII), his mother became very ill. She consulted a Catholic doctor, who saw her condition as a way to kill this Protestant. The doctor told her to take a long trip to the mountains and rest. Before she could get on the bus, her appendix burst and the doctor was forced to do surgery.

The doctor invited some witnesses into the surgery to see that her abdomen was totally infected inside. He declared that he could not be held responsible for her death. The next day he took out his pocketknife and opened her abdomen again but without anesthesia. He pulled out her intestines then washed them in a dishpan. Jim's mom held on to the bedpost and tried not to scream, but from that day on she would not trust doctors.

Jim, for his part, feared Catholics. After some physical abuse from the pacifist Protestants in his school, he distrusted them as well. Spiritual beliefs might get him killed. Political views were obviously getting his neighbors killed. When Cuban Marxist guerrillas were added to the mix, Jim was greeted on the streets by, "Yankee imperialist, go home" and racial insults. The way he looked might get him killed. Enemy mode was all around him, and enemy mode was growing within. At the same time, a sense of indignation, that it was all unfair, was also growing. Compassion was motivating him to find a better way for people to live, for political differences to be resolved, for the common good to have value, and for Christians to humanize life for others.

ESCAPING ENEMY MODE IS
MORE THAN COMPASSION BUT NOT LESS

After he survived the genocide in Rwanda that killed his mother and many family members, Father Ubald Rugirangoga returned there to practice and teach peace. For him, confession and forgiveness were core steps to freedom from the past and the way to avoid repeating it. Genocide was a public horror that required public confession by those who committed the violence and forgiveness by the survivors. For Fr. Rugirangoga, those who would not confess their crimes were not Christian, although they might be members of his parish.

The word forgiveness (*imbabazi*) in the Kinyarwanda language means "to suffer with." Compassion, to suffer with the other, is central to escaping enemy mode for both perpetrators and survivors. Fr. Rugirangoga once told Jim that it was impossible for anyone to follow Jesus and not have compassion. No one with compassion could commit genocide.

Sharing the suffering that we produce (even accidentally) can be very difficult. The brain is ready to produce moral-sounding reasoning about why it is not our fault. *We had to! They had it coming!* The left brain can make up justifications on the spot. Self-justifications and blaming others only increase the pain we produce in order to win.

Not sharing suffering equals not having compassion. No shared suffering means no correction will be made. Merely observing suffering without feeling it ourselves makes us better predators. No shared pain makes domestic violence, rape, child abuse, genocide, torture, and murder something we learn to do better. Hurt easily turns to hate.

Shared suffering means we accept pain we might have avoided. Shared suffering creates an attachment. Shared suffering teaches our brain to look for a less harmful alternative next time. Shared suffering means we learn each time we injure others not to do that again.

Sharing the suffering we produce teaches us to stop in time before we hurt someone whose pain we will share. Our mirror neurons, cingulate, PFC, and insula take the pain as ours and make a better plan for next time.

When we hurt others during our enemy mode, we must go back later and share the pain we have caused if we are to learn better ways. Sharing pain begins by validating the impact the pain has on the victim of our enemy mode. Beyond acknowledging what we have done, we deliberately feel the impact. One way Ray knew he was escaping enemy mode was that he was beginning to be able to feel the pain he had caused others.

Escaping enemy mode and going back to share the pain is different from going back later to talk our way out of responsibility. We are not trying to talk our way back into a relationship as happens in the domestic abuse cycle. Sharing pain is different from promises to change, do better next time, never do that again, or to make it up to someone. Nice promises teach the brain nothing. Ray had always asked forgiveness after hurting his wife while in enemy mode, but to sit with her in her pain and share it with her was retraining his brain.

One caution about building compassion relates to intelligent enemy mode. If we tell sociopaths that we are looking for them to develop compassion, clever sociopaths will fake compassion if they have anything to gain by it. Usually, their gains involve keeping access to relationships and resources those relationships provide. The sociopath's partner runs home and says, "My doctor says that if you will just show compassion, we can get back together." Kiss your assets goodbye, but buy a body bag first.

HATE IS A STATE OF MIND, NOT AN OPINION

Differing opinions are not the cause of enemy mode. Being right or winning an argument is not an escape from enemy mode. In chapter 5, we saw Dr. Haidt and others demonstrate how emotions come before beliefs, religious thoughts, and moral opinions in the brain's process. Hate also comes before beliefs in brain operation. This means that trying to change people's beliefs will not resolve the brain's hate state. Hate creates beliefs, not the other way around. We develop moral sounding opinions to justify our enemy mode to others. Moral thinking is about persuading others we are right. Beliefs are how we find other people like ourselves.

As tempting as it is to blame hate on certain beliefs, those beliefs don't start the hate. Disagreeing with those beliefs will not correct hate. Compassion, not enlightenment, opens the door to change. Compassion comes with a degree of relationship attached. Attachment and compassion move us to love, not hate.

Enemy mode is a brain state. Staying in enemy mode is a good way to develop hate. We only focus on enemy mode in this book long enough to understand how enemy mode works. Understanding and recognizing enemy mode helps us escape. We are looking to produce a different state of mind, not change opinions as our path forward.

The sustainable way to escape enemy mode is through a relational life. Life does not start in enemy mode and trying to escape. Life starts by building relationships through joy. Joyful people know when they crash into enemy mode that it isn't their norm. But suppose that we are generally in the company of people who are not on our side, or we made our early attachments to people who generate stress hormones in our bodies. Now our brain will predict that enemy mode life is normal, standard, and our default operating condition. Joy becomes as rare as finding gold nuggets in our yard. Here is a good garden for growing some hate and beliefs that will justify it. Once we see a way to win, a weakness to exploit, or social status to gain, someone is going to lose or die.

Joy is rather easy to "start" in Western cultures. We meet, we smile, someone smiles back, and a spark of joy happens. Joy can start in a hospital, grocery store, school, workplace, dating app, recovery group, hiking trail, or anywhere. We do not need to be the same age, gender, race, culture, religion, social status, political affiliation, or ethnicity to see joy blossom. If joy keeps growing, we develop attachments. So, why isn't life all peaches?

Keeping joy going is not easy because sooner or later enemy mode is going to happen. Once we experience people who we do not feel are for us, the lower stages of our brain make predictions about what is about to go wrong or right. The thalamus and amygdala (with related structures) watch for signs that someone will not be on our side or wish us well and fire up enemy mode responses in anticipation. If we can stay relational, our PFC will update those predictions in real time and shut off the false alarms. Staying relational with upset feelings must be learned from people who stay attached even when we are upset.

My Right Brain Helps Me

Between the temporal and parietal lobes of the right brain are the systems that construct what may be going on in another person's mind at the moment. This Theory of Mind (ToM) system helps us figure out people's motives and intentions. Our "mindsight" fills in what is going on behind another face and voice by sort of hitchhiking a ride. These systems can get it wrong during paranoia or during enemy mode. We often "sense" when someone's ToM is in trouble. When a brain we are trying to track is running too slowly, we are likely to feel they are not "tuned in" to us but are lost in their own reality. If our brain is running too slowly, we are not likely to notice that we are reading others incorrectly. We should not be surprised that this system can make mistakes.

By forming attachments to two or more people with whom we develop and test our mindsight, our ToM system becomes more accurate and also understands a broader spectrum of other minds. With two trusted attachments, we can use one to verify the other when we are not sure.

"Is Dad mad at me?"

"No. Dad is just tired and lost his glove in the snow."

This process of correcting mindsight allows an external point of view to be represented in the right dorsolateral PFC, where we also keep the views of our identity group. Once two people get their mindsight readings wrong (a misunderstanding), they need a correction from a trusted third source. The mind or minds we trust in our dlPFC can help us pull out of enemy mode by updating mindsight.

Updating mindsight can also contribute value to people we have never met before. For instance, our brother says, "I'd like you to meet my new girlfriend." Our mindsight begins shifting. We see the signals that this couple really like each other, and suddenly their joy starts becoming our joy. Their attachment starts becoming my attachment to this stranger. This process of sharing someone's attachment through our ToM is called "acquired value."

Acquired value can help us escape enemy mode *or* enter enemy mode:

"I'm sorry. That is my rescue dog, and I am trying to train it to stop."

"Quit picking on my sis. You made her cry, you big bully."

A very powerful force, once we enter adolescence, is the point of view of our identity group as understood by our dlPFC. This external reference is faster than conscious thought and provides us with the list of "our" options at the moment. From these options we can figure out the least harmful alternative.

Having an attachment to a friend, family, tribe, or other outside observer can increase our response flexibility and creative options. Having a toxic shaming or rigid controlling third perspective will not help us 1) get out of enemy mode or 2) think relationally about how we treat our enemies.

Helping My Right Brain

I can help my right brain make some friends. Enemy mode is a state that does not usually stop to notice itself. Giving someone I trust permission to tell me they think I am in enemy mode can really speed my recovery. This is particularly true for simple enemy mode.

My initial response to being told I am in enemy mode is defensive. But, if I am going to continue getting help, then thanking my observer-friend for telling me is necessary. Maybe I need to take a deep breath first. After thanking my friend, we take a minute or two for celebration. My friend is helping me find my best self, and that is enough cause for joy. If I am grumpy, perhaps a quick hug and a few seconds of quiet time together substitutes for celebration.

Because my brain is not trained to check my enemy mode status, it can help to set up standard times to check. If I have a coach, we may meet once a week. When I check in with my coach, I can report if I have been in enemy mode since my last visit. I can also do a nightly check on myself. At first, I only become aware of my day's enemy mode moments during the nightly checks. Soon I will start noticing enemy mode as I leave a situation. As my mind gets faster, I will catch myself halfway in, then just as enemy mode starts, and finally when I see enemy mode coming.

In enemy mode I want to win. In relational mode I want the least harmful alternative. I help my slower conscious mind participate with escaping enemy mode by naming the *win* I was focused on and the *least harmful alternative*. Making my conscious mind name my objective and my alternatives increases my ability to steer my thoughts.

In enemy mode I want to win. In relational mode I want the least harmful alternative.

Let's consider a couple of conditions where we might need extra help. Attachment pain is one condition that makes everything harder. When we are feeling attachment pain, everything that goes wrong will feel more intense. Attachment pain makes enemy mode of every kind more likely and harder to escape.

Another common condition that exacerbates enemy mode happens when the anterior cingulate becomes too activated or starts to slow its operating frequency. When that happens, my mind experiences two seemingly contradictory things at the same time. First, I can only sense my own reality, and second, I cannot see my part in what is happening. "I am so into me, I can't think of nothin' else!" I am not a bad person. My brain is locking up.

The result of having my cingulate frequency slow or lock up is that I will want people to totally agree with my perspective and feelings. I want them to say I am right, plus take full responsibility for the problem. Anyone who disagrees with me makes me more upset. Anyone who tries pointing out my part in the problem sounds like they are blaming me for everything. Enemy mode will tell me loudly and convincingly that they are not on my side. They don't get it! They are avoiding their part of the problem and just trying to win! Of course, my own enemy mode brain is just trying for a win that will stop the upset—or so it thinks.

Think of that blocked cingulate like a dam in the stream. With my cingulate blocking the flow toward resolution, the past floods in. I start thinking about (remembering) every time this feeling has happened before and who I think caused it. Since the flow to the PFC has been blocked, the PFC cannot shut off the alarms from the amygdala or update these feelings in real time. My brain concludes that these feelings must ALL be from the present. The VLE in my left brain looks around and sees the person in front of me and provides many proofs that it is your fault, not mine. It is really essential for me to know if my brain does this to me, because otherwise I will defend and explain myself to the death—perhaps the death of this relationship.

If you or someone you know has this kind of cingulate lock-up, you will know just what we are talking about. A cingulate malfunction is not anyone's fault. It may take professional help and possibly medication or neurofeedback to correct. You can start by practicing quieting.

REFRIENDING DURING OR AFTER SIMPLE ENEMY MODE

Simple enemy mode is being nonrelational at a moment when I should connect to someone who is important to me. When nonattachment is a way of life, waking up my attachment can sound mysterious. In this case, the cure is simple. I ask the people in my life to tell me when they are feeling ignored or dismissed by me and do all the preparations in chapters 7, 8, and 9.

Using the RC test in chapter 3 to start my afternoon and evening will be helpful until I begin noticing the state of my RCs spontaneously.

It also helps to deliberately start the first interaction of the day (particularly with people I know) with a smile and something I appreciate. My appreciation can be general, "This sure is a good day for coffee!" or personal (about them), "I like your smile this morning!"

It can really help us escape simple enemy mode when we recognize what usually causes the state. Let us consider three common causes: intense focus, excessive activity, fatigue.

Being focused on a nonrelational task tends to shut down the RCs. We saw in chapter 3 that Jim's wife called it his "computer brain" when Jim went into simple enemy mode whenever she interrupted his writing. They arranged that when Kitty entered the room, she would wait a moment for Jim to change his "annoying interruption" reaction into a grateful smile and tell Kitty how he appreciated her letting him finish his sentence. By then his RCs were on.

The second of the common causes for simple enemy mode comes from excessive activity. Too much talking, work, time on the internet, or shopping blunts our social engagement system. Excessive activity can be a distraction from a low joy state inside while contributing to that low joy life at the same time.

Fatigue is the third common cause for simple enemy mode. Jim worked twelve-hour days plus commuted an hour each way on Los Angeles freeways. When he arrived home, his family was eager to see him, but he was in enemy mode with the world. He just wanted to sit down and have some quiet. His family agreed that Daddy came home ten minutes after his body arrived. Ten minutes after he collapsed in the chair, everyone's RCs were ready for some joy.

CHANGE MY BRAIN—
Objectives for escaping simple enemy mode

Below are three objectives in changing our brains to escape simple enemy mode:

1. My conscious slow track recognizes when I should be having an attachment response. For example, "This is my child greeting me after my return from a long day at the office. They love me and missed me."

2. My procedural memory knows how to restart my attachment system.

    a. Say aloud, "Give me a moment to get my relational mind back."

    b. Make a note to myself about where I left off with the task.

    c. Recall an important joy moment (preferably with the person in front of me).

    d. Greet them warmly once my face starts a slight smile.

3. I thank people for waiting for me or reminding me to become relational.

REFRIENDING DURING OR AFTER STUPID ENEMY MODE

Quieting practice is essential for recovery from stupid enemy mode. We get stupid when our brain becomes too active. Brain scans would show that our anterior cingulate is way too intense and is blocking the flow to our PFC and our better judgment. We need to be able to quiet our brain on the spot. Once a storm starts, it is not the time to teach a sailor how to tie a knot. The only way to be able to quiet a raging brain is with practice before the next occurrence.

There are three kinds of quieting we need to practice: baseline, instant, and together. We need to take ourselves down to as calm a state as possible each day. If we don't get down to some basic quiet, each day adds a little more tension. When Jim was training in a biofeedback lab, he measured muscle tension on the forehead when the client was as relaxed as possible. Sure enough, when stress increased in that person's life, so did the base level of muscle tension. Each day the levels were higher than the day before. It was like a boat slowly filling with water. Each day it would be easier to sink. Daily bailing out some tension with quieting practice was needed to keep overall tension levels low.

Baseline quieting is like a lizard on a rock in the warm sun just taking it all in. Lying still and letting our muscles relax while we picture an inviting scene or memory for fifteen minutes will usually accomplish lowering our baseline for the day.

The second kind of quieting works the top end of arousal. This kind of quieting is like hitting the brakes when the car is going too fast. We do not reach our lowest quiet for the day, but we don't go off the road either. One method for instant quieting is a few minutes of four-count "box breathing," which we discussed earlier.

Colonel Tom Kolditz served in combat in the streets of Baghdad in 2003, and for twelve years was head of the Department of Behavioral Science and Leadership at West Point. His 2007 book *In Extremis Leadership* talks about how to lead in dangerous situations, such as combat, sport parachuting, flying airplanes, or even daily life. From personal experience and the stories of soldiers and SWAT teams, Kolditz highly recommends deep breathing. He says:

Of all the autonomic responses to an adrenaline rush—including heart rate, respiration, skin conductivity, and muscle tension—the one that we can best control consciously is respiration. Deep, controlled breathing is largely incompatible with the other elements of the fear response. Physical relaxation can get you to the point where mental relaxation, and therefore outward focus, can be reestablished and maintained.[3]

Jim and Ed Khouri developed another method using the brain science ideas from Schore and some advice from the neuropsychologist Suzanne Day we met in chapter 6. Schore insists that emotional regulation requires alternating the sympathetic arousal system and parasympathetic quieting system. If both are on at the same time, we quickly get exhausted. Jim observed that telling his biofeedback patients to relax caused an immediate rise in tension. Using this reaction to our advantage meant triggering a sympathetic reaction first. Start alternating arousal and quieting cycle with arousal.

Suzanne pointed out that fear (the basic sympathetic reaction) began in all children as the Moro reflex. Triggering the Moro reflex should start a sympathetic reaction. Other sympathetic responses were learned over that reflex even when it was no longer visible. During the Moro reflex, an infant throws its arms up, its head back, and sucks in a lungful of air in a startled way. Jim and Ed used this sympathetic system motion as step one.

They added the following steps: exhaling slowly and lowering the arms until the hands rest upon the belly, which triggers the parasympathetic phase. Jim and Ed called the sequence *Shalom My Body.*

The method worked rather well but looked ridiculous. People often began laughing. A couple who fought frequently learned *Shalom My Body* at a THRIVE training (relational brain skill training conducted by thrivetoday.org). No sooner were they back in their room than the usual stupid enemy mode fight started. While one was getting stupid, the other one started the Moro reflex. Both began laughing.

Jim's relative had a four-year-old who put on a demonstration of stupid enemy mode every time she didn't get her way. Her mother taught her *Shalom My Body.* When the little girl began to lose her temper, she and Mommy would escape enemy mode doing the exercise together.

A few weeks later, Mommy began to lose it. Her daughter ran to her and said, "Mommy! Mommy!" then threw her hands up and her head back, inhaled deeply, and exhaled slowly. Her mother was startled into laughing, so they did *Shalom My Body* together a few times. While this gets into the next chapter on how to help others escape enemy mode, it shows that the brain can learn to escape.

The third kind of quieting is called "quiet together," and it helps our entire relational cluster to calm down. We want to be like a box full of sleeping puppies. A quiet together time before bed or on weekends is a great way to resist the trend toward getting stupid. A few quiet together minutes helps when our children are getting wound up or our group energy is getting overwhelming. A quiet together time is as simple as sitting and enjoying being together without saying a word.

Taking Precautions

Pain (particularly attachment pain), diminished capacity (often alcohol related), and going too long without quieting are the common triggers for getting stupid. In general, these come from trying to be stronger than we actually are. Before long we feel like the world is asking too much or listening too little.

Stupid enemy mode reactions may also follow feeling dishonored, disrespected, or disregarded by someone who wants to lower our social standing. Unlike the first cluster, these episodes of stupid enemy mode will usually be suppressed toward anyone with the power to hurt us and get expressed toward someone who is weaker than we are. We go home and kick the dog. Sapolsky points out that this targeted attack on someone weaker reduces stress for rats and baboons.[4] Humans who do the same thing may develop a police profile instead.

Escaping enemy mode when we are attached to the person who gets stupid will require finding an identity group that provides safety. Trying to prevent the natural consequences of someone else's stupid enemy mode is called codependence. It is also not uncommon to end up injured, dead, or with our family swimming in toxic shame that continues generation after generation. We need to find a group identity that does not see enemy mode as either who we are or what we must put up with in others. We must admit when we are powerless—that is, too small to do everything we expect of ourselves. We need our "box full of puppies" times and places we can rest quietly together.

Simply escaping stupid enemy mode is not going to be enough to correct the damage I produced. Escaping stupid enemy mode requires going back to share the pain I have created. Rather than trying to blame as much of my behavior on what others did, I want to maximize compassion and share every bit of pain I contributed to other people.

Trying to prevent the natural consequences of someone else's stupid enemy mode is called codependence.

The pain others experience often includes remembered pain from the past. Maybe I caused that pain, or maybe I had nothing to do with it. I brought that pain back up for

them when I got stupid. Yes, I share that old pain too, so my brain will learn to get out of enemy mode faster.

If it turns out that substances like drugs and alcohol increase my chances of stupid enemy mode, I am going to need to get sober and not justify myself. Shifting even a little of the responsibility for my stupid enemy mode to the substance or whatever "made me" do it reduces what my brain will learn about finding a less harmful alternative. The more I share the pain I create, even unintentionally, the better my brain recognizes harmful alternatives it will avoid next time.

CHANGE MY BRAIN—
Objectives for escaping stupid enemy mode

1. I use the instant quieting method (such as controlled breathing). I have been learning to get quiet.
2. If I cannot quiet, I go to a place I can cool off and use my quieting method there.
3. I follow the steps for escaping simple enemy mode.
4. I go back and share any pain I have created without justifying myself.

REFRIENDING DURING OR AFTER INTELLIGENT (PREDATORY) ENEMY MODE

NOTE: *If you are reading this section trying to keep yourself safe from or help someone who is in intelligent enemy mode—those solutions are not here. Get out of harm's way and find help for yourself.*

Hello, all focused winners! We are going to have a harder time getting motivated to escape than people with other enemy mode weaknesses. If I don't really feel much when other people get hurt,[5] I may have a genetic insensitivity that will make change harder.[6] The baseline issue is that my brain is set on winning, and other alternatives sound like losing. Perhaps the most intelligent part of enemy mode is how well my brain fools me.

People with an impaired rPFC have trouble winning in relationships. The impact of this impairment is a poor to nonexistent appraisal of the actual cost of losses when relationships weaken or fail. One member of most couples Jim has counseled didn't see trouble coming or know they were an inch from a big loss. Relationship failures in families and businesses are expensive, but only those who already feel the pain will be persuaded.

At its core, setting out to be *the* winner means I must surround myself with losers. When relationships become bigger than problems, I bring out the best in everyone. When everyone in my life is cheaply replaceable, there is no reason to bring out the best in others. Keeping the relationship bigger than the problems provides the big relational win.[7]

Keeping a relationship bigger than a problem works when I help everyone become their best self. It is hard, probably impossible, to want to stay connected to someone's worst self. Trying to overlook problems is also not going to work. Instead of using people's weaknesses to make them lose, I use those weaknesses to help them find a better self. In return, I request help with my biggest weakness—the tendency toward enemy mode—so that we all find our best selves.

Finding our best selves is a group project. Group identity statements that are worth fighting for and living to achieve can really help us once we are fourteen or older. For example, *We are a family/team/business/ community who find our best selves when something goes wrong.*

Awareness of my body helps me lessen my tendency toward enemy mode. Being present in my body and in the moment is needed to avoid living an "as if" life with an image rather than an identity.

When the vmPFC function is well connected with our insula we are generally present in the moment; we can feel our bodies and have compassion for others. You may recall that "embodied identity" was what was lacking in Nazi doctors and prescribed by Dr. Robert Lifton (who researched the doctors after WWII) for anyone who wanted to find a better self.[8]

Intelligent enemy mode is actually kind of ugly, and I need to let people I am attached to see it for what it is. Really! I stop self-justifications, as they simply put sheepskin on my wolf-self. When I combine becoming more authentic with making relationships more important than problems, I find my best self.

Jim and Ray get honest 360s regularly. It is difficult at first to tell the difference between "my best self" and "my good image." A good image is not a better or best self. Image is pretense for the sake of a win. Image is about raising my perceived social standing. My best self is not a fantasy. Who I really am does not always show up when needed. An honest 360 evaluation that includes input from family or coworkers will expose the places where image has blocked the growth of my real best self.

CHANGE MY BRAIN—
Objectives for escaping intelligent enemy mode

1. Identify the relationships I have that are worth keeping.
2. Ask these people to tell me if they see me in enemy mode.
3. Thank and reward everyone from my "keeper" list who tells me when I am in enemy mode.
4. Find a coach I respect who can call me on any ways I fool myself.
5. Invest myself in helping each of my keepers develop their best self in one area of weakness.

One major caution is that a narcissist will insist that tests and corrections for intelligent enemy mode be applied to others. A narcissist will generally have proof of who (other than the narcissist) is in intelligent enemy mode. Corrections are only reasonably safe when applied to the person who is asking for them. I must ask for my own intelligent enemy mode to be examined.

Finding Spiritual Reasons for Christians to Escape Intelligent Enemy Mode

A variety of individual and group practices for self-examination have long histories in Christian communities. One in particular is seeing recent growth. Father William Watson developed resources for personal discovery through research in neuroscience, medicine, and psychological theory for Christians from every tradition.[9] Fr. Bill is a Jesuit priest who served as vice president at Gonzaga University and is currently president of the Sacred Story Institute. Fr. Bill explained the purpose of his research and programs to Jim and why the Ignatian daily self-examination was part of Ignatius's own way out of enemy mode. Ignatius lived near the start of the Protestant and Catholic separation, and he instructed his followers to avoid topics that would produce enemy mode reactions in Protestants and, instead, to focus on spiritual exercises that transformed character.

On the Protestant side, reformer John Wesley developed twenty-two self-examination questions with their related group practices for his followers to repeat each year. His groups were labeled "methodists" because of this practical approach. Systematic spiritual practices that reveal intelligent enemy mode suggest that both of these reformers embraced a life free from treating others as enemies.

HELP WITH PREDATORS

"You haven't been taken until you have been taken by a Christian."

At the time the local businessman voiced this warning, Jim was just a twenty-year-old in the market for a new car. Jim had voiced appreciation for buying a used car from someone he knew. Mr. Vogel looked at Jim as if he thought the young man was way too trusting.

Understanding intelligent enemy mode helps us spot predators, particularly the benevolent sounding predators who promise to eat the rest of the world but protect us. Since a brain in enemy mode cannot tell who is really on their side, it is safe to say that predators are planning how to win and not promising loyalty. When the winning strategy changes, so does who will become lunch or get thrown under the bus.

Intelligent enemy mode knows how to look nice, track what others want, say what others want to believe, and get themselves elected, appointed, in front, and on top. When we understand intelligent enemy mode, we see a nice winner who will make our *dreams come true* as the threat they actually are.

WHAT IS IN IT FOR ME TO GET OUT OF ENEMY MODE?

Friends. The great part of refriending is that my best self attracts friends, and my friends bring out my best self. Lasting friendships are not based upon holding all the same opinions. Friendships last because we build joy. We discover what is best in one another. We escape enemy mode quickly, refriend, and find our way back to joy together.

We generally underestimate the impact our friends have on our emotions. We tend to see enemy mode reactions as caused by too much testosterone or a menstrual cycle. Sapolsky indicates that much of what we attribute to hormones does not match the science.[10] When we escape enemy mode, our nervous system is less reactive to hormones and amygdala surges and less prone to misinterpreting what others are thinking. Friends help provide relational stability with far-reaching effects.

HOW DOES ESCAPING ENEMY MODE
WORK IN THE BRAIN?

By now we are all familiar with the lack of attachment during all forms of enemy mode. We also know that a brain in enemy mode does not perceive others as important attachments—that is, people who are on our side. As long as my brain sees attachments as unimportant, those attachments will not help me. Asking my brain to think of what it cannot see at that moment won't help me escape enemy mode.

If you and I are in enemy mode with each other, the work-around in the brain is finding a third mind to help. Let's say Adam, Bob, and Chris have attachments to one another. Adam and Bob are in enemy mode and cannot feel their attachment at the moment. By activating their attachment to Chris, both Adam and Bob can come out of enemy mode instantly. Chris is a rescue attachment.

The brain can go in and out of enemy mode in a flash, so when Adam looks at Chris, attachment is on, but looking back at Bob reactivates enemy mode. More than attachment with Chris is needed. Adam must see Bob the way that Chris does at that moment. Adam uses the ToM system with Chris to let Adam's own mind acquire value for Bob. Acquired value brings individuals, families, and groups out of enemy mode.

Spiritual people who are attached to (love) a God who is attached to (loves) everyone will find that everyone they meet has acquired value. If enemy mode develops with anyone, a rescue attachment is available. Of course, attachments in the brain's fast track have very different effects from beliefs in the slow track. Believing that God loves everyone (as a conscious thought alone) will not substitute.

JOY AND MY BEST SELF

Jim learned about the importance of joy and a healthy identity in 1997 from the science of Dr. Allan Schore. Schore laid out how the infant's brain developed through high joy states that formed attachments. It was not at all clear if the same could be done with adults who needed to develop a better self. Schore said joy means *we are glad to be together*, so people whose default personality was in enemy mode would not be attracting joy. Jim figured that if he could help people find their best self, they might be able to build joy and a stronger brain. What he needed now were some actual people to practice with him.

Jim met Chris Coursey when Chris was rebuilding his life after two DUIs. Meanwhile, Jim's wife Kitty was on antidepressants and experiencing considerable conflict with people she felt were not on her side.

She was in therapy trying to recover from her experiences in Christian boarding schools. While Chris and Kitty considered themselves Christian, neither was particularly happy about it. Perhaps out of desperation, they both eagerly agreed to experiment with the joy building exercises that Jim created from Schore's brain science. The results were immediately encouraging.

About that time, Chris met Jen, who was twenty and on SSI disability for depression. She had first been hospitalized and suicidal at eleven. Within two years of practicing joy exercises, the two were married and Jen was teaching school. Chris, Jen, Kitty, and Jim used the exercises that they had tested for building joy and a better identity and developed a program called THRIVE. Since Jen was a teacher by education, she broke the training into nineteen skills and sequenced them so they build upon each other.

CAN CHRISTIANS BE PERSUADED TO PARTICIPATE?

THRIVE became an experiment in training Christians to have relational skills and joyful identities that would help their communities. Training was held in hotel conference centers and quickly became a favorite event for hotel staff. Training included a nonverbal day. Curious hotel patrons asked the concierge why all these people were gesturing but not speaking to one another. The concierge explained, "You have to understand. These people are Christians, and Christians don't listen very well. They are not allowed to speak for a whole day so they will learn."

As THRIVE grew, a psychiatrist teaching addiction recovery internationally came for training. Dr. Darv Smith soon had Jim teaching joyful identity skills in India, then for a recovery program in Korea, where Onnuri Church regularly reached over a hundred thousand people through satellite TV. Pastor Kiwon Lee oversaw recovery at Onnuri. He took THRIVE training, then trained his community as his doctoral research project. His goal was a joyful and resilient community.

Smith brought Jim to Brazil, and then sent him to Chile. Along the way, he introduced Jim to Ed Khouri and his wife Maritza, who developed training for recovery leaders and community building. This pair has trained people from at least seventy nations. Ed was an officer of the International Substance Abuse and Addiction Coalition (ISAAC) Secretariat representing people from over a hundred nations. Ed immediately recognized the way that addictions and craving take over the brain's attachment system. Ed and Maritza soon became THRIVE trainers along with teaching joy-based brain skills for addiction recovery.

Perry Bigelow soon joined the community joy building effort. Bigelow was a developer who designed and built people-friendly, energy-efficient communities planned so that children could play safely. Bigelow had a particular interest in rebuilding homes in an African American neighborhood in Chicago in partnership with the Christian Community Development Association (CCDA).

Dr. Bill Atwood is an Anglican bishop whose work covered six continents and a personality that is a cross between Santa Claus and a bulldog. Bill was an ex-Air Force pilot with experience in Vietnam and during the Cold War. The bishop was raised in great part by his grandfather, Brigadier General James A. Pickering, while his own father was in the Korean conflict. Bishop Bill took THRIVE training from Chris, Jen, Kitty, Ed, and Maritza and immediately grasped the importance of joy. General Pickering taught him as a boy to stay out of enemy mode with family, neighbors, and bullies. Eventually these skills helped him in combat, with the CIA, and in KGB confrontations. In addition to introducing joy into his churches, Bishop Bill wrote books on spiritual life and applied brain science like *The General, The Boy, & Recapturing Joy*.[11]

Thomas, whose grandfather was a Nazi SS officer involved in the arrest of Thomas's hero, Dietrich Bonhoeffer, met Jim at a conference. Thomas has spent much of his life countering the damage caused by his grandfather's enemy mode. Thomas arranged for Jim to teach trauma recovery and joy in Sudan and Poland where his SS grandfather had been deployed. Most recently Thomas invited Jim to help Muslim refugees in Germany recover from the traumas they had suffered. Thomas also used the science of joy to correct the Us versus Them (enemy mode) developing between some of his German neighbors and refugees.

Dr. Julia Moore is an associate professor of African American religion at UNC Charlotte. She teaches courses in African American religion, religions of the African Diaspora, and racial violence in America. She and her husband, Ricky, (both ordained ministers) are dedicated to bridge-building between racially diverse groups within the church. They help facilitate meaningful attachments through engaging the presence of God, identity sessions, truth-telling utilizing healthy shame, and journaling. They began an experiment to overcome the long history of racial separation on Sunday mornings between two churches in the same town. One church had the descendants of the slaveholders. The other church was home to the descendants of the slaves. They wanted to apply the spiritual and brain resources outlined above to help people come together and escape enemy mode. Church communities were asked to share the sufferings of others, developing group identities reframed through the Golden Rule as a way for communal healing. The brain issues they needed to resolve included navigating a whole range of triggers for enemy mode including powerful social status triggers and attachment pain.

As relational spirituality continued to spread, Dr. Chris Shaw, an Argentine native, picked up on the science of joy and began publishing material to his over forty thousand readers, most of whom were pastors. Gerard Feller of the Netherlands published *Promise Magazine* for Christian healing professionals. Gerard was soon publishing recovery materials on joy and the brain. Meanwhile in Egypt, the Coptic Church was consulting with Jim on how to help orphans develop strong joyful identities. Orphanages in Mexico and Nicaragua were seeking similar answers.

Michel Hendricks was an associate pastor in a megachurch in Colorado when he discovered the need for relational brain skills from talking with Jim. Together they wrote a book on how churches could build joyful communities. Hendricks now works full-time helping churches build joyful communities.

Escaping enemy mode was also seeing early implementation. Ray consulted with Chaplain Kerry Haynes on relational ways to lead his department at the VA hospital. Kerry began seeing success helping staff stay out of enemy mode with each other and with the vets they supported. Dr. Naomi Paget was using the concepts of staying relational and reminding her chaplain trainees to be their best self when providing pastoral care with disaster victims. Coach Greg Hiebert began seeing how escaping enemy mode could help him in his marriage, with his children and grandchildren, and in his work with executives. Consultant and former Congressman Geoff Davis was using his military experience, relational skills, and ability to be flexible in dynamic situations to help in the workplace. He intervened with a plant foreman whose job was in danger and showed him a way to escape enemy mode with his plant manager. Experienced leaders were becoming early adopters.

Ray began making changes in the culture at Life Model Works. He organized a yearlong study of how to stay relational as a team which was well-received by the board and executives. He changed the meeting rhythm, so meetings began relationally. He also got a leadership coach and requested a 360 from his team.

Ray's changes were deeper than just professional, however. Ray began noticing his emotions and paying closer attention to them. He rediscovered the joy of relational connection with his wife, family, and friends. At his request, Deborah began to help him recognize when he was slipping into enemy mode. She found this challenging because his old neural pathways would often kick in.

One evening during the writing of this book, Deborah had told him, "You are in enemy mode," and Ray retorted, "No, I am not." This was not his best self! He remembered feeling angry, defensive, and not at all curious about his wife's observation. He was also determined to convince her that she was wrong. Sadly, the time and focus required to write this book have occasionally made enemy mode more likely for Ray. Deborah's love for him, personal courage, and willingness to fight for his best self constantly inspired Ray.

After incidents like this one, Ray found he needed deeper help, and so began meeting with a therapist who specializes in attachment pain. He began growing a deeper awareness of his emotions, but also of the pain Deborah feels when he slips into enemy mode.

He was beginning to be able to share the pain he had caused. Ray began this quest aware of his enemy mode tendencies, but only occasionally able to give them up. He was now experiencing a more relational way of living, more joy in relationships, and much more connection with his wife, family, and friends. He was also surprised to learn how much more productive he could be by working with his whole brain, no longer blindly in enemy mode.

JOYFUL IDENTITY

With growing evidence that the global Christian community might be open to relational joy and identity building, Jim and his partners continued writing books. How would the other four-fifths of the world like the plan? Jim joined Dr. Marcus Warner, who had been a professor and loved making important things simple. Marcus reduced relational brain science to four habits under the acronym RARE:

R = remain relational
A = act like yourself
R = return to joy quickly
E = endure hardships well[12]

With additional help from Chris Coursey, Marcus and Jim launched a series of RARE/Four Habits books for the workplace, marriage, and children, and another on how to get our joy restarted using relational brain skills. It's evident that learning a joyful identity will help us escape enemy mode of all kinds. The reader may find the books listed below address personal interests for growing a joyful identity. In our next chapter we will see how interest continued spreading and how these skills can be used to help others.

Joy Books

The Joy Switch, Chris Coursey (Northfield, 2021)
RARE Leadership in the Workplace, Marcus Warner and
    Jim Wilder (Northfield, 2021)
The Four Habits of Raising Joy-Filled Kids, Marcus Warner
    and Chris Coursey (Northfield, 2021)
The Four Habits of Joy-Filled Marriages, Marcus Warner
    and Chris Coursey (Northfield, 2019)

Joy and Spiritual Life

The General, The Boy, & Recapturing Joy, Dr. Bill Atwood
    (Ekklesia, 2020)
The Other Half of Church, Jim Wilder and Michel Hendricks
    (Moody, 2020)
Becoming a Face of Grace, Ed Khouri (Illumify Media Global,
    2021)

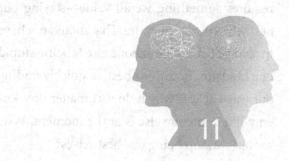

HELPING OTHERS ESCAPE ENEMY MODE

THE LIFEGUARD CERTIFICATION INSTRUCTOR was emphatic. Jumping into the water with a drowning person was a good way for two people to drown. "They will grab you by the neck, try to climb up, and push you under." He paused, looking around at Jim and the class. "Unless you grab them first and push them up." Similarly, helping others out of enemy mode has only one objective: staying solidly in our relational identity while we push others up to theirs. We are running on the ragged edges of existing brain science in this chapter. What we do know suggests that if we keep our brain relational, our brain provides a stabilizing model of proper function for others to mirror.

Our relational identity is grown and strengthened through secure attachments that stabilize our sense of who we are and how we act when things get rough emotionally. Helping others escape enemy mode

If we keep our brain relational, our brain provides a stabilizing model of proper function for others to mirror.

requires something we all value—staying our best selves under pressure. That should not have to change because someone else is being stupid or a predator. Being our best, or quickly finding our way back, is why it doesn't matter how enemy-like someone else is at the moment. Why should we stop being our best selves?

My secure attachments develop a reliable presence of my relational self in my brain. Healthy attachments in our past develop strong and stable identity systems. Helping others escape enemy mode uses our attachments to people who are not physically there. The best people in our past built our relational identities, and implicit memories of them sustain us if others cannot see our best selves because they are in enemy mode. We can grab someone who is relationally unresponsive and flailing and push them up toward their living self. "In a situation like this, I like to be my best and best self" is a very short story with lifting power.

Arthur Brooks of the Harvard Business School wrote *Love Your Enemies*. In it, he tells how sharing personal stories can help one brain mirror another. Brooks credits this discovery to Professor Uri Hasson of the Princeton Neuroscience Institute.[1] Hasson had one person tell a personal story while another listened, and both were brain scanned. Not only did they show similar brain activity, sometimes the listener would anticipate what the teller was about to say and show the brain activity first. Hasson used both English and Russian speakers to show that the brain activity matched the meaning rather than the words used.

Personal shared stories synchronize brain activity between two people. The weaker brain follows the stronger brain whose patterns are not easily disrupted. In this way, a stable identity can provide stability for someone whose identity system is becoming unstable. If the stronger brain is in enemy mode, both will go down.

Ray discussed this dynamic with General Jack Briggs, who you'll recall is CEO of the Springs Rescue Mission. Jack has actively helped others escape enemy mode. He dealt daily with hundreds of homeless clients, mission staff, and volunteers from every walk of life, many of whom had widely diverging views. He found a model which was making a difference.

Briggs said, "It could be clients, staff, donors, or community members. If it's clients, I know what the mindset is. If it's community partners, their mistrust of us is sometimes because we're big and we're Christian, and they may be small and secular to the point of being anti-Christian. How do they fit in the continuum of care in the community? So how do I work with them? I have to remember that I'm not there to make them believe the way I do. I'm there to find common ground for collaborative work."

Briggs resonated with what we were discovering and told Ray, "What you described as enemy mode is the mentality at a homeless shelter. There is very little trust, and there is a transactional mindset: if you do this for me, I'll do this for you, or if I do this for you, you have to do this for me. That goes to the limited bandwidth our clients have."

He faced pressure in two directions: Christians of all backgrounds who strongly disagreed with each other, and secular organizations suspicious of the motives of the Mission. Ray asked, "How do you help your staff, volunteers, and clients escape enemy mode?"

Briggs worked to keep the relationship bigger than the problems that would cause enemy mode. The Mission was successful in getting cooperation. Briggs intuitively began to use story and modeling to get Christians and secular people out of enemy mode to work together relationally and help the most vulnerable.

Briggs admires the mission volunteers and their compassion, empathy, and resilience and notes the change in their preconceived ideas that occurs after they begin their work. "When volunteers first come to the Rescue Mission, they are amazed at all the things that we're doing. Initially, they come with a certain mindset or a picture about what a rescue mission should be like," Briggs said. "Once here, they begin to see things differently. Our volunteers see that clients aren't what they thought they were going to be. Some think clients are going to be incredibly appreciative and very engaging. In many cases clients are appreciative, but they have a hard time articulating it because they live in a world of transactions."

Jack brought out the best self in everyone: clients, staff, and volunteers. "I talk about the different faith backgrounds volunteers bring to the Rescue Mission. When they get here, volunteers realize that we're much more focused on the basics of Christian compassion and Christ loving all the broken people."

Briggs pointed out a modernistic bronze sculpture of Christ in the mission courtyard. He helps volunteers escape enemy mode with each other and with clients by using the sculpture as a unifying metaphor. He tells them, "Before you saw that statue, you had a picture in your head of what Christ looked like, what you've always thought he looked like. This statue probably doesn't match your vision of what Christ should look like."

Briggs then compares that perception to their perception of those they serve. "Have you thought about how you think our clients should look versus what you're seeing? How does that make you think about your vision of what Christ should look like? Could it be that Christ doesn't look the way you think that he does, and still is Christ?"

Briggs said that despite perceptions and appearances, there's one shared commonality. "Everybody here is broken, whether staff or clients or me. We help the volunteers understand that their simple mission is to love clients unconditionally, just the way Christ loves us. So, Christ knows that we're going to disappoint him, and he still loves us.

"Taking that perspective, wherever you come from in your particular background of faith, that's really where we boil it all down. One of the most interesting things is volunteers, after they've been with us for a while, often come up to me and say, 'You know, this has been such a great experience for me and my faith to realize how to apply it. I had this book knowledge, maybe, but I wasn't applying it.'"

Jack Briggs helped mission volunteers and staff experience acquired value for others, loving people like Jesus did. That was their best self, their identity.

IDENTITY IN THE BRAIN

Let us review. Our relational identity, our best self, sits at the top of our brain system. Keep in mind that the neurological "top of the brain" does not stick straight up, but rather is tucked around and under the way we might wrap our fingers around the thumb of the same hand.

Acting like ourselves is the height of full brain function. Identity is assembled stage by stage, starting at the bottom of the brain and following the arcing path up and around. We reinvent who we are many times a second. If this process in the right brain fails, our identity stays incomplete and unstable. Enemy mode is likely.

By matching levels of the right brain with the stages of identity assembly, we see where failures produce enemy mode. The goal is to maintain a stable brain and identity all the way from the bottom to the top.

Obviously, we want the brain that keeps it all together from the bottom to the very top. If our attachment system (A) is off, we are not going to be relational. If our cingulate (B) is not handling emotions and memories relationally, our overwhelmed feelings become an artificial ceiling "top of the brain" operation. When we go no farther than our "as if" simulator in the dorsomedial PFC (C), we will do whatever works rather than behaving as who we really are. When the identity process reaches all the way to include the ventromedial PFC (D), we will use everything from A to D to choose the least harmful option that will maintain our best self—my relational identity.

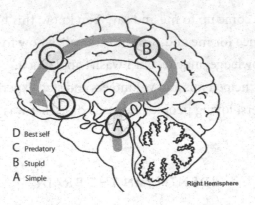

D Best self
C Predatory
B Stupid
A Simple

Right Hemisphere

RELATIONAL IDENTITY AND RIGHT BRAIN (DYS)FUNCTION

TOP OF THE RIGHT BRAIN	MY IDENTITY	ENEMY MODE
D	My relational ID	*My best self* (non-enemy mode)
C	"As if" ID	Intelligent/predatory
B	Emotionally overwhelmed ID	Stupid
A	Inactive ID	Simple
BOTTOM OF THE BRAIN		

Taking the Elevator to the Top Floor

There is obviously little chance that we will be able to, or even want to, initiate an attachment with people we don't know who are in enemy mode. Reactivating an existing attachment we already formed is a better starting point. Once attachment is activated, we might go to their top brain floor and find their best self.

In simple enemy mode, a smile, a small kindness, or a bit of personal interest might be enough to get attachment restarted. A person who is on fire and in stupid enemy mode clearly requires us to have excellent self-quieting skills. Affirming what is very important to them may restart their attachment. Starting the attachment system for someone in intelligent enemy mode is difficult. Conversations about keeping relationships bigger than problems may help. Self-disclosure will be seen as a weakness, but self-disclosure may also help show the person in intelligent enemy mode how my best self values my attachments in this kind of situation.

Keeping our brain running in a stable relational self condition is our main objective. With our right brain identity functioning at every level, we provide an opportunity (not a certainty) for another mind to mirror ours. With our relational identity (A-D) quietly in charge, we become a beacon of hope. Meanwhile, our left PFC is working like mad encouraging the other mind to see its way out of enemy mode.

Both Ray and Jim were strongly convinced, with no brain studies to back their impressions, that many high status Christian leaders were stuck in "as if," and therefore, in intelligent enemy mode. The path to my best self means getting out of who I am trying to act like (C) and up to who I actually am (D). The more a person identified with their status-gaining, performance-based self (C), the more difficult it was to find their real self. Their elevator almost always stopped at their image (C) and went no higher. Left unattended, a best self begins looking more like a skeleton in a closet.

Ray and Jim have known people with high status lives who manage their image by rules, checklists, and goals. They are typically quite disciplined and controlling of themselves and others. They normally have no idea who their best self is and may have a shameful secret they are hiding. This is how living from the "as if" self can look and is a manifestation of intelligent enemy mode. Many are not even aware that they are living nonrelationally and without their whole brain.

Here are some examples to show how the "as if" life contrasts with the "best self" life:

PROBLEM	"AS IF" SELF	BEST SELF
Leader learns daughter was molested by brother	Protects reputation of the leader and organization as top priority	Protects the girl and seeks family healing as top priority
Pastor's work-life is out of balance with care for family	Prioritizes the church's mission and vision; during a family crisis minimizes time lost for family healing	Prioritizes protecting the family, allowing the pastor time to work on the family crisis
Four of six senior staff members resign in one month	Finds replacements to "keep the ship moving" and celebrates a new season with new executives to fulfill his/her mission	Prioritizes learning how he/she can become a better CEO and leads more relationally, while hiring a new team
Many followers but little change of character	Prioritizes easy applause-line numbers like "buildings, baptisms, and budgets" or follows what is trending and attracts community interest to new activities	Prioritizes more important but harder-to-measure trends like "How am I loving my enemies like Jesus does?" or "How are lives being developed so people are their best selves?"

FULL-BRAINED ESCAPES FROM ENEMY MODE

Our left brain can help us. The left brain normally pays almost no attention to whether the right brain is running. First, the right brain is faster, and the left cannot catch up. Second, the left brain is not wired to watch the right. Our left brain doesn't do any better watching other people's right brain activity. The left brain is like a passenger on a whale-watching trip who must start looking for signs that something big is down there that it cannot see directly.

Ways the Left Brain Can Help

Helping others: This book is a guide for how to watch ourselves and others for enemy mode, and we know how many pages that has taken. But, when we know what we are watching, we can start taking steps to help ourselves and sometimes others. Since we need our relational identity to be in charge, the first step is always a self-rescue by our left brain.

Self-rescue: By knowing the signs of where a brain can get stuck (from A to C), the left PFC can initiate escape from enemy mode if our own right brain starts to churn and burn at less than our relational best self.

Language: Communication-based (conscious slow track) solutions have become the "talking cure" to many problems that do not resolve well by talking. People in enemy mode generally talk rather well, often rapidly and rabidly. However, using language really helps when agreeing on a plan, listening to others, and explaining ourselves.

Jim and his friends have made "I am in enemy mode" part of their conversation. When one of them feels ready to get stupid, they don't hide it or "make nice," or get stupid. In one week, a hair stylist, a mean neighbor lady, a husband, a store clerk, a driver of a painting company van, and a surgeon inspired the phrase, "I am in enemy mode with . . ." There was no need to insult ancestry, focus on the culprit, or tell a long story. Jim and his friends turned their attention immediately to encouraging their friend's best self. They don't team up to hate; they are immediately on the same side because they are escaping enemy mode. That is a full brain escape.

STAYING CREATIVE

With our relational identity (A-D) quietly in charge, there is work for our left brain. The left brain is always too focused on procedures to be left in charge. But, if the right brain is staying cool with all systems operational and the RCs are working, we can do a bit of problem-solving to help someone stuck in enemy mode.

Procedure: Procedures in the left brain are not state-dependent. We can learn procedures at any time. We do not have to be in enemy mode while we learn. Jim learned self-rescue sequences for scuba diving in a classroom, not underwater. Learning what procedure to use is different from actually becoming proficient. Skill practice is state-dependent learning. Jim rehearsed diving self-rescue in the pool, then reviewed his efforts with the instructors. Working cooperatively to escape enemy mode is something we can talk about ahead of time and return to after the fact, maybe even after we cool down and get a night's sleep. Like anything new to the brain, escaping enemy mode is learned through a lot of failed attempts and partial successes.

Speed: Helping others depends in large part on how well we know our stuff. Since the brain is a learning machine, the more times we practice escaping enemy mode, the faster we are. We will need some speed and skill because being around people in enemy mode tends to pull us in too. We say something helpful and are told where we can put our advice. We need to be able to pull ourselves out of enemy mode again and again quickly.

Here's an example: Ray's doorbell rang urgently at 6:30 a.m. twice one Thursday morning. He hurried to the door, wondering, "What on earth?" A scruffy, young, barefoot stranger in pajamas stood on the porch, yelling furiously, "YOUR DOG HAS BEEN BARKING FOR AN HOUR AND A HALF!" Spit flew as he yelled. He was in stupid enemy mode.

Ray responded calmly, his relational circuits on. "Good morning. Actually, we don't have a dog." In years past, Ray would have responded in stupid enemy mode. This time was different. Ray stayed out of enemy mode and was able to keep his RCs online.

Ray's rapid but calm response slowed the young man down. Ray saw a shift of awareness in his eyes before the man stomped over to the neighbor's house. Ray helped him back down from his stupid enemy mode for a few seconds, and possibly helped slow down the spread of enemy mode on his street.

Relational practice: Mutual practice in our good relationships helps us when we are with strangers who are in enemy mode. Strangers have never heard of enemy mode and have no significant attachment to us, so we need creativity. If we practice talking about our best selves with people we trust, we will not be at a loss for words with strangers.

Have a team: Expert enemy mode operators resist relationships with us even if they know us. Helping them escape enemy mode is nearly impossible as an individual effort. These semi-professionals respond better to an identity group effort to help them escape enemy mode. We will have more on identity groups in our next and final chapter.

Group identity: We will have a far better time helping others out of enemy mode if they are affiliated with an identity group that supports the idea. Bhutan has a national group identity as the happiest kingdom on earth. Himalayan life was not easy, but Jim noticed few signs of enemy mode when roads were blocked, rooms were unheated during the winter, and events did not go according to plan.

Reduce dependence on fear-based motivation: When we discuss a problem while feeling connected and looking out for one another, it will be a different experience than discussing the same problem while we feel afraid and distrustful. Helping others out of enemy mode is more about correcting fears that block real relationships than a series of steps or good techniques.

Raise their social standing with me: Enemy mode is frequently fueled by the perception that we are being seen or treated as less important than others. The human brain is very sensitive to any signal of disrespect. Pointing out what we value about the person in enemy mode helps. Arthur Brooks suggests in *Love Your Enemies* that feeling needed creates dignity.[2] We want people to know how much their best self is needed.

Tell mini and micro stories: When we think about storytelling, we may envision long, elaborate tales told around a fire. No one does much listening with their brain in enemy mode. Mini stories are a sentence or two about something personal. Micro stories can be nonverbal or just a few words that also make a connection. Here are a few examples:

- Say! Aren't you the girl I married?
- So, you have a son living at home too.
- Make eye contact, grimace, and shake your head when someone is rude (micro).

Brooks applied Hasson's research on storytelling between brains to encourage stories as a way to help one brain track another. If our brain is relational, we want someone in enemy mode to track us, but we need to be quick about it.

Sharing pain: Compassion plays a big part in keeping us out of enemy mode. Focusing on what our body feels for the other person and putting that in words helps. When we show shared pain on our face, it helps even more. By contrast, laughing is particularly unhelpful. When something painful has been shared, many people become nervous and laugh. We also know that attachment pain increases the chance of enemy mode. Talking may not help. "There just aren't words for what you are going through" is probably the wisest thing to say.

Sharing any pain that we have caused is a priority. We might even say, "I really want to know and feel any pain I caused you. It will help my brain learn a better way for next time. I really want to be on your side."

Helping others prepare: Most of our enemy mode events are repetitive. We have been here before. We are going to be here again. We can prepare reminders of our stable and relational identities. This may sound strange at first. People we know don't say these things, but here are some examples:

- I want to be on your side, and I know you want to be on mine.
- We seem stuck, but we are the kind of people who figure out what we both need.
- We are too tired to find a satisfying solution, but we can rest together and then find a way.
- Next time I get in enemy mode, do the Moro reflex movement and I will too.

Making refriending mutual: Falling into enemy mode can and will happen again with people we know. It makes it a lot better when we can agree together that the first person to dig themselves out from under the avalanche will help dig the other out too. Cooperative effort and empathy both use our anterior cingulate. Let's train our anterior cingulates to work together!

DANGEROUS POPULAR CURES FOR ENEMY MODE

We will need to eliminate some popular ideas of how to deal with emotions that are not safe when facing enemy mode. Two solutions don't work and usually backfire: 1) expressing my feelings, and 2) making you understand.

Psychology fads have created the impression that mental health and good relationships come from getting in touch with our feelings and expressing them. This emotional ventilation theory turns mental health into something like passing gas. One person's momentary relief is not appreciated by the people around.

For the therapists of wealthy psychotherapy patients with big "as if" personas, knowing what their patients really felt was necessary. When psychiatrist R. D. Laing and his doctors let themselves and their patients get in touch with feeling and simply express themselves, the group descended into dysfunction. Laing's goal was helping people discover their true self. Laing's son expressed the result as, "everyone became a patient" rather than the patients getting better.[3]

The ultimate emotional expression psychology cure was called Primal Scream and is documented in *Therapy Gone Mad*.[4] The therapeutic community disintegrated into depression, violence, and even suicide. Simply letting feelings out is a cure that resembles how doctors let out "bad" blood to cure diseases. Brain science is bringing the days of bloodletting psychology to an end. We are not getting healthy or escaping enemy mode by telling everyone how we feel.

Identity (self) is formed by learning *emotional regulation* in relationships that bring joy. Being able to quiet ourselves while having our feelings keeps the relational attachment bigger than the problem. Relationships grow our best self. Hide emotions or avoid attachment, and we become "as if" people. Let emotions define our identity and we become an unguided missile. We are relational people who feel, quiet ourselves, and stay present to others in ways that express their value as well as ours.

The second popular solution that fails to work is "making you understand." Pressing our point only works when there is mutual mind and compassion—both are missing during enemy mode.

Making others understand easily becomes tainted with self-justifications that can intensify enemy mode. Consequently, the drive to make others understand does not help people escape enemy mode.

ENEMY MODE IMPACT

During enemy mode we enjoy when others lose. Win-win arrangements become lose-lose with one side smugly thinking "I win" while losing relational capital.

Former Congressman Geoff Davis, who we met in chapter 5, told Ray about a company he advised, working directly with CEO Bob. Davis noticed right away that Bob lacked emotional intelligence and operated in enemy mode. Bob was out to win and wasn't sharing the pain of anyone he hurt on the way to the top.

"He could be pretty mean, yet he wanted to be the center of attention and essentially be worshiped," Davis said. "Bob could be very mercurial. One day he lost his temper with me and then with some of my team. I haven't heard anybody talk like that in twenty-five years."

Bob's instability weakened the team around him. He inflicted pain on others in a failed attempt to create corporate momentum, and he tried forcing wins through stupid enemy mode. Davis's trust in him began to drop that day.

The company was having an off-site a week later. Bob evidently felt disrespected by the lead engineer. Bob saw it as a status challenge and told Davis, "I'm going to really give it to him in there."

Davis warned Bob, "You don't need to do that. I don't think that's going to be helpful to the program you support. I don't think it's going to be helpful to the effectiveness of the business."

The off-site had barely started when Bob verbally attacked his enemy, the subcontractor. "He just lit into this other guy and amped up," Davis said. "They were screaming at each other, looking around the table and saying, 'Right, am I right?'"

Intelligent enemy mode had slid into stupid enemy mode, but was still seeking allies to force the other side to lose. Sometimes stupid does what stupid does. Bob permanently harmed the relationship with the subcontractor, divided the team, and blew up the meeting.

Relational capital was wasted and never regained. With Davis's help, everyone calmed down and got back to what Davis called a functional meeting. After that, Bob saw Davis as an enemy. The final loss was Bob's job. He was let go several months later.

Davis had learned to stay relational and to help people out of enemy mode. He and his firm were building relational capital with the business owners who hired them. "Our team stock went up with the people that own the business over time." Davis attributed the trust he gained to his identity. "I had always been a person who would say what I believed was the truth, even if it ticked someone off." By patiently defusing the situation, Davis's credibility rose dramatically.

WHAT IS IN IT FOR ME TO GET OUT OF ENEMY MODE?

"Think globally, act locally," is attributed to Scottish town planner Patrick Geddes. There is less enemy mode in the world when I escape enemy mode myself and refriend you out of enemy mode. Awareness is the first step.

Most of the world's Christians are Catholic, and Jim was in personal enemy mode with Them. He would need to act locally with his own enemy mode. On a trip to Cologne, Jim's friends suggested they visit the cathedral. Jim was surprised by the degree of terror that seized him as he approached the doors. Only after considerable persuasion that this was a tourist destination, and no Catholics would be watching him, did Jim enter. He left as quickly as possible. Jim could usually act "as if" Catholics didn't exist by avoiding them. But his enemy mode reaction and fear embarrassed him. This was not his best self.

Jim followed Geddes's advice. When Kitty wanted a spiritual weekend at a Catholic retreat house, Jim went along to get over it. The only decoration in their room was a crucifix. Jim's heart pounded as he lay awake a good part of the night, telling himself it was nuts to be afraid. Jim's Level Two amygdala alarms did not turn off by ignoring them.

The next evening Jim pushed himself to go with Kitty to vespers. They sat in a small room with about twenty people. A priest came in and asked if anyone played guitar. Kitty said that Jim did.

"Good," said the priest looking at Jim, "You can play for the mass."

Having never seen a mass, Jim didn't have a clue how to fake an "as if"-looking Catholic guitar player. He started trembling, sweating, checked where the exit was, and stuttered, "But I am not Catholic."

"That is fine," said the priest. "I am here recovering from my alcoholism," and he began the mass. The priest's short story about himself and his need for Jim to help out were a nudge out of Jim's enemy mode. Jim played the guitar.

ENEMY MODE ERUPTS

Thinking globally led Jim to speak at an international trauma conference in Medicine Hat, Canada. The organizers thought an ecumenical service would be a nice touch, so they arranged for Father Francis and Baptist pastor Billy Ray to conduct a joint service. Before long, Fr. Francis had Pastor Billy Ray cornered on the platform trying to put a Catholic communion wafer in the Baptist's mouth. One of Jim's friends stayed outside, shouting loudly about Catholics.

Someone invited participants of any faith to the front for the Eucharist. Marilyn Grant, who was sitting near Jim, had taken vows as a member of the Madonna House Apostolate. Neither of them joined the chaos in the front. As they left, Grant expressed to Jim that she was not at all sure she should participate, citing some reason he could not understand.

Grant was not a bit bashful about what she thought. When the chaos ended, Jim saw his chance to find out what Catholics think. This was Jim's first "me Protestant, you Catholic" conversation after a public exhibition of enemy mode. Since Grant was "almost a nun," she could explain anything Catholic. Both agreed that their identity groups had long histories of being enemies "for God's sake."

Grant was well educated and both interested and knowledgeable in science and medicine. She and Jim went on a long walk down a dirt road and across a bridge. Both had a passion for trauma recovery and a desire to see much less enemy mode in the world. They were doing their best to understand together what they had just witnessed. How had this enemy mode erupted?

Grant said her father was a Catholic doctor in a Protestant town that did not care for Catholics. A Catholic doctor in a community that did not care for Protestants had tried to kill Jim's mother and caused her severe pain. Returning across the bridge, Grant and Jim shared pain, expressed compassion, and admitted distrusting each other. They agreed to make refriending mutual and have continued almost daily email discussions of relational spirituality and growth.

GOOD FOR EVERYONE IS
THE LEAST HARMFUL ALTERNATIVE

Dr. Bill St. Cyr, who was also at Medicine Hat, mentioned that he, a Catholic, was on the board of Protestant organizations. Bill invited Jim to a guided tour of an actual mass in a Catholic church, with no guitar playing or being chased with a wafer.

Bill studied the same relational brain science as Jim did, first for healing, and then for education. Bill and his wife, Maryellen, created the Ambleside Schools International. These schools taught students to escape enemy mode by restoring relationships. Relational living, attachment, compassion, group identity, being our best self, and raising the status of others were all part of the Ambleside education system from administrators to teachers to children and their families. The school in South Africa helped children escape enemy mode in the country where two giants, Bishop Desmond Tutu and Nelson Mandela, escaped enemy mode.

Meeting Dr. George Bebawi, an Egyptian Jew who became a Coptic Christian, helped Jim understand a group identity. Bebawi told vivid stories about his times giving and receiving enemy mode, even being poisoned by the secret police. Bebawi was invited by the Vatican to teach Catholic seminarians to be the best Catholics possible. Jim was shocked. He anticipated that George would want to be right and win. Bebawi's message to Christians everywhere was, "What is wrong with you people? You don't seem to have a group identity." He was all about helping people find their best self.

James Martini liked applying relational brain skills to business, home, and parish life. After going to masses and then meeting priests and a bishop together with Martini, Jim noticed his reaction shifting to a warm and interested feeling.

By the time trauma counselor Katsy Long suggested Jim meet Fr. Ubald Rugirangoga of Rwanda, Jim was ready but still nervous. Long invited Jim's help with the documentary about Fr. Ubald's story of betrayal, genocide, and forgiveness. It hit Jim hard that Fr. Ubald's family was killed by Catholics.

Fr. Ubald and Jim spent almost a week together in Long's home. That week the world changed for Jim. He formed a strong attachment to Fr. Ubald. With his mind clear of enemy mode, Jim realized he had trauma from Catholics early in life, but that most of his traumatic experiences came from fellow Protestants. Everyone seeking a "win" hurt others and justified their actions with their beliefs. Enemy mode said, "Vote for me—I am Christian. Kill with me—I am Christian. Cover for me—I am Christian." Those whose life was relational did not use beliefs for a win but to find the least harmful alternative that was good for all.

When Jim was invited to teach at Duke University's School of Divinity's Summer Institute for Reconciliation, Long helped lead the class. Next, she introduced Jim to Dr. Christina Lynch, a staff member at a Catholic seminary in the Denver Archdiocese. Lynch's goal was joyful, protective priests who nurture joyful communities. She arranged for Jim to give lectures at the seminary and speak at retreats. Lynch and Jim become coauthors of *The Joy Workbook* for Catholic seminarians.

They did not agree to disagree about beliefs. In fact, outside of constant discussions with Marilyn Grant, beliefs had not entered the picture. Grant helped Jim find his best self. Jim no longer hid in an "as if" self around Catholics. Jim was introduced as a Protestant and the topic went to relational and spiritual brain skills. Jim's enemy mode was gone, and attachments were forming. Jim wanted every Catholic to become their best self. Thanks to Grant, Jim understood Catholic vocabulary, structure, and beliefs. Jim did not escape enemy mode through information or compromise. His intelligent enemy mode melted away through lasting attachments.

Around this time, Jim was challenged by a friend to pass everything he had learned to the next generation. Lynch recommended a Catholic priest who was open to building joy through relationships. Father Matthew had been a priest for fifteen years, but his default mode of operation included a negative filter. Fr. Matthew walked around every day in enemy mode, feeling rejected, unappreciated, and with no sense of clear purpose. He retained a passion for seeing transformative parish communities.

Once Fr. Matthew understood the science of how the right brain develops character through relational joy, loving attachments, group identity, and healthy correction, Fr. Matthew started to "light up" whenever he saw someone, calling them by name and taking an interest in their intrinsic value. Even if encounters only lasted a few seconds, Fr. Matthew wanted authentic moments that mattered and made a difference. He learned to smile at strangers so they knew he saw them and cared about them as fellow human beings.

Fr. Matthew learned to stay calm, curious, and compassionate whenever someone launched an attack against him because of their issue with the Catholic Church. His personal escape from enemy mode paved the way for turning people's pain into positive encounters.

Fr. Matthew felt he had a whole new operating system to live life the way it is meant to be lived. His role, as one of the missionaries of mercy, was delegated by Pope Francis to extend God's closeness and tenderness to those in particularly difficult situations, reconciling them and restoring them to peace. People told him that he has given them hope in dark situations and helped them find healing and share the love of Jesus for greater joy and a more impactful experience of community.

Now that Fr. Matthew knew how to get himself out of enemy mode and build joy, he spent much of his time traveling from church to church as a consultant helping people achieve interior freedom and joy in a life well lived.

Jim was also celebrating his own escape from enemy mode. With his amygdala quiet and his PFC updating in real time, Jim recalled that the Cardinal of Colombia had asked his mother, in her old age, to design a curriculum for children in all the public schools of the country. Yes, escaping enemy mode can help us shape whole countries and generations as well as fulfill dreams.

Deborah and Ray reflected on the changes he had made. Enemy mode had been normal, and escaping enemy mode would take time. They both felt it was the "end of the beginning," to quote Churchill. The journey had begun. Ray knew he had a long way to go becoming a relational husband and father. Repairs were beginning with his children. Deborah felt hope for greater connection.

WHERE DOES ENEMY MODE SCIENCE TAKE US?

Jim was running out of science when it came to the actual study of hate, enemy mode, attachment, brain activity, group identity, and how they fit together. Usual social psychology studies focused on ethnocentrism, social conformity, pacifism, or specific emotions such as disgust, anger, and occasionally hate. Solutions were even less studied and seemed to need trained therapists, specialized awareness, or summer camps for the children of enemy groups. Studies usually represented very skewed population samples and immature brains.

Some of the challenges with the science thus far have included:

- If loving enemies is developed in mature brains, those are missing from most brain studies. Most social science uses primarily young WEIRD (Western, Educated, Industrialized, Rich, Democratic) subjects.
- Brain frequency and activation levels are not often studied together.
- What the brain does well is not being studied in scans.
- Most brain scan interpretations are modular (looking for hot spots), not sequential (looking for how the process flows through).

- Interventions that involve attachment (Schore) are primarily individual.
- Interventions that involve groups rarely consider individual or group attachment activity in the brain.

Some of the less (even poorly) researched topics include:

- The impact of attachment or group identity on enemy mode has not been studied.
- Dr. Kaiser reports dropping brain frequency in the medial-frontal brain with increasing loss of differentiation of brain regions as predicting criminal as well as psychotic processes. Can these relationships be verified? And what is their relationship to interpersonal hostility, misunderstanding, and alienation? What triggers and solutions can be developed?
- The studies on hate in the brain are very small and scarce.
- Is group identity the same as ethnocentrism or conformity?
- Deference and social status in the brain (and their contributors) are poorly studied.
- The division between "as if" self and "best" self is not well defined or studied.

Scanning a brain to detect enemy mode is obviously difficult. Studying social situations where people are in enemy mode is not only difficult but likely dangerous. Getting into the areas of the world where enemy mode is armed and active is unlikely. Yet, when we think of solutions, we tend to think in terms of conscious sequences—instructions to follow. Enemy mode operates in the fast track of the brain where the influence of instructions is minimal. Everyone from social scientists to religious leaders to educators and rulers would like to see steps we take to get results. The right and left hemispheres do not lend themselves to that solution.

This is the trouble with steps and sequences. Literature on the brain and its treatment is really quite confusing when it comes to how the right and left brain work together. Consider the question of whether we should encourage left PFC or right PFC activity. Neurofeedback treatment providers have found that elevating rPFC activity (where our relational identity would be active) makes people more depressed. Happier people have elevated lPFC activity (where McGilchrist says our mean actions originate). On top of that, we saw that Kaiser found undifferentiated activity in the rPFC region at lower frequencies associated with violent criminal behavior—definitely not our best self.

Then there are the rookie mistakes. The brain does not use much energy when doing nothing, but it also does not use much energy when doing what it does well. The brain burns fuel, generates blood flow, and has lots of nerves firing when it is doing something it needs to do but does not do well. As we saw from Sapolsky, people who habitually tell the truth showed no brain activation while telling the truth but burned fuel telling lies. If the rPFC was burning and churning, it is not doing what it does well. When the right brain was running calmly, the rPFC was doing what it does well without much activation. What the rPFC does well is joyful identity. If there is no struggle with identity, we are no longer depressed.

People who are developing treatments like rewarding brain frequency, heating spots in the brain with infrared lights, sending electrical signals into the brain through the skull, and other methods take a "try it and see what happens" approach. Some track frequency, some track blood flow, some track differentials or voltages. Figuring out where brain waves come from is like trying to locate which smoke alarm in the house is making that beep. We hear it everywhere in the house, but turning our heads and going from room to room eventually accomplishes what having wires all over our head does for brain activity. From these results, they form an explanation that makes sense to them and sells their treatment system.

The next step depends on where the brain's relational process was blocked but also on how well the different parts of the brain are working together. If that isn't enough, we must add the influence of our group mind and identity. It all adds up to staying relational and finding the least harmful solution for a life of joy, but it does not fit well into steps.

The Pacifist and the General

Is there any time when our best selves will not want the least harmful solution? Enemy mode thinking never considers the least harmful solution. Stupid and intelligent enemy modes go farther and calculate that more harm to you is better for me. All three enemy modes produce reduced or nonexistent compassion for the suffering of others. Is that ever desirable?

No matter the scale of military intervention that Ray and Jim discussed (police actions, Hitler and the Nazis, the bombing of Dresden, Putin's invasion of Ukraine, or use of the atomic bomb as examples), Ray consistently wanted the least harmful solution. He could not help it. Jim asked if Ray ever wanted to see the military operate without concern for the least harmful solution. No! Ray was emphatic. He was greatly distressed about times when anyone's armies or soldiers had destroyed all they could. Even enemy forces and populations mattered when Ray was considering the least harmful solution to conflict.

The conclusion both Ray and Jim reached was that there was never a time or place for military men, political leaders, law enforcement, courts, civil authorities, religious leaders, crowds of people, social movements, educators, neighbors, parents, children, or any human to disregard the harm they might cause. The least harmful solution should always be valued. Since enemy mode does not value the least harmful alternative, enemy mode thinking should be understood but never be in charge.

Opposing enemy mode thinking and actions was the reason retired Brigadier General Ray Woolridge was proud of his military service. Ray and the officers he admired had sometimes put their careers on the line to reduce enemy mode thinking during military operations. The language of brain science was not in their minds but explained what they were keen to accomplish. The places where enemy mode had crept into his service weighed heavily on Ray. Any avoidable harm to civilians, fellow soldiers, or even opposing soldiers caused moral injuries that tormented veterans, noncombatants, and their families. Every time a win became crucial, however, it was very hard to escape enemy mode and find the least harmful solution.

Jim examined his conflicted relationship with Christians, both Catholic and Protestant. Much of the physical and emotional abuse he experienced came from Mennonite pacifists in enemy mode. Jim's other horrifying experiences had come from Catholics in enemy mode. Beliefs provided little if any capacity to take a brain out of enemy mode. During enemy

Since enemy mode does not value the least harmful alternative, enemy mode thinking should be understood but never be in charge.

mode, religious people stopped considering the least harmful solution, disregarded relational costs, and went after a win for God.

In Europe, pacifism developed in groups of Christians who wanted to stop killing other Christians over differing beliefs. Belief in pacifism began as efforts to find the least harmful solution to religious wars. Over time, these groups showed a tendency to isolate. Not killing is not the same as forming attachments to enemies or discovering our best selves. Many pacifist groups emerged, including Anabaptist, Quaker, Amish, Hutterite, Bruderhof, Brethren (the group that ordained Jim as a minister in 1984), and the Mennonites with whom Jim was raised.

Belief does not keep us from enemy mode. History provides us with many groups of pacifists from different religions. Some wear white, saffron, brown, or black robes. Pacifism, like all beliefs, will not keep us out of enemy mode. Jim was greatly bemused when he saw young

Buddhist monks playing war games on cellphones in their Himalayan monastery. All beliefs and their symbols can easily take over the brain's "as if" circuit and produce a sort of avatar identity worn on the outside.

In the end, if Christians and the military had something in common, it was the difficulty of escaping enemy mode when status or winning were involved. Both were failing to produce best selves, although each believed they were making improvements. Soldierization overcame fear of engagement and built group cohesion. Christianity generally failed on those two points and improved beliefs instead. Exactly which beliefs mattered could not be agreed.

Jim and Ray were both seeking the least harmful solution and wanted to see their friends and enemies find it too. Losing sight of the least harmful solution produced people who were not their best selves and encouraged growth of avatar-like personalities. A winning image subverted true human attachment. Avatars are gathered easily but cannot really escape enemy mode. In the next chapter, we see what we find to help whole groups escape enemy mode.

12

HELPING MY IDENTITY GROUP ESCAPE ENEMY MODE

DID YOU SKIP RIGHT TO THE LAST CHAPTER? If you followed along with us, you noticed we didn't talk about ways to avoid enemy mode. What we need is skill and lots of experience escaping enemy mode. Our brains take us into our particular style of enemy mode in a flash. We can even wake up in simple enemy mode. What we are looking for now is how a "herd" escapes together. Some group identities isolate. Some attack. Some build defenses. Some follow leaders who protect Us from Them with the promise that Us will win. Some simply try to recover from the damage enemy mode has done to their people.

Enemy mode is best escaped together. Coaches Jamie Magalei and Heather Roberts were on that journey together and shifting to a relational coaching style. The two had retained Lori Mateer, the leadership coach, to guide them. They had just begun their journey on learning how to escape enemy mode.

Magalei reflected with Ray on her years as a coach and escaping from enemy mode in her work: "I do look back. We had a lot of great moments, years, and experiences. I wish we would have had better attachment relationships with those players.

"This year has been a complete transition into just staying relational as coaches. Lori always goes back to the number one thing: to 'stay in relational mode' for that tough conversation. That is the toughest part, having tough conversations at tough moments but doing it relationally. We're at the very beginning of the change."

Roberts talked about how she has changed, saying, "We still have wins or losses, right? Those are still going to come into play, but how we're choosing to handle those has changed. Am I able to keep a relational switch on, or even realize my switch is off right now?"

During a recent pre-game practice, Magalei and Roberts slipped into that older enemy mode neural pathway. Before the game, Susie, a leader on the team, told the whole team, "Well, we all know what we're thinking could happen in this match!" hinting at a previous loss. Both coaches were frustrated with her for verbalizing "old tapes from last season." Mateer arrived before the game and saw Magalei and Roberts were trying to figure out how to get back into relational mode.

She grabbed a quick courtside chat with them. As they filled her in, Mateer said, "Actually it's a really good thing Susie said that." The coaches gasped. She continued, "Now we know what Susie is thinking, and probably other players also."

Magalei asked, "Should we correct Susie in front of the team?" Mateer countered, "You could, or you can bring it to the team and say, 'Who else thought this?' Maybe Susie is just stating the obvious. You can continue to be curious. How will we all be our best selves in a hard place?"

After the courtside brainstorm, the coaches took a much more relational approach. Their intervention was light, engaging, and even humorous. In the past, Magalei and Roberts would have stayed in enemy mode.

Another relational coaching win came mid-season. Mateer met with Magalei and Roberts at a restaurant. Both coaches were feeling the pressure to win and the fear that goes with it. They said, "Okay, we have to win the next couple of games." Mateer surprised them with, "Wait, what did you bring me in for—to win or to be better relational coaches?"

The coaches were stunned. "That did not go the way we expected it to go," Magalei told Ray with a grin. She added, "It's not that I don't want the girls to play their best game and be themselves out there, but if we go into this with 'fear' motivation, we're going to lose the players. Either we go back to the way we used to coach or we're going to continue to transform."

By that point in the volleyball season and the academic semester, the players were tired and midterm exams loomed. Magalei made a courageous decision and tried something new. She said, "Okay, you have the day off. Let's rest."

The players were blown away and felt their coaches' care for them. In the past, a day off would have never been an option before a game. The next night the team played a stunning game. Magalei and Roberts felt their joy of coaching returning as they led relationally.

WHAT ABOUT THOSE CHRISTIANS AND THEIR BRAINS?

We proposed at the start of the book that, according to their beliefs, Christians should spontaneously attach to their enemies. Nearly two and a half billion people (representing one-fifth of the world's population) should be out there loving their enemies. Obviously most don't.

Ray and Jim set out to find a working solution for enemy mode. What would the brain reveal about the process? Would any Christians be interested? Would what the brain required fit Christians' beliefs and values? Would any Christians begin escaping enemy mode?

The brain proved to be highly relational. Our identity and spontaneous reactions developed through attachments. Relationships with people whose brains we mirror developed both our individual and group identities. Attachments, not beliefs, developed a relational identity that knew how my people would act under the current circumstances. Enemy mode was a weakness, a failure of the brain to stay relational. Enemy mode was a relational blindness that produced relational injuries.

Only attachments of joy with relational people can teach us to escape enemy mode. After the critical apoptotic period at about age thirteen, the identity center in the PFC shifts from survival as an individual to the survival of my identity group—my herd, my people. Wars are made possible by this shift because now individuals will die for *my tribe* or *my country*. However, if my identity group brings out the best self in others by attaching to them, even when they feel like enemies, we bravely face enemies with compassion. We escape enemy mode and offer that option to others. When we see an enemy, we are never seeing their best self.

While the brain experts we consulted could not say how to produce a hive/tribe/people/identity group that did not attack Them, soldierization provided clues to an identity group that will attack Them. Thousands of years and millions of soldiers later, we know it is really hard to teach soldiers to kill Them, but training soldiers to protect Us develops readily and deeply. Unfortunately, soldierization promotes enemy mode and damages the relational life of veterans.

A hive/tribe/people/identity group with a mission to love enemies would need to escape enemy mode rapidly. Their attachment response to enemies would express acquired value. Soldierization shows us that people would seek, engage, and even die helping others out of enemy mode if that was their group identity.

Rev. Ariel Babikian's grandparents escaped the Armenian genocide as orphaned children. Armenians lay claim to being the oldest

Christian civilization.[1] Babikian told Jim that the Armenians isolated and polarized rather than forming attachments to the Turks of the Ottoman Empire—a failure to seek, engage, and attach to their enemies. Babikian travels back to Armenia teaching relational joy—how we can be glad to be with others. Babikian sees his effort as both recovery and prevention.

BRAIN SCIENCE AND THE IDENTITY GROUPS THAT ESCAPE ENEMY MODE

Jim collected the characteristics of a group identity that foster escaping from enemy mode. Ray examined whether Jim's list would match the teachings of Jesus and carry weight with all Christians. The characteristics and teachings matched in the following ways:

Enduring: Identity groups, like all attachments, are lifelong. The brain does not expect to have them change. The better attachments fare, the less attachment pain there will be. We are predisposed to be part of a group that will outlive us and whose welfare is our welfare. Identity groups are becoming harder to recognize as relationships become virtual.

Jesus taught: *I am with you always.*[2]

Attachment based: Relational living that allows people in a group to attach and know one another is required to help others out of enemy mode. From time to time we must trust someone more than we trust our own thoughts and feelings. Trust in other minds disappears for people we don't know. Every group has their own trusted sources while ignoring others. This kind of trust in other minds is disrupted for people with schizophrenia and bipolar disorders.

Jesus taught: *Love one another as I have loved you.*[3]

Joyful: Attachments develop strong and resilient identities when they form around joy rather than shared fears. Fearful people have very active amygdalas, and their nervous system must keep working hard to quiet itself. Entering enemy mode becomes easy, but escaping is hard. Joyful groups develop hopeful children with an eagerness to be relational—the opposite of enemy mode. Joyful girls are particularly impactful on the creativity of the next generation.

Jesus taught: *I have told you this so that my joy may be in you and that your joy may be complete.*[4]

Protective: Predators operate in intelligent enemy mode. Winning takes precedence over finding the least harmful solution for relationships. Fearful group identities will select predatory "winners" for their leaders, leaders who foster enemy mode for their own power and status. In the short run, predators often win. Attachment with a Them is not an option to predators. Enemy mode is how the predatory win.

Jesus taught: *I am the good shepherd.*[5]

Raises the social standing of others: Feeling that one's social standing is being lowered is a major contributor to enemy mode. Ed Khouri attributes many of the reactions he received as a police officer to the expectation by the person he was approaching that they were about to be taken down a notch. Contesting and fighting for social standing are common.

Jesus taught: *If anyone would be first, he must be last of all and servant of all.*[6]

A group identity that encourages members to raise the social standing of others relative to their own reduces the reasons for enemy mode. Haidt suggests that conservatives will more easily value a social order hierarchy than would liberals. However, liberals seem just as likely to visit enemy mode if their social standing is being lowered and boost social status for women, minorities, LGBTQ, workers, pets, and animals.

Jesus taught: *If I then, your Lord and Teacher, have washed your feet, you also ought to wash one another's feet.*[7]

Compassionate: Our brain learns the least harmful alternatives by sharing the pain of others and particularly the pain we created ourselves. Stupid enemy mode creates pain and often does whatever will hurt most. Intelligent enemy mode tracks the pain of others to use against them for a win. Simple enemy mode fails to see the attachment pain others feel. A compassionate group identity will not allow this insensitivity in group members. Members escape enemy mode and find the least harmful alternative.

Jesus taught: *Blessed are the compassionate, for they shall receive compassion.*[8]

Present as my real self: Our identity in the PFC is connected to our awareness of our bodies in the insula. Being present means our brain is not off in the past. We are not in the "as if" world of the future. We are not nonattached observers. Group identities who promote enemy mode do a great deal of image management. My "as if" image uses your "as if" image to win and raise my status. All three types of enemy mode do fairly well in an "as if" world of avatar selves.

Jesus taught: *I know my own and my own know me.*[9]

Bring out the best self in myself and others: Why should I attach to avatar selves? We are certainly not going to suggest attaching to harmfulness. If there is a better self in people who are in enemy mode, then finding that better self is something we all desire. We want people who are disrespecting us and treating us like enemies to treat us relationally. Only the relational person in us has a chance to help our "enemies" find their better (relational) self and escape enemy mode.

Jesus taught: *I have come to save the world and not to judge it.*[10]

Acquired value for Them: When we are angry or alienated from other members of our group, anyone who values us both offers a way to escape enemy mode and restore relationships. In the same way, if our group values Thems, anyone we meet gains preexisting value. The attachments of people we love acquire value to us simply because someone we love also loves them. If we are part of a people who share life and care for strangers and the weak, then we approach Them by offering attachment to us.

Jesus taught: *Love your enemies and pray for those who persecute you . . . For if you love those who love you, what reward do you have?*[11]

The teachings of Jesus indicate that raising the status of others, taking the lower status places, and serving (very low status) rather than being served reverses social status expectations. The last were first and the first last. Loving attachments in a spiritual family replaced attachments to clothes, position, wealth, and power, revealing the true status of the soul. God was lovingly attached to everyone, so people we consider enemies should acquire value for his spiritual family members. Jesus said, "Then you will become children of your Father in heaven. For he makes his sun shine on good and bad people alike, and he sends rain to the righteous and the unrighteous alike."[12]

Loving attachments and goodness are offered to enemies. Jesus' most attached follower went so far as to say that people could not claim to be attached to God if people had not acquired value for them.[13] Religious self-justification was not allowed in this identity group. The winner was the one with a soul rather than the one who owned the world. All these elements are incompatible with living in any form of enemy mode.

Believing and teaching all the above in the left brain without attachment creates a religious avatar that can be very useful for intelligent enemy mode. Enemy mode thinking uses beliefs to justify itself and persuade others to cover its actions. Beliefs do not create or remove enemy mode and hate in the brain.

Ray had been interviewing leaders at the center of the military, government, law enforcement, business, medicine, church, and recovery structures that maintain society. He found Christians were a significant percentage of the leadership. Ray also found that relational Christians (Christians on the inside) looked for the least harmful alternative that was good for everyone. A surprising number had quite high status, which they used to raise the status of others. This group did not stay in enemy mode very long. Leaders who cared about the least harmful alternatives and the good of the group were subdued about what they believed while actively building relationships.

Ray had always wondered why some high status Christians looked so good on the outside and were so hard to be around. He discovered, after his search, that status-seeking Christians (Christians on the out-side) were looking for the win using intelligent enemy mode. These religious avatars were relationally blind most of the time. They did not share the pain they created for others. Those who were most vocal about their beliefs were looking for higher status and the win. The noisy leaders attracted more followers, but there were bodies under the buses. Church staff and members became replaceable parts on the assembly line of organizational progress.

In chapter 8, we met Pastor Frank who lamented staff turnover while hearing, "It is a privilege to serve in this first-class church." Frank saw many staff leave the church's enemy mode culture following relational breakdowns.

FINDING SUSTAINABLE GROUND

Author and inspirational speaker Bob Goff provides indications that loving one's enemies has traction with young Christians. Goff was a lawyer who taught in Southern California, but his personal adventures learning to love his enemies, including criminals he had prosecuted, are international. His book *Love Does* and his *New York Times* best-seller, *Everybody Always*, tell the stories.

While Goff inspires readers to find their best selves as individuals, sustaining our best selves under upsetting conditions requires grow-ing within an identity group that also values escaping enemy mode.

Ray, Jim, and friends are constantly being asked where joyful, attachment-based groups worthy of survival can be found. The human brain is waiting, wanting, and asking to belong. The answer will not come from finding a utopian group. The intersection of utopian vision and strong personal attachments to the leader or group creates cults and wackos. Sustainable identity groups will need to grow from the people in our lives.

"Ray," Jim said, "I think that where Christians have prided themselves on their beliefs, they have fragmented their identity into groups by fighting. This fighting has created a terrible tendency to select predatory leaders. Rationalistic, nonrelational, status-seeking, religiously justified, intelligent enemy mode practitioners will circle the wagons against the evil world of Them. Our mission will be difficult."

"Disgusted people are leaving the church in droves—particularly the young," Ray answered.

"Leaving creates another problem," Jim added. "We really need an identity group to escape enemy mode reliably. For our attachments to bring out the best self in others, we need people who stay attached to us when we drop into enemy mode. And," he said wistfully, "it doesn't pay for us to get into enemy mode with 2.4 billion people."

Ray was thinking about how many churches need leadership that stays out of enemy mode. He remembered a conversation with General Halstead. She had a toxic leader in one of her brigades. A colonel was commanding from intelligent enemy mode. She'd told Ray, "Everything revolved around that colonel, who was very manipulative both for good and bad."

Getting to the truth was tough. Halstead had heard the rumors and conducted two challenging investigations. The brigade was afraid to speak up. She said, "They just wouldn't answer the questions. We discovered that nothing illegal or immoral was going on there, but it was clearly a very toxic environment. That colonel could turn it on and off. I had a hard time communicating to my two-star general boss what that commander was like. Why? Even if the colonel was being toxic, the brigade successfully performed their mission. The commander was a smart logistician and was intellectually very strong but displayed little to no emotional intelligence."

Halstead recalled: "What this colonel constantly communicated to the team was 'I don't care what you think, I don't care if you like me, I don't care. I don't care anything about you. We're just here with a mission to do, so get it done.'"

Morale was extremely low, and people were being affected personally and professionally, so Halstead stepped in continuously and kept a close eye on the organization and its people. "That colonel had to retire after the deployment. It was a very challenging situation, especially in combat."

Intelligent enemy mode is very deceptive and smart. How we choose leaders needs to change if we want to escape enemy mode as a group.

DELIBERATELY UPGRADE YOUR GROUP IDENTITY

Ray had discovered narcissism and enemy mode in his organization, Life Model Works, and set out to do something about it. As his own mode of working shifted, the team established a rhythm of connecting relationally whenever they met and making decisions collaboratively. The team studied narcissism for fourteen weeks and did corrective exercises. Ray said, "I am seeking input and asking the team what they see as the next steps. We held a three-day off-site twice last year, and our relationships with each other have grown a great deal. We are repairing the relationships damaged by our enemy mode. I noticed last spring our differences are complementary. One executive is always thinking. Another is feeling and networking. I am always devising ways to 'do it better' and designing 'how' we do what we do. That makes a good team."

Helping our identity group out of enemy mode required a relational way of leading. Ray remembered two senior generals he observed personally. Ray watched the first general get the team moving together in the right direction and accomplishing their strategy. Without stopping the work, she was able to build relationships with the team. Morale soared, even among the generals and senior civilians who worked directly for her.

The general who followed her was as nonrelational as can be imagined. The only thing that mattered to him was the task and mission. He was entirely transactional. His direct reports were only contacted when the work was not going well. He didn't make time for personal connection and criticized his direct reports publicly. Morale plummeted.

When Ray was a young officer, he served on the staff of a three-thousand-soldier Army brigade commanded by a colonel. The staff had a bad reputation for always saying no to requests from subordinate units. The commanders of those subordinates complained frequently. This was bureaucracy and enemy mode together.

A new brigade executive officer changed the organization's culture, which made an impression on Ray. Major Monroe gathered the brigade staff and talked about their work. "When one of our units asks us to do something for them, we will find a way to say 'yes' to them, because we support them. So we will say, 'The answer is yes. Now, what is the problem and how can we help?'"

Without knowing it at the time, Ray saw modeled a powerful example of a relational group identity that stayed out of enemy mode.

CONSIDERATIONS FOR DEVELOPING A GROUP IDENTITY

Using attachment-building activities to strengthen group identity will both form attachments and provide motivation to do so. A short list of activities will get us started, although attachment-building is not the topic for this book. These are some well-known ways for building attachments.

Playing together is one of the best activities for attachment between peers.[14] In real play, there are no serious consequences. Playing has a pretend sort of winning, but the real fun is the game. Predators end the game. Players avoid winning decisively to keep the game going. An ancient prophet said that good leaders take even the strong out to play while predatory leaders drive everyone with ruthless severity.[15]

Some other attachment activities are:

- Feeding visitors in our own home
- Making music together
- Celebrating accomplishments
- Storytelling
- Helping individuals in need as a group

A group identity that treats enemy mode as a weakness helps us escape enemy mode. Four general practices are needed:

1. **Simple** enemy mode needs our attachment awakened. We learn to awaken our body and spirit to the presence and value of others. We have our RCs on.
2. **Stupid** enemy mode needs to be quieted to get our brain back into a working zone. We learn to quiet ourselves and rest protectively together.
3. **Intelligent** enemy mode needs to experience pain others are feeling in order to escape. We share the pain of others.
4. **Attaching to enemies** needs group examples. Attachment-building activities with people outside our identity group give us the feeling of how "we" treat "them." We are not talking about charity, or neighborhood cleanup, or anything that might make us feel superior. Attachments are made between people who feed, are fed, give shelter, share joy, and play.

HOW DOES ENEMY MODE IMPACT MY GROUP?

When my people are the target for enemy mode, the full impact spans generations. When a slave becomes king, the winners and losers are reversed. The French Revolution is a clear example of this reversal. Very rarely do these changes end enemy mode. In enemy mode, groups take sides, don't listen, and work hard so others lose or look bad. This relational alienation and partisanship will change hands as oppressed and oppressors switch places. Having new intelligent enemy mode predators in charge will not end enemy mode. Only the justifications will change.

Sapolsky detailed how the infant's attachment system suspends stress hormones following birth to allow attachment.[16] During that moment without stress hormones, children can form attachments to scary predators. Without refriending, these predators roam freely, creating a predator culture. Control, power, winning, and avoiding pain for myself at your expense become the cultural norm. These are dangerous places to live. Enemy mode has become the way of life.

As Jim was lamenting how his guitar playing had languished while researching and writing this book, a thought crossed his mind. "Wherever Christians are building their status, they lose the chops to transform predators into protectors. Status-seeking Christianity will continue disappearing from the earth. If Christians become a people who escape enemy mode, form attachments, and bring out the best in others, they will last."

WHAT IS IN IT FOR MY GROUP TO ESCAPE ENEMY MODE?

Refriending moves our world away from domestic violence, terrorism, racism, human trafficking, genocide, and other human rights abuses. None of these hideous human practices can function without enemy mode thinking by the perpetrators.

Even the best groups will have moments of all three styles of enemy mode. Groups that refriend can smile, see that weakness, and say, "We can do better." Keeping relationships bigger than problems helps us find our best selves.

HOW DOES GROUP IDENTITY IMPACT ENEMY MODE?

A strong group identity built around shared fears intensifies enemy mode and will become tyrannical, oppressive, threatening, and deadly. In a fear-based group identity, the joy levels drop, intelligent enemy mode prospers, and world class predators may result. Whether a strong group identity brings out our best self depends on: 1) how our group shares the pain of others, and 2) how we treat those who feel or act like enemies.

CONCLUSION FROM HISTORY

Status enforced by power emerges as the biggest block to escaping enemy mode. Creating a winning avatar-self that does what it takes to win characterizes corporate environments and leadership selection. Image, spin, results, and control build nonrelational government, businesses, and religious groups. Winning and power are unbuffered by attachment or compassion and driven by vision and mission.

History links intelligent enemy mode to winning predators who tell fearful followers that some terrible Them will harm Us unless the followers appease and support the predator. Humanity then suffers. Status seeking appears to be the active force behind the rise of enemy mode nations, businesses, and churches. Those who seek status build enemy mode empires.

Less obvious bits of history suggest that attachment and compassion build relational brains where enemy mode does not last as long. Our best self receives support from our relational identity group and learns to escape enemy mode. Those who raise the status of others are rare but iconic in their impact. Lifting the status of others rarely remains an identity group characteristic for long. Second and third generation leaders in any movement usually seek status.

CONCLUSION FROM BRAIN SCIENCE

Humans have relational brains. The very things that make us human make us relational. The relational brain is born predatory and must learn to be protective. As the infant brain matures, it learns that not everything is there for lunch. Attachment is the corrective factor that helps us correct enemy mode at all levels of brain activation.

When it came to enemy mode, three distinct failures in relational thinking emerged. We named them: simple, stupid, and intelligent enemy mode. Enemy mode patterns were easily recognizable for many people we interviewed. Enemy mode patterns have received very little research.

Beliefs did not cause enemy mode thinking. Beliefs did not prevent the three forms of enemy mode. Beliefs could gather people who were in enemy mode or people who wished to escape. Belief in the value of relationships encourages us to seek relational solutions so we can escape enemy mode.

The most important consideration for humans after the apoptotic period at about age thirteen is: Who are we and who are our people?

Belief in the value of relationships encourages us to seek relational solutions so we can escape enemy mode.

Identity groups become more important than personal survival but create an Us and Them division. Identity groups that practice attachment through joy, bring out our best selves, raise the status of others, offer compassion, and support rescue attachments might provide the training needed to escape enemy mode.

Enemy mode experiences were much more common with Us than with Them.

Escaping enemy mode and refriending people who felt like enemies was needed for both Us and Them. When escaping enemy mode, differences between Us and Them are less important than whether Us stays relational with Them.

Human sensitivity to status challenges and status losses produces many enemy mode reactions. Social status enforcement during critical periods leaves multigenerational effects on brain development. Challenges to status usually result in violence, wars, and traumas. Both status and attachment have immediate and long-term impact on brain operation.

The brain has a very fast "as if" simulator in the dorsal PFC capable of avoiding strong feelings while still predicting how others will feel. This simulator system provides a theoretical explanation of how people create and maintain an avatar-self capable of winning without compassion. Intelligent enemy mode; leading a genocide; becoming a manipulative religious, business, military, or political leader; and supporting predators develop from this "as if" life. Little brain research is available on the topic.

Current brain studies tend to focus on what the brain does poorly in immature brains. The speed and flow of information is rarely considered in brain scan studies. How the brain develops an identity group and expresses its best self are barely understood. How the brain fails to be compassionate, hates, and passes enemy mode using identity groups is basically unknown.

CONCLUSION FROM CHRISTIANS

Christians could provide an identity group compatible with escaping enemy mode and forming attachments to enemies. Central to Christian belief, but tragically not to practice, is that people have no human enemies. Seeing other humans as enemies is failing to see a full reality. We are not experiencing our own value or finding their best self. A Christian response would form an attachment with enemies in trouble and help them find their best selves rather than stay in enemy mode.

The authors' interactions with Christians revealed a widespread knowledge of religious beliefs and near total astonishment that escaping enemy mode was a real possibility. How can people change? For centuries we have relied on beliefs and moral thinking, but that is building on a weaker part of the human brain. Our best chance for transformation is to build on attachment.

Avatar Christians are wildly successful and very noisy about their beliefs. Upon closer inspection, everyone we investigated showed strong signs of seeking higher status for themselves. Since the brain uses beliefs to justify itself and find support from others, there is a strong tie between Christians looking for a win, losses of relational capital, and leaders loudly promoting their beliefs, mission, and vision. Only Christians who face their own enemy mode and inner predator can help their identity group protect and raise the status of others. Identity groups need to seek, engage, and transform their own high status leadership. You know, all the winners.

Ray found that relational Christian leaders were quite clear that their beliefs supported their best selves but led through identity (being themselves) rather than talking about beliefs. Peter, an original follower of Jesus, said we become one people through compassion: "For once you were not a people but now you are the people of God. Once you had not received compassion but now you have received compassion."[17] Compassion grows a people from former enemies.

CONCLUSIONS FROM MORAL REASONING

The five professors looking at the brain and moral behavior—Haidt, Sapolsky, Sasse, McGilchrist, and Schore—gave evidence that moral behavior is a feature of group identity and attachment before it ever becomes belief and explanations. Beliefs are quite helpful for justifying judgments and finding like-minded people. We have reached the point in this book where we are looking for like-minded people who would like to escape enemy mode thinking and help others refriend.

It appears to us that humans have suffered more from the destruction caused by enemy mode than from all cancers combined. We don't say this lightly. Ray has battled melanoma for years and lost an ear. Jim's wife, Kitty, battled leukemia and lost her life. Yet, both Ray and Kitty have expressed far more regret about their enemy mode moments than their cancers.

Kitty and Ray received a great deal of help from associations supporting research and treatment for their cancers. Should we not support an escape from enemy mode for everyone on the planet? When we combine what we have learned from history, science, and spirituality, recovery from enemy mode includes a relational life, compassion, attachment, and group identities that encourage our best selves. We teach each other to escape enemy mode and become relational once again. It took generations to get in this mess, and it will take generations to escape.

Believing that we have no human enemies is a blatantly Christian value. The chances are that you know a Christian. Encourage him or her to escape enemy mode and be their best self. Quote a little from Jesus if you need to. You know what he said.

Human value is invisible to relationally blind people in chronic enemy mode. Treating others as enemies is a weakness. We would like to see identity groups learning to overcome this weakness. Staying in enemy mode is a failure to be our best human selves. Jim and Ray were hopeful about the brain science behind enemy mode, but they were even more hopeful about escaping enemy mode within themselves and with their community.

Humanizing the planet will require compassion and attachment to everyone, but particularly those who see the world as their enemies. We begin by knowing that escaping enemy mode is learned and that enemy mode takes different forms: we wake up the simple, quiet the stupid, and call for compassion from the intelligently predatory. We refuse to promote, keep in power, or enable the status-climbing avatars who do not attach with compassion.

We long to rehumanize the planet around the elements of a relational life by forming identity groups that help us attach to each other's best selves and raise the status of others. When we affiliate as identity groups who bring out the best self in ourselves and others, we can escape enemy mode.

Will you join the escape?

APPENDIX

TYPES OF LOW ENERGY RESPONSES

Distinguishing simple enemy mode from other muted responses

RELATIONAL CIRCUITS (RCS) AROUSAL ISSUES

TYPE	DESCRIPTION
SIMPLE ENEMY MODE	
The **Suppressed** Response Spectrum	A lack of energy in response to others (Level One) is accompanied by a non-pleasurable tone (Level Two) about connecting. Some justification of the negative response is often mentalized (VLE) but not always expressed. If the response is energized or amplified, something that Level Two considers BAD will become energized as well. The motives attributed to others will be negative in some way. Occasional episodes of simple enemy mode are easily recognized, but those with chronically low joy may be completely unaware.

The **Untrained** Response Spectrum	Person with a well-trained relational system uses emotions to improve their relationships. Many people enter simple enemy mode when facing one or more of the six non-pleasurable emotions hardwired in the brain. These emotions are: sadness, fear, anger, disgust, shame, and hopelessness. The trigger emotions produce a "not on my side" reaction and may even escalate into saying and doing stupid things.
NON-ENEMY MODE	
The **Fatigued** Spectrum	Depleted physical and emotional energy, whether momentary or prolonged, deadens the response to others. However, if the person regains energy, a joyful response emerges. Lack of sleep, illness, exertion, prolonged work, and even too much fun can drain the energy available and mute the RCs. This response is not enemy mode, but it creates a heightened potential for misunderstanding.
The **Impaired** Spectrum	Traumatic brain injuries, autistic spectrum, strokes, concussions, loss of oxygen, high fevers, diseases, and toxins are some of the causes for impaired responses from the RCs. While these may result in non-pleasurable emotional reactions, the individual's ability for social engagement is limited.
The **Unregulated** Spectrum	An energetic, somewhat louder, and positive engagement with others with little regard for the context (places people are generally quiet) or degree of familiarity. Familiarity generally strengthens this response.

ACKNOWLEDGMENTS

JIM AND RAY WOULD LIKE TO THANK the Life Model Works Board of Directors for their support and adjustments needed to find the time to research and write this book. Our colleagues and community helped bear the load of exploration and discovery needed to understand and explain enemy mode and its varying expressions. Many people participated in uncomfortable and vulnerable conversations in order to explore the topic.

We have deep gratitude for all who shared your stories, whether named or anonymous, to illustrate this book. We would particularly like to thank those who agreed to be interviewed by Ray or Jim and have their interview included here. Thank you also to those who reviewed the book contents in its development and checked for accuracy and clarity.

Thanks to our editors from Northfield: Duane Sherman, who championed the project, and Amanda Cleary Eastep, who oversaw the combination of the science with the story.

Thanks to Jim and Judy Ebbitt for the use of their cabin in the Rockies for a week of editing.

Ray is especially grateful to his wife, Deborah, and children, Andrew, Jonathan, Kimberly, Philip, and Kathleen. They endured patiently as Ray worked to escape enemy mode, document what he was learning, and lead a nonprofit. It felt like two jobs at times. Ray's gratitude to his wife, Deborah, is boundless, for all of her sacrifices these past thirty-six years, and for her advanced relational skills, which every day remind Ray to stay relational by escaping enemy mode.

NOTES

PAGE 13

1. Ecclesiastes 9:15, author translation/paraphrase.

INTRODUCTION

1. "Most Christian Countries 2022," World Population Review, https://worldpopulationreview.com/country-rankings/most-christian-countries.

CHAPTER ONE

1. Jim Collins and Jerry Porras, *Built to Last: Successful Habits of Visionary Companies* (New York: HarperBusiness, 1994).
2. Matthew 5:44.
3. Jonathan Haidt, "Why the Past 10 Years of American Life Have Been Uniquely Stupid," *The Atlantic*, April 11, 2022, https://www.theatlantic.com/magazine/archive/2022/05/social-media-democracy-trust-babel/629369/.

CHAPTER TWO

1. The amygdala also produces a FREEZE response when no amount of energy will help. The FREEZE response is not part of enemy mode.

CHAPTER THREE

1. Chris Coursey, *The Joy Switch* (Chicago: Northfield Publishing, 2021), 56.
2. This pattern is often called a dismissive attachment.
3. Karl Lehman, *Outsmarting Yourself* (Libertyville, IL: This Joy Books, 2011), 23.

4. "On the evening of May 25, 2020, white Minneapolis police officer Derek Chauvin kills George Floyd, a Black man, by kneeling on his neck for almost 10 minutes. The death, recorded by bystanders, touched off what may have been the largest protest movement in U.S. history and a nationwide reckoning on race and policing." "George Floyd Is Killed by a Police Officer, Igniting Historic Protests," History.com, May 25, 2020, https://www.history.com/this-day-in-history/george-floyd-killed-by-police-officer.

CHAPTER FOUR

1. James Wilder, Edward Khouri, Chris Coursey, and Shelia Sutton, *Joy Starts Here: The Transformation Zone* (East Peoria, IL: Shepherd's House Inc., 2013).
2. Anne Trafton, "Newly Discovered Neural Connections May Be Linked to Emotional Decision-Making," *MIT News*, September 19, 2016, https://news.mit.edu/2016/neural-connections-linked-emotional-decision-making-0919.
3. Karen Zauder Brass, *Trauma Filters Through* (Pine, CO: Chazak Publishing, 2018), 346.
4. Cold Spring Harbor Laboratory, "Reversing a Genetic Cause of Poor Stress Tolerance," SciTechDaily, May 9, 2021, https://scitechdaily.com/reversing-a-genetic-cause-of-poor-stress-tolerance.
5. Wilder et al., *Joy Starts Here*, 193.

CHAPTER FIVE

1. John Feinstein, *A Season on the Brink* (New York: Macmillan Publishing Company, 1986), 336–37.
2. *The Rise and Fall of Mars Hill* podcast, *Christianity Today*, 2021.
3. "Piling Dead Bodies Behind His Bus," uploaded by Dear Driscoll, YouTube, May 31, 2021, https://youtu.be/11Q5K26bup0.
4. Kate Shellnutt and Morgan Lee, "Mark Driscoll Resigns from Mars Hill," October 15, 2014, *Christianity Today*, https://www.christianitytoday.com/ct/2014/october-web-only/mark-driscoll-resigns-from-mars-hill.html.
5. Interview with Martha Stout of Harvard Medical School, author of *The Sociopath Next Door*, quoted in Jon Ronson, *The Psychopath Test* (New York: Riverhead Books, 2011), 113.
6. Jonathan Haidt, *The Righteous Mind: Why Good People Are Divided by Politics and Religion* (New York: Vintage Books, 2013), 52 (emphasis in original).
7. Ibid., 31.
8. Ibid.
9. Ibid., 105.

10. Ibid.
11. Haidt quotes Michael Tomasello, the expert on chimpanzee cognition, as saying, "It is inconceivable that you would ever see two chimpanzees carrying a log together," *The Righteous Mind*, 237.
12. Haidt, *The Righteous Mind*, 344.
13. Robert Sapolsky, *Behave: The Biology of Humans at Our Best and Worst* (New York: Penguin Books, 2018), 479.
14. Ibid., 56–57.
15. Ibid., 58.
16. Ibid.
17. Ibid., 481.
18. Ben Sasse, *Them: Why We Hate Each Other and How to Heal* (New York: St. Martin's Griffin, 2019), 74.
19. Ibid., 85.
20. Iain McGilchrist, *The Master and His Emissary: The Divided Brain and the Making of the Western World* (New Haven, CT: Yale University Press, 2010), 22.
21. Ibid., 88.
22. Allan Schore, *The Science of the Art of Psychotherapy* (New York: W. W. Norton and Co., 2012), 1–20.
23. Ibid., 87.
24. Ibid.
25. Sapolsky, *Behave*, 387–425.
26. Ibid., 85.
27. Ibid.
28. Ubald Rugirangoga, *Forgiveness Makes You Free* (Notre Dame, IN: Ave Maria Press, 2019), 29–39.
29. Jon Ronson, *The Psychopath Test* (New York: Riverhead Books, 2011), 85.
30. Sapolsky, *Behave*, 179.
31. Ronson, *The Psychopath Test*, 113.
32. Dave Grossman, *On Killing* (New York: Back Bay Books, 1995), 182.
33. Dave Grossman, "On Sheep, Wolves and Sheepdogs," Killology Research Group, https://www.killology.com/sheep-wolves-and-sheepdogs; from the book *On Combat* by Lt. Col. Dave Grossman (Seattle: WSG Research Publications, 2004).
34. Sasse, *Them*, 105.
35. "Lt. Gen. Sean MacFarland: Building Better Arab Armed Forces | LIVE STREAM," YouTube, March 18, 2019, https://youtu.be/EWHffWl0DUY?t=4013.

CHAPTER SIX

1. Joseph Henrich, *The WEIRDest People in the World* (New York: Farrar, Straus and Giroux, 2020), 112.
2. Semir Zeki and John Paul Romaya, "Neural Correlates of Hate," *PLOS ONE* 3(10): e3556, October 29, 2008, https://doi.org/10.1371/journal.pone.0003556.
3. Robert Sapolsky, *Behave: The Biology of Humans at Our Best and Worst* (New York: Penguin Books, 2018), 519.
4. Gerald Edelman and Giulio Tononi, *A Universe of Consciousness* (New York: Basic Books, 2000).
5. Douglas Noll, "Why Can't We All Just Get Along?," *Mediate*, December 16, 2003, https://www.mediate.com/articles/noll9.cfm.
6. Tom Holland, *Dominion* (New York: Basic Books, 2019), 403.
7. G. K. Chesterton, *Orthodoxy* (United Kingdom: J. Lane, 1909), 5.
8. Matthew Bigler and Judson L. Jeffries, "'An Amazing Specimen': NFL Draft Experts' Evaluations of Black Quarterbacks," *Journal of African American Studies* 12, no. 2 (June 2008): 120–41, https://www.jstor.org/stable/41819165.
9. Michael Hirsh, "He Just Couldn't See Past My Color," *Foreign Policy*, June 4, 2020, https://foreignpolicy.com/2020/06/04/dana-pittard-interview-army-pentagon-institutional-racism-black-lives-matter-protests/.
10. Ibid.
11. Sapolsky, *Behave*, 306.
12. Ibid., 616.
13. Ibid., 615.
14. Ibid.
15. Holland, *Dominion*, 209.
16. Ibid.
17. Ibid., 210.
18. Ibid., 16.
19. Ibid., 99.
20. Ibid., 528.
21. David Hancock, "Clinton Cheated 'Because I Could,'" *CBS News*, June 16, 2004, https://www.cbsnews.com/news/clinton-cheated-because-i-could-16-06-2004/.
22. Daniel Silliman and Kate Shellnutt, "Ravi Zacharias Hid Hundreds of Pictures of Women, Abuse During Massages, and a Rape Allegation," *Christianity Today*, February 11, 2021, https://www.christianitytoday.com/news/2021/february/ravi-zacharias-rzim-investigation-sexual-abuse-sexting-rape.html.

23. Ruth Malhotra, "My Work Almost Crushed Her Family. Now I'm Welcomed at Her Table," *Christianity Today*, December 20, 2021, https://www.christianitytoday.com/ct/2021/december-web-only/christmas-restoration-ruth-malhotra-rzim-lori-anne-thompson.html?utm_medium=widgetsocial.

24. Justin Taylor, "Driscoll, Schaeffer, and Packer on the Size of Your Church and the Idolatry of Your Heart," TGC, December 10, 2021, https://www.thegospelcoalition.org/blogs/justin-taylor/driscoll-schaeffer-and-packer-on-the-size-of-your-church-and-the-idolatry-of-your-heart/.

25. Holland, *Dominion*, 452.

26. David Kaiser, "Introduction to Kaiser Neuromap Part 2," YouTube, June 24, 2020, https://www.youtube.com/watch?v=2P_mtAvC9dw.

27. "Veteran Population," US Department of Veterans Affairs, https://www.va.gov/vetdata/veteran_population.asp.

28. Dave Grossman, *On Killing* (New York: Back Bay Books, 1995), 190.

29. Ibid.

30. Ibid., 120–22.

31. Charles Brandt, *I Heard You Paint Houses* (Lebanon, NH: Steerforth Press, 2016), 38.

32. Sapolsky, *Behave*, 85.

33. Zeki and Romaya, "Neural Correlates of Hate."

34. Jonathan Haidt, *The Righteous Mind: Why Good People Are Divided by Politics and Religion* (New York: Vintage Books, 2013), 70.

35. Sapolsky, *Behave*, 454, 562.

36. Michael Regner et al., "The Insula in Nicotine Use Disorder: Functional Neuroimaging and Implications for Neuromodulation," *Neuroscience and Biobehavioral Reviews* 103 (August 2019): 414–24, https://doi.org/10.1016/j.neubiorev.2019.06.002.

37. Nasir Naqvi et al., "Damage to the Insula Disrupts Addiction to Cigarette Smoking," *Science* (January 2007): 315, 531–34, https://doi.org/10.1126/science.1135926.

38. Allan Schore, *The Science of the Art of Psychotherapy* (New York: W. W. Norton and Co., 2012), 100.

39. Ibid., 83.

40. Robert Jay Lifton, *The Nazi Doctors* (New York: Basic Books, 1986), 497–500.

41. Ibid., 499–500.

42. Ibid., 500.

CHAPTER SEVEN

1. William Watson, *Sacred Story: An Ignatian Examen for The Third Millenium* (Seattle: Sacred Story Press, 2012), 2–3.
2. Robert Morris, speaking at the 2014 Gateway Church Conference, "Mark Driscoll at the Gateway Conference October 20, 2014," YouTube, October 20, 2014, https://youtu.be/2ZVtuOIrrDg.
3. Mark Jurkowitz and Amy Mitchell, "A Sore Subject: Almost Half of Americans Have Stopped Talking Politics with Someone," Pew Research Center, February 5, 2020, https://www.journalism.org/2020/02/05/a-sore-subject-almost-half-of-americans-have-stopped-talking-politics-with-someone/.
4. Amina Dunn, "Few Trump or Biden Supporters Have Close Friends Who Back the Opposing Candidate," Pew Research Center, September 18, 2020, https://www.pewresearch.org/fact-tank/2020/09/18/few-trump-or-biden-supporters-have-close-friends-who-back-the-opposing-candidate/.
5. Tovia Smith, "'Dude, I'm Done': When Politics Tears Families and Friendships Apart," *NPR*, October 27, 2020, https://www.npr.org/2020/10/27/928209548/dude-i-m-done-when-politics-tears-families-and-friendships-apart.
6. Robert Sapolsky, *Behave: The Biology of Humans at Our Best and Worst* (New York: Penguin Books, 2018), 673.
7. Eamonn Brennan, "Seth Davis on Larry Bird and Bobby Knight," *Inside the Hall*, March 5, 2009, https://www.insidethehall.com/2009/03/05/seth-davis-on-larry-bird-and-bobby-knight/.
8. Stuart Brown, *Play: How It Shapes the Brain, Opens the Imagination and Invigorates the Soul* (New York: Avery, 2009).
9. Job 29:12–17.

CHAPTER EIGHT

1. Robert Sapolsky, *Behave: The Biology of Humans at Our Best and Worst* (New York: Penguin Books, 2018), 88.
2. Ibid.
3. These names are fictitious, but the scones were actual.
4. *Merriam-Webster*, s.v. "jus primae noctis (*n.*)," accessed June 22, 2022, https://www.merriam-webster.com/dictionary/jus%20primae%20noctis. Most historians consider this custom to not be a historical fact.
5. Sean Jones, "Virginia Attorney General Sues Town over Discriminatory Police Practices after Caron Nazario Investigation," *USA Today*, January 4, 2022, https://www.usatoday.com/story/news/nation/2022/01/04/virginia-ag-sues-town-where-police-pepper-sprayed-caron-nazario/9091894002/.

6. Pamela Wible, "Why Three MDs From One Hospital Died by Suicide Within 8 Months: Can We Stop This?," Medscape, July 19, 2021.
7. Elizabeth Cooney, "Salary Gap between Male and Female Physicians Adds Up to $2 Million in Lifetime Earnings," Stat, December 6, 2021, https://www.statnews.com/2021/12/06/male-female-physician-salaries-gap-2-million-lifetime-earnings/.
8. Curt Thompson, *The Soul of Shame* (Downers Grove, IL: IVP, 2015).
9. Brené Brown, *The Gifts of Imperfection* (Center City, MN: Hazelden Publishing, 2010).
10. Will Oremus et al., "How Facebook Shapes Your Feed," *The Washington Post*, October 26, 2021, https://www.washingtonpost.com/technology/interactive/2021/how-facebook-algorithm-works/.

CHAPTER NINE

1. *The Joy Switch*, pages 52–54, does a masterful job of spelling out "how I can tell when my relational circuit is on."
2. Wendy Maltz, *The Sexual Healing Journey: A Guide for Survivors of Sexual Abuse* (New York: HarperCollins, 2012), 147–63.
3. Daniel Wegner, "How to Think, Say, or Do Precisely the Worst Thing for Any Occasion," *Science* 325 (July 2009): 48–50, https://doi.org/10.1126/science.1167346.
4. Charles W. Colson, *Born Again* (Tappan, NJ: Fleming Revell Company, 1977), 57.
5. Charles Brandt, *I Heard You Paint Houses* (Lebanon, NH: Steerforth Press, 2016), 51.
6. "Mike Tyson – Fear Is My Best Friend!" YouTube, September 23, 2020, https://www.youtube.com/watch?v=OXkQr4C2lfo.

CHAPTER TEN

1. Ed Khouri, *Becoming a Face of Grace* (Littleton, CO: Illumify Media Global, 2021). The Greek word "grace" can be misunderstood. In context, anyone who was "graced" in Greek culture would get gifts from the benefactor to show how special they were. Before theologians made it solely about the undeserved favor of God and focused on salvation, the word meant to be "special." God "graces" us because we are special to Him. Ed Khouri makes this point admirably in his book *Becoming a Face of Grace*.
2. "Wesleyan and Keswick Models of Sanctification," Bible.org, https://bible.org/article/wesleyan-amp-keswick-models-sanctification.

3. Thomas A. Kolditz, *In Extremis Leadership* (San Francisco, CA: Jossey-Bass, 2007), 122.

4. Robert Sapolsky, *Behave: The Biology of Humans at Our Best and Worst* (New York: Penguin Books, 2018), 131–32.

5. Megan Brooks, "The Psychopathic Brain: New Insight," Medscape, May 18, 2022. Stimulation seeking and impulsivity partly mediated the striatal-psychopathy relationship, accounting for 49.4 percent of this association. We examined striosomes briefly in chapter 4 in connection with de-escalation of stupid enemy mode.

6. A few people only feel alive while they are hurting others. This book does not cover that extreme condition.

7. This point is discussed in Marcus Warner and Jim Wilder, *RARE Leadership in the Workplace* (Chicago: Northfield Publishing, 2021).

8. Robert Jay Lifton, *The Nazi Doctors* (New York: Basic Books, 1986), 500.

9. William M. Watson, *Discovery: A Disciple's Journey* (Seattle, WA: Sacred Story Press, 2021), 11–13.

10. Sapolsky, *Behave*, 101–36.

11. Bill Atwood, *The General, The Boy, & Recapturing Joy* (Frisco, TX: Ekklesia Society Publishing, 2020).

12. Marcus Warner and Jim Wilder, *RARE Leadership: 4 Uncommon Habits for Increasing Trust, Joy, and Engagement in the People You Lead* (Chicago: Northfield Publishing, 2016), 19.

CHAPTER ELEVEN

1. Arthur C. Brooks, *Love Your Enemies* (New York: Broadside Books, 2019), 131–33.

2. Ibid., 74.

3. Jon Ronson, *The Psychopath Test* (New York: Riverhead Books, 2011), 71.

4. Carol Lynn Mithers, *Therapy Gone Mad: The True Story of Hundreds of Patients and a Generation Betrayed* (Reading, MA: Addison Wesley Publishing Company, 1994).

CHAPTER TWELVE

1. "Armenian Apostolic Church," *Britannica*, accessed June 23, 2022, https://www.britannica.com/topic/armenian-apostolic-church.

2. Matthew 28:20.

3. John 13:34.

4. John 15:11.

5. John 10:11.
6. Mark 9:35 (esv).
7. John 13:14 (esv).
8. Matthew 5:7 (wnt). *Weymouth New Testament* (public domain).
9. John 10:14 (esv).
10. John 12:47 (nlt).
11. Matthew 5:44–46 (esv).
12. Matthew 5:45 (cjb).
13. 1 John 4:20.
14. Stuart Brown, *Play: How It Shapes the Brain, Opens the Imagination, and Invigorates the Soul* (New York: Avery, 2009).
15. Ezekiel 34:4, 16 (tneb). The New English Bible Cambridge University Press, New York Copyright the Delegates of the Oxford University Press and the Syndics of the Cambridge University Press 1962-1970. Corrected impression 1972.
16. Robert Sapolsky, *Behave: The Biology of Humans at Our Best and Worst* (New York: Penguin Books, 2018), 193.
17. 1 Peter 2:10, author's paraphrase.

REVIVE YOUR LEADERSHIP. GROW HEALTHY TEAMS. SEE GREAT RESULTS.

LIFE IS HARD WHEN YOU'RE NOT YOURSELF.

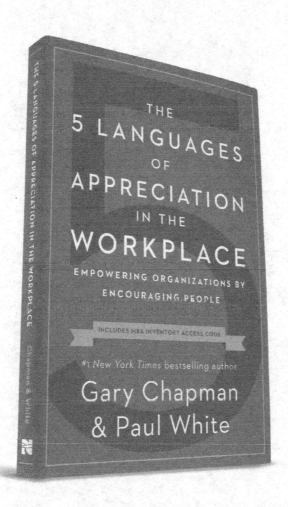